Al-Qaeda's Revenge

Al-Qaeda's Revenge
The 2004 Madrid Train Bombings

Fernando Reinares

Woodrow Wilson Center Press
Washington, D.C.

Columbia University Press
New York

Woodrow Wilson Center Press
Washington, D.C.
www.wilsoncenter.org

Columbia University Press
Publishers Since 1893
New York   Chichester, West Sussex
cup.columbia.edu

Library of Congress Cataloging-in-Publication Data

Names: Reinares, Fernando, 1960– author.
Title: Al-Qaeda's revenge : the 2004 Madrid train bombings / Fernando
    Reinares.
Other titles: ¡Matadlos! English
Description: Washington, D.C. : Woodrow Wilson Center Press ; New York :
    Columbia University Press, [2016] | Includes bibliographical references
    and index.
Identifiers: LCCN 2016043284 (print) | LCCN 2016057069 (ebook) |
    ISBN 9780231704540 (cloth) | ISBN 9780231704557 (pbk.) |
    ISBN 9780231801409 (ebook)
Subjects: LCSH: Madrid Train Bombings, Madrid, Spain, 2004. |
    Terrorism—Spain—Madrid—History—21st century. | Terrorism—Religious
    aspects—Islam. | Qaida (Organization)
Classification: LCC HV6433.S7 R4513 2016 (print) | LCC HV6433.S7 (ebook) |
    DDC 363.325/93884094641—dc23
LC record available at https://lccn.loc.gov/2016043284

Cover photo: Rescue workers work around the destroyed intercity train at the Atocha train station in
Madrid on March 11, 2004. AP Photo / Peter Dejong
Design and layout: Station 10 Creative

W | Wilson Center

The Wilson Center, chartered by Congress as the official memorial to President Woodrow Wilson, is the nation's key nonpartisan policy forum for tackling global issues through independent research and open dialogue to inform actionable ideas for Congress, the Administration, and the broader policy community.

Conclusions or opinions expressed in Center publications and programs are those of the authors and speakers and do not necessarily reflect the views of the Center staff, fellows, trustees, advisory groups, or any individuals or organizations that provide financial support to the Center.

Please visit us online at www.wilsoncenter.org.

Jane Harman, Director, President, and CEO

Contents

Maps and Figures

Maps

Figures

Acknowledgments

This book was made possible thanks to the affection and support of many people, ranging from uniquely loving intimates and relatives, to whom I offer my deepest gratitude, to friends and colleagues, who in many cases, most fortunately, belong to both categories. All of them know personally the depth of my gratitude. Thanks are also due for the collaboration of many judicial, police, and intelligence senior officials, both inside and outside Spain, who, if not explicitly mentioned, it is because they prefer to remain anonymous. The research for this book was done between 2008 and 2013, and was conducted in a good number of countries across the world, mainly while I was based at the Elcano Royal Institute (Real Instituto Elcano) in Madrid. But I also strongly benefited from the help provided by the Universidad Rey Juan Carlos, also in Madrid, and by the Woodrow Wilson International Center for Scholars, as well as by the Center for Security Studies at Georgetown University, in Washington. When it comes to people I can name, I am especially grateful to Carola García-Calvo, Emilio Lamo de Espinosa, Bruce Hoffman, Rob Litwak, Charles Powell, and Bruce Riedel. And I am also grateful to Isabel Bazaga, Rut Bermejo, María Cifuentes, Lee Hamilton, Javier Jordán, Maite Pagazaurtundua, Joan Tarrida, Pedro González-Trevijano, and, last but not least, Peter Waldmann. I was privileged to participate in exchanges on 3/11 with, among others, Bruno Megale, Rafael Gómez Menor, Jesús de la Morena, María Ponte, and Javier Zaragoza. A true gift for me was the assistance provided by Antoine Garapon, Juan Antonio Jabaloy, Carolina Jiménez, Ángel Llorente, Marco Lombardi, Francisco de Miguel, Álvaro Vicente, Cristina Villa, and Christopher Wall. Gracias, muchas gracias, to Joe Brinley and Shannon Granville of the Woodrow Wilson Center Press, to Alfred F. Imhoff, and to Anne Routon of Columbia University Press. The memory of the victims of the March 11 attacks was and is always present in my mind and in my heart.

Foreword

Bruce Riedel

On March 11, 2004, at about seven-thirty in the morning, ten explosive devices were detonated on four commuter trains in Madrid, killing 191 and wounding more than 1800 people. It was the deadliest terrorist attack in Europe since the downing of the Pan Am Flight 103 jumbo jet in December 1988 over Lockerbie, Scotland. Since the Madrid attacks, terrorist attacks have struck across Europe from London to Paris, Brussels, Nice, and elsewhere. Madrid began the carnage that al-Qaeda and its offspring, including the Islamic State, have waged relentlessly since that morning rush hour in Madrid.

Assigning responsibility for the attack in Madrid has been a source of intense controversy. The bombings took place only three days before national elections in Spain. The ruling government, led by Prime Minister José María Aznar, initially sought to blame the attack on the Basque separatist group ETA (Euskadi ta Askatasuna). It rushed to the United Nations Security Council and had a resolution, number 1530, adopted unanimously that same day, blaming ETA for the attack. It quickly became apparent, however, that the attack was the work of Islamic extremists with ties to al-Qaeda. Aznar's party lost the election, and the new Spanish government withdrew its troops from the American-led occupation of Iraq, in a move widely seen as an early vote of no confidence in the Iraq war.

Now we have this fabulous piece of history by Fernando Reinares, which provides the first in-depth account of the plot behind the 3/11 attacks. Contrary to the accounts circulating at the time, which emphasized that the plot was the work of a loosely organized, self-recruited group of local jihadists without any real organizational connection to al-Qaeda, this definitive account shows that the plotters were from a long-established al-Qaeda cell with strong connections to the senior al-Qaeda leadership then hiding in Pakistan, including Osama bin Laden.

This cell had played an important role in the attacks on the United States on September 11, 2001. The Spanish cell had helped Mohamed Atta, the leader of the nineteen 9/11 hijackers, to meet with his al-Qaeda contacts in Spain twice before the attack. In January and July 2001, Atta had traveled from Miami to Madrid and consulted with bin Laden's messenger from Afghanistan. The cell had survived a crackdown by the Spanish authorities after the September 11 attacks. It maintained regular contact with the senior leadership even after the fall of the Taliban in Afghanistan in late 2001. In December 2001, in Karachi, Pakistan, the remnants of the original cell decided to attack Spain in revenge for Spain's counterterrorism operations.

This account of the plot reveals in detail that al-Qaeda was alive and actively plotting its revenge in Europe before and after President George W. Bush had proclaimed that the mission had been accomplished in the war against al-Qaeda and had pivoted his attention to Iraq. It was essential for the Bush narrative that the Madrid attack not be linked back to the senior al-Qaeda leadership, because that link would expose the reality that Washington had taken its attention off the jihadist threat prematurely by the invasion of Iraq. It would demonstrate that instead of destroying al-Qaeda in 2003, Bush's invasion of Afghanistan had simply moved it across the border into Pakistan. From his Pakistan hideout, in October 2003 bin Laden had publicly promised that Spain would be attacked, and later took credit for the attack several times before he was finally brought to justice by US Navy SEALs in Abbottabad in 2011. It was also in Pakistan where the mastermind of the Madrid attack was killed by an American drone missile strike.

This book puts the Madrid attack in its proper perspective. It clearly shows that, rather than being the work of some autonomous and leaderless local extremists, the Madrid attack was the work of al-Qaeda and its top leaders directing a global jihad after 9/11. Its extensive and detailed research takes the reader inside the plot and inside al-Qaeda. The role played in the conspiracy by Moroccan, Libyan, and Algerian terrorist groups affiliated with al-Qaeda is explored. And the importance of the Belgian capital, Brussels, as a hub for terrorist planning also is highlighted.

This account of the Madrid attack is thus a superb case study in why it is important not to rush to judgment about national security crises in general and terrorist attacks in particular. All too often, the morning-after assessments of horrific events can prove to be flawed and misleading. Hastily assigning responsibility for a terrorist plot can lead to disastrous policy decisions. Careful and meticulous analysis of a plot and its conspirators can instead provide crucial insights into how terrorism works and how to defeat it effectively. Intelligence professionals and law enforcement experts need to be given time and authority to do the detective work necessary to understand a threat and counter it, not rush to misjudgment.

Al-Qaeda's Revenge: The 2004 Madrid Train Bombings is one of the most important books written on the subject of radical Islamic terrorism in Europe and North America since 9/11. No other book has taken such an in-depth look at the way a plot was conceived and how a conspiracy of plotters came together to execute their plan. This kind of patient reconstruction of a terror attack is a model for intelligence and security services around the world to emulate in order to better understand the challenges they face. It is also a benefit to average citizens who want to understand the world we all now live in. Since the carnage of the global jihad is unfortunately likely to stay with us for some time to come, this book should be essential reading for understanding the dangers ahead.

Abbreviations

AECI	Agencia Española de Cooperación Internacional (Spanish Agency for International Cooperation)
AQM	Al-Qaeda in Mesopotamia
CGI	Comisaría General de Información (General Commissariat for Intelligence, Spain)
CNI	Centro Nacional de Inteligencia (National Intelligence Center, Spain)
CNP	Cuerpo Nacional de Policía (National Police Corps, Spain)
DGP	Dirección General de la Policía (Directorate General of Police, Spain)
ETA	Euskadi ta Askatasuna (Basque Homeland and Freedom)
FATA	Federally Administered Tribal Areas (Pakistan)
FBI	Federal Bureau of Investigation (United States)
FCSE	Fuerzas y Cuerpos de Seguridad del Estado (State Security Forces and Corps, Spain)
GEO	Grupo Especial de Operaciones (Special Operations Group, Spain)

GIA   Groupe Islamique Armé (Armed Islamic Group, Algeria)

GSPC   Groupe Salafiste pour la Prédication et le Combat (Salafist Group for Preaching and Combat, Algeria)

LeT   Lashkar-e-Taiba (Army of the Pure)

LIFG   Libyan Islamic Fighting Group

MAK   Maktab al-Khidamat (Afghan Services Bureau)

MICG   Moroccan Islamic Combatant Group

NCTC   National Counterterrorism Center (United States)

RER   Réseau Express Régional (Paris train system)

UCIE   Unidad Central de Información Exterior (Central Unit for External Intelligence, Spain)

Map 1. The Madrid Metropolitan Area

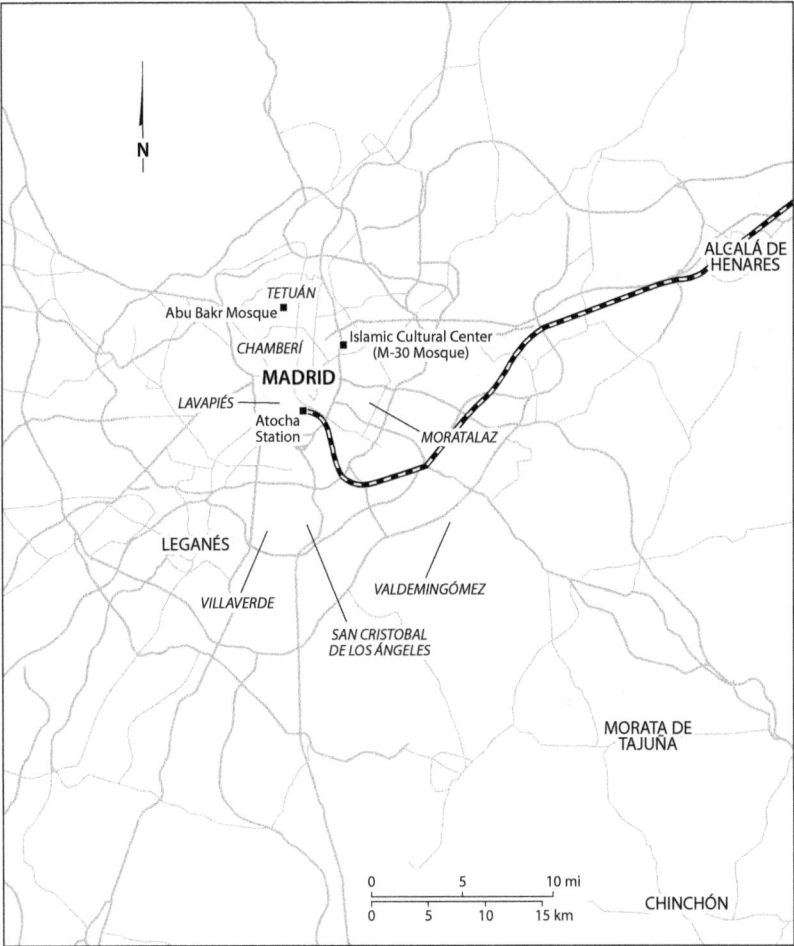

N

ALCALÁ DE
HENARES

TETUÁN
Abu Bakr Mosque ■

Islamic Cultural Center
(M-30 Mosque) ■

CHAMBERÍ

MADRID

LAVAPIÉS

Atocha
Station

MORATALAZ

LEGANÉS

VALDEMINGÓMEZ

VILLAVERDE

SAN CRISTOBAL
DE LOS ÁNGELES

MORATA DE
TAJUÑA

0   5   10 mi

0   5   10   15 km

CHINCHÓN

Map 2. Key Cities and Locations in Spain

Map 3. Western Europe and the Mediterranean

N

Manchester

UNITED KINGDOM

London

Hamburg

BELGIUM

Molenbeek-Saint-Jean

Brussels

GERMANY

ATLANTIC OCEAN

Mantes-la-Jolie

Paris

FRANCE

Milan

Brescia

Bilbao

ITALY

Zaragoza

PORTUGAL

Madrid

Barcelona

Lisbon

SPAIN

Valencia

MEDITERRANEAN SEA

Tangier

Tétouan

Algiers

Larache

Tunis

Kenitra

Rabat

Casablanca

MOROCCO

TUNISIA

Tripoli

ALGERIA

LIBYA

| 0 | 100 | 200 | 300 mi |
| 0 | 100 | 200 | 300 | 400 | 500 km |

Map 4. The Madrid Train Bombings

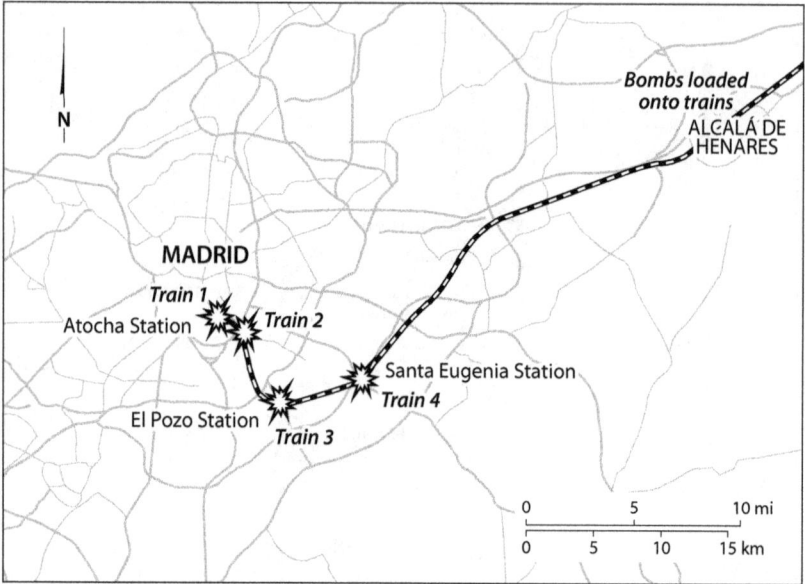

Figure 1. Diagram of the Madrid Train Bombings

Atocha Station | Convoy 21431

Calle Téllez | Convoy 17305

El Pozo Station | Convoy 21435

Santa Eugenia Station | Convoy 21713

Note: All ten bombs in the four commuter trains exploded almost simultaneously, between 7:37 and 7:41 a.m. on March 11, 2004. Three additional explosive devices were found after the bombings. Two of these, found respectively in rail carriages in the Atocha and El Pozo stations, were detonated by bomb disposal teams in controlled explosions that same day. A third bomb, which failed to explode, was also found in El Pozo station, and was successfully defused, providing crucial evidence to further the police investigation of the 3/11 attacks.

Figure 2. The Composition of the 3/11 Network

Initial component that evolved from
the remnants of Abu Dahdah's
al-Qaeda cell

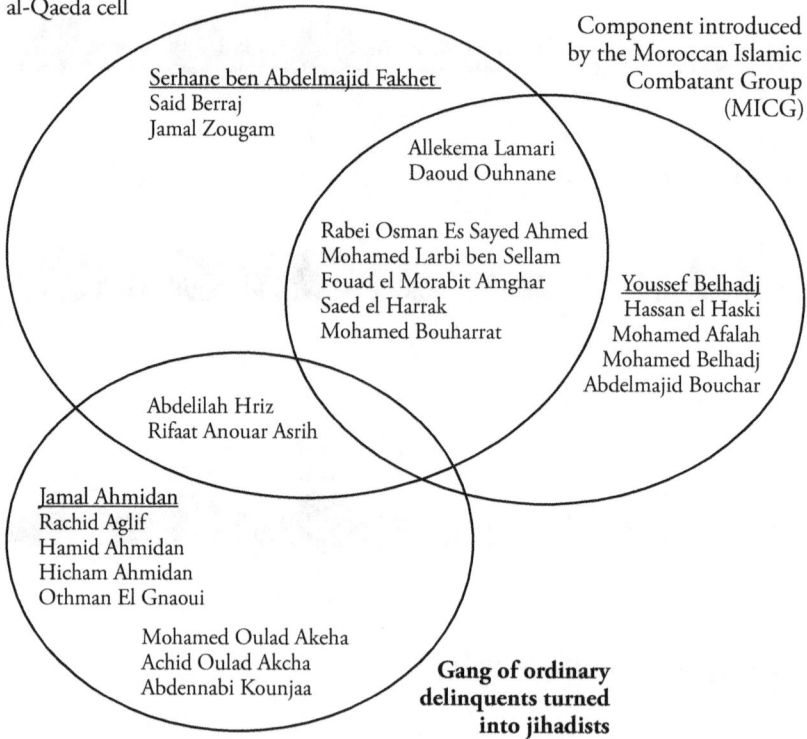

Component introduced
by the Moroccan Islamic
Combatant Group
(MICG)

Serhane ben Abdelmajid Fakhet
Said Berraj
Jamal Zougam

Allekema Lamari
Daoud Ouhnane

Rabei Osman Es Sayed Ahmed
Mohamed Larbi ben Sellam
Fouad el Morabit Amghar
Saed el Harrak
Mohamed Bouharrat

Youssef Belhadj
Hassan el Haski
Mohamed Afalah
Mohamed Belhadj
Abdelmajid Bouchar

Abdelilah Hriz
Rifaat Anouar Asrih

Jamal Ahmidan
Rachid Aglif
Hamid Ahmidan
Hicham Ahmidan
Othman El Gnaoui

Mohamed Oulad Akeha
Achid Oulad Akcha
Abdennabi Kounjaa

**Gang of ordinary
delinquents turned
into jihadists**

Note: Twenty-five members of the 3/11 network were free when the Madrid train bombings took place (although an arrest warrant had been issued for Allekema Lamari). Each of the three component nodes is underlined. The terrorist network was connected to Amer Azizi, who was the adjunct to the then–chief of al-Qaeda's external operations command, mainly through the initial component coming from the Abu Dahdah cell, which was dismantled in November 2001. The formation of the 3/11 network started in March 2002 and was completed by August 2003.

Prologue

On March 11, 2004, two and a half years after the September 11, 2001, terrorist attacks on the United States, another spectacular act of mass-casualty jihadist terrorism took place. But this attack was on the other side of the Atlantic, in Western Europe, and against a much softer target: commuter trains on the railway line connecting the city of Guadalajara with Madrid—more concretely, on the stretch between the historic city of Alcalá de Henares and Madrid's downtown Atocha Station. On March 11, thirteen bombs, each containing no less than 10 kilograms of dynamite and about 650 grams of shrapnel, were placed inside plastic bags and backpacks in twelve different carriages on four trains filled to rush hour capacity.[1] Ten of the bombs exploded almost simultaneously between 7:37 and 7:41 am. They were detonated by means of the synchronized alarms of cellular telephones. The blasts in the commuter trains killed 191 people and injured 1,841.[2] Though the attacks caused immediate material damage calculated at €17.62 million, the minimum direct economic cost has been estimated at more than €211.58 million.[3]

In the decade following the 9/11 attacks on New York and Washington, there was an ongoing controversy within scholarly and intelligence circles about whether the real global threat of jihadist terrorism, concretely in the context of Western open societies, was posed by al-Qaeda, with its burgeoning decentralized territorial branches and affiliated organizations, or by individual and collective actors inspired by, but unconnected to, entities related to al-Qaeda.[4] In the context of this debate, the March 11, 2004, Madrid train

1

bombings—known as the 3/11 attacks—have been held up as the arche-type of an independent local terrorist cell at work, and the perpetrators have been depicted as self-recruited terrorists exemplifying leaderless jihad, only aroused by the propaganda of al-Qaeda in the context of the Iraq war initi-ated in 2003.[5]

However, conclusive evidence connecting some of the Madrid bombing network's most notorious members to the external operations command of al-Qaeda's central organization, located in Pakistan—and also to prominent members of the Moroccan Islamic Combatant Group and the Libyan Islamic Fighting Group—along with the 3/11 terrorist network's distinctive features, imply that these assumptions are misleading. The groundwork for the 3/11 attacks began with a meeting in Karachi in December 2001 and extended into February 2002, involving al-Qaeda's other Maghreb associate entities, whose delegates gathered in Turkey that month. The terrorist network behind the 2004 Madrid train bombings came together between March 2002 and the summer of 2003. Also, the decision to perpetrate a major terrorist attack in Spain, which culminated in the 2004 Madrid train bombings, was initially motivated by revenge but, as is explained in this book, was unrelated to Spain's participation in the Iraq war.

That decision to perpetrate a terrorist attack in Spain led three relatively small, separate, and partially overlapping clusters of people to coalesce. As I substantiate in the following pages, the first of these clusters had evolved from the remnants of a very important al-Qaeda cell that had been established in Spain a decade before the 3/11 attacks and was dismantled as a result of the major antiterrorist operation launched in November 2001. This cell was linked to the Hamburg 9/11 cell led by Mohamed Atta. The second cluster within the Madrid bombing network was linked to the structure established by the Moroccan Islamic Combatant Group, mainly across Western Europe, particularly in France and Belgium. The third cluster, the last to be incorpo-rated and a rather unexpected component of the 3/11 network, brought to the effort a bunch of former delinquents active throughout Spain who specialized in trafficking in illegal drugs and stolen vehicles.

This evidence comes not only from the extensive criminal proceedings for the Madrid attacks but also from other relevant sources, such as police and judicial documents, including intelligence collected since the main sentence convicting those responsible for the attacks, though not the only one concerning 3/11, was pronounced in 2007 by Spain's Audiencia Nacional (National Court), which has the country's centralized general jurisdiction over terrorism offenses.[6] The evidence also indicates that al-Qaeda's senior leadership approved, facilitated, and even supervised the operation through a key intermediary connecting its central organizational structures in Pakistan with the 3/11 terrorist network and its operational nucleus in Spain. In addition, the accumulated evidence helps us better understand what the Madrid train bombings really tell us about al-Qaeda and global terrorism in transition, along with the changing nature of the threat they pose to open societies in general and to the Western European countries in particular.

The records of the criminal proceedings for the Madrid train bombings fill 241 volumes and 30 separate additional tomes, including previously secret records and restricted documents, comprising 93,226 pages of files. The available judicial documentation relevant to the case includes, in addition to court and attorney records, the records of several related criminal proceedings on jihadist terrorism in Spain initiated in 2001, 2003, and 2009, along with a number of sentences handed down by the National Court and the Tribunal Supremo (Supreme Court) in Spain, or delivered by courts in Milan and in Rabat or Salé in Morocco. This book also relies on police and intelligence documents from Spain, Italy, the European Union, Morocco, and the United States, as well as on personal interviews conducted by the author, both inside and outside Spain, between 2007 and 2013, with knowledgeable senior officials of various Western and non-Western nations as well as with other key informants, among whom were former leading jihadists.

Far from being perpetrated by an independent cell of self-radicalized individuals only inspired by al-Qaeda, the 3/11 Madrid attacks were a coordinated, complex manifestation of al-Qaeda's capabilities in Western Europe after 9/11. The 3/11 explosions evidenced the existence of jihadist networks or cells prone to direction and support, and even supervision, from al-Qaeda's external operations command through intermediaries with first-hand knowledge of the concrete operational scenario and close ties to local operatives. Networks or cells that eventually incorporated individuals ascribed to al-Qaeda's affiliated entities had a significant presence in some Western European countries. They were able to perpetrate sophisticated, coordinated, and highly lethal attacks in the region that followed al-Qaeda's general strategy and had originally been devised as al-Qaeda's revenge.

Overall, the Madrid train bombings revealed much about global terrorism as a polymorphous phenomenon—with diverse, heterogeneous interacting components—whose leaders recognized a top-down hierarchy of command and control. But in the years after the 2001 attacks on New York and

3

Washington, this phenomenon became flexible and was adapted to specific circumstances, producing extraordinary combinations when necessary and allowing the strategies of international actors and the aspirations of local activists to converge at the operational level. Furthermore, the 2004 attacks illuminate the changing nature of the jihadist terrorist threat inside—but not only inside—Western Europe. The Madrid bombing network speaks for itself as a composite source of threats, whereby individuals from different groups and organizations converge. Al-Qaeda's general guidelines, the decisions made by associated organizations, and the subordinate visions of local cells all converged in the 3/11 attacks to make the best of favorable opportunities and successfully execute an act of terrorist revenge in the context of a broader terrorist strategy.

The research upon which this book is based was initiated in December 2008, when documents from a Crown Court in Manchester gave me the first indication that a former prominent member of the al-Qaeda cell dismantled in Spain in November 2001 was occupying a prominent position inside al-Qaeda's external operations command at the time of the Madrid train bombings. My research formally concluded some five years later, in November 2013, when I had the opportunity to interview the assistant director of Indonesia's national counterterrorist agency concerning the same essential phone-triggered device used to detonate bombs in both the 2004 Madrid attacks and the 2002 Bali attacks. Tentative, provisional, and partial results of the ongoing research were opportunely offered in the meantime, before this volume was finalized.[7]

This book is divided into two parts. Part I deals with, among other topics, several basic questions: Where did the Madrid bombing network come from? What individual and collective components coalesced in the 3/11 network? When was this terrorist network initially formed, and how was it finally completed? In part II, I address another series of questions, such as: Why was Spain initially targeted, and who made the decision to attack? What was the connection between the 3/11 network and al-Qaeda's external operations command in Pakistan? What were the social and political consequences of the Madrid train bombings?

Valvanera, La Rioja, Spain, and
Old City, Jerusalem, Israel
September 2016

Part I

The 3/11 Terrorist Network: Origins, Components, and Formation

1

Osama bin Laden's Man in Spain and His Associates

On March 11, 2004, the same day that the Madrid train bombings took place, twenty-four individuals were about to be prosecuted before a tribunal of Spain's National Court (Audiencia Nacional). This court, based in Madrid, is the Spanish judicial body that deals with terrorism offenses. The defendants were charged with belonging to or collaborating with an al-Qaeda cell that was active in Spain.[1] Ostensibly, the timing of the trial seemed to be a coincidence. Nonetheless, to understand where the 3/11 network originated, why Madrid was targeted, who had instigated the massacre on the commuter trains, and what international connections had facilitated the terrorists' plans, it is necessary to know that in 1994—a decade before the train bombings—al-Qaeda had established an important cell in Spain.

Six years earlier, in 1988, Osama bin Laden, Ayman al-Zawahiri, and Abdullah Azzam had founded the organization that soon would become the entity of reference for global terrorism.[2] Indeed, al-Qaeda emerged in a specific context: the end of the armed conflict triggered by the Soviet invasion of Afghanistan in 1979. During the decade-long conflagration, Pakistan, then undergoing an accelerated process of Islamization, provided the Afghan insurgents with military aid. The insurgents also benefited from the financial support of Saudi Arabia, which was interested in extending its official fundamentalist version of Islam, and of the United States, still immersed in the bipolar dynamics of the Cold War. Moreover, tens of thousands of volunteers from

7

many Islamic countries and from Muslim communities in Western societies went to Afghanistan to join the insurgents. Their involvement was a response to religious edicts calling for a defensive jihad, understood as the individual obligation of every Muslim to become involved in the fight against the occupation of Muslim lands.[3] After the Soviets withdrew from Afghanistan in 1988 and 1989, a limited but sizable number of these former insurgents clustered around the emerging organization known as al-Qaeda, which maintained facilities in the border region between Afghanistan and Pakistan. These facilities remained even as al-Qaeda consolidated itself as a terrorist organization in its Sudanese sanctuary between 1991 and 1996.[4] During this period, al-Qaeda expanded its international presence and penetrated Western European countries such as the United Kingdom, Germany, Italy, and also Spain.

Although the al-Qaeda cell in Spain had formed in 1994, the Spanish National Police Corps (Cuerpo Nacional de Policía; CNP) were able to arrest most of the cell's members in November 2001 during a counterterrorism operation codenamed Operation Dátil (Operation Date), by far the most important police sweep against jihadist terrorism in Spain until then. The operation's main effort came during its first phase that November and had wide international resonance, but the full sweep was not completed until its fourth and final phase in September 2003. By the start of the autumn of 2005, the National Court had convicted eighteen of the twenty-four defendants in *Sumario* (*Criminal Proceedings*) *35/2001*.[5] Of the eighteen convicted, twelve were from Syria, five were from Morocco, and one was from Spain. Almost all of them resided in Madrid, though a few lived in Granada. In May 2006, Spain's Supreme Court (Tribunal Supremo) upheld the sentences for fifteen of them—including their leader, Imad Eddin Barakat Yarkas, better known among his followers and other jihadists outside of Spain as Abu Dahdah.[6]

These arrests aside, one extremely important fact about Operation Dátil is directly related and highly relevant to the 2004 Madrid train bombings: During the operation, the CNP did not arrest all of the members or collaborators of the al-Qaeda cell led by Abu Dahdah. Five individuals inside Spain eluded arrest in November 2001: Mustafa Maymouni, Driss Chebli (who would be arrested in the third phase of Operation Dátil in June 2003), Serhane ben Abdelmajid Fakhet (nicknamed "El Tunecino," or "the Tunisian"), Said Berraj, and Jamal Zougam. There were a number of reasons why these five individuals eluded the Spanish police. In some cases, the judicial authorities, with limited knowledge of the emerging jihadist phenomenon, did not consider the evidence sufficient to incriminate certain individuals associated with the cell. These legal

8

considerations were affected by Spanish counterterrorist laws at the time, which did not change significantly until the end of 2010. Perhaps, too, the Spanish authorities had political considerations in mind, wanting to avoid the impression that they were reacting solely to the dictates of US counterterrorism efforts following the September 11 attacks in New York and Washington. A sixth and prominent member of Abu Dahdah's al-Qaeda cell, Amer Azizi—an individual whose history and activities will be examined extensively in the second part of this book—also escaped capture during Operation Dátil. The authorities could not arrest him simply because he was not in Spain at the time.

The fact that these six individuals were not arrested during Operation Dátil, even though they had actively participated in the cell led by Abu Dahdah, proved crucial in the formation of the network that would carry out the 3/11 attacks. These six individuals, and their relationships with Abu Dahdah's cell, are essential to understanding how the massacre on the commuter trains was planned, prepared, and executed.

From Soldiers of Allah to Abu Dahdah's Cell

Two individuals formed the initial core of the al-Qaeda cell established in Spain in 1994. The first, the Palestinian Anwar Adnan Mohamed Saleh, also known as Chej Saleh, was around twenty years old at the time. The other was the Syrian Mustafa Setmarian Nasar, or Abu Musab al-Suri, then in his mid-thirties, who would become a key figure in global jihadism.[7] In 1987, about two years after first arriving in Spain, al-Suri had married a Spanish Islamic convert, Elena Moreno, and subsequently became a naturalized Spanish citizen. Between 1988 and 1991, he spent time in Afghanistan, where he served as an instructor in various al-Qaeda training camps.[8] In 1991, he returned to Spain, and with Saleh he disseminated an extremist vision of Islam that attracted Muslims living in and around Madrid, especially among those who frequented the Abu-Bakr Mosque in the Tetuán district in central Madrid. Soon after, al-Suri and Saleh formed a small group calling themselves Soldiers of Allah.

The Soldiers of Allah adopted the extremist view of Islam propagated by Saleh and al-Suri, a Sunni Muslim doctrine known as Salafist-jihadism. Salafism is a fundamentalist conception of the Islamic creed whose adherents argue that it is necessary to follow the rigorously observant behaviors of the first Muslims—the term *Salaf*, or "ancestor," refers to the earliest generations of the prophet Muhammad and his followers—hence the notion of "Salafism." However, proponents of this movement also reduce the meaning of the Quranic term *jihad*, or "struggle," to mere bellicosity, providing the "jihadist" adjective. For the adherents of Salafist-jihadism, or jihadism for short, jihad in the form of violence against infidels and apostates is justified, on both moral and utilitarian grounds, to advance and defend Islam. Indeed, the jihadists regard violence against enemies of the faith as a religious duty for every believer in Allah. Salafist-jihadism is the ideology of al-Qaeda.[9]

Both Abu Musab al-Suri and Chej Saleh abandoned Spain in 1995. The former moved to London in June of that year to take over *Al-Ansar* magazine, the propaganda arm of the Armed Islamic Group (Groupe Islamique Armé; GIA) of Algeria. The GIA had formed around Algerians who fought in Afghanistan during the 1980s, as well as individuals who had become radicalized within Algeria. Based in Algeria since its foundation in 1992, the GIA established strong ties to al-Qaeda.[10] It extended its network across various European countries throughout the 1990s, notably on the northwest shore of the Mediterranean, including Spain. Abu Musab al-Suri had been in close contact with the leaders of the GIA since at least 1993, well before he left Madrid. In February 1994, he had become an adviser to GIA leader Cherif Gousami, and remained in that post at least until Gousami was killed by the Algerian security forces in September 1994 and Djamel Zitouni stepped up to take Gousami's place.

In 1994, al-Suri—who was still focused on developing an al-Qaeda cell in Spain—advised the GIA leadership that they should "strike deep in France."[11] The GIA made an initial attempt in December 1994, when four GIA members hijacked Air France Flight 8969 at Algiers International Airport, intending to crash it into Paris. French security forces thwarted the plot during a layover in Marseille. French security also saw the effects of Abu Musab al-Suri's advice on July 25, 1995, when timed bombs exploded on board a Réseau Express Régional (RER) train at the Saint-Michel station in central Paris. Eight people died in the bombing, and around a hundred were injured. The Saint-Michel bombing was the first and the deadliest of several attacks that the GIA executed that year in France, and the first act of jihadist terrorism in Western Europe against commuter trains. The 3/11 network members would choose a similar target for their own attack nearly a decade later.

During his stay in London, al-Suri was in direct contact with Khaled al-Fawwaz, a Saudi businessman whom Osama bin Laden had appointed as his delegate in the United Kingdom in 1994. To this end, al-Fawwaz established an office in London, presenting it as a Saudi political group called the Advice and Reform Committee. The office took advantage of the official tolerance toward radical Islamists in the city, a tolerance that helped coin the derisive nickname "Londonistan." Through this office, the directors of al-Qaeda channeled instructions to the organization's cell in East Africa, most notably in 1998 when the cell was planning suicide bombings against the US embassies in Kenya and Tanzania. These attacks, which took place on August 7, killed more than 220 people. A month after the US embassy bombings, the first of such spectacular and lethal plots prepared and executed by members of al-Qaeda, British police arrested Khaled al-Fawwaz after the US authorities accused him of being involved in the attacks.[12]

Abu Musab al-Suri, however, carried out most of his daily activities with Abu Qatada, one of the most influential contemporary ideologue propagandists of Salafist-jihadism.[13] Born in Bethlehem as Omar Mahmoud Othman, Abu Qatada had lived in Amman and taught Islamic law in Peshawar before settling in the United Kingdom in 1993. He received political asylum there, even though he was still leading a terrorist organization in Jordan and disseminating edicts and treaties that incited hatred toward the West. Sentenced in absentia to life imprisonment by the Jordanian courts for his connections to terrorist activity, the British arrested him only after 9/11 and finally extradited him to Jordan in July 2013.

In spite of their close working relationship, Abu Qatada and al-Suri did not always concur over ideological positions, which led to some very public clashes between them.[14] Despite their tactical and strategic disagreements, both shared the same vision of Salafist-jihadism. As a doctrinaire of religious violence, Abu Qatada had tremendous influence on the members of the al-Qaeda cell established in Spain in the mid-1990s and, by implication, on the 3/11 attackers. The following passage is a succinct yet eloquent example of the kind of ideas that Abu Qatada propagated safely from London, thanks to his status as a political refugee in the United Kingdom:

> Let them say we are terrorists. Yes, that is what we are. The word is in Islamic terminology. Let people call us enemies of thought and opinion. Yes, we should raise the Islamic state with fire and steel, as Allah prescribed to purify gold impurities and rubbish.[15]

Abu Musab al-Suri moved back to Afghanistan in 1996, joining Osama bin Laden's inner circle.[16] Later, he led his own terrorist training camp in Kabul. At this camp in August 2000, he made a series of twenty-eight audiovisual recordings, with the generic title "Jihad Is the Solution." He made these videos to share one of the intensive courses he taught on terrorist indoctrination and training. In the twenty-second recording he made, he shared with his students—mainly well-educated Arabs—ideas such as "Terrorism is an obligation and murder, a rule"; "All young Muslims should become terrorists"; and "You, as a university student, what do you lose if you commit a terrorist act once a year, or once in your life?"[17] In his videos, al-Suri advised his students to attack Western countries to cause "collective massacres" against "personalities contrary to Islam," "Jews in Europe," "train stations," "airports," "nuclear installations," or even cause a "wildfire."[18] His videos also provided suggestions for funding the creation and maintenance of a jihadist cell:

> Any tourist carries a good amount of money, [perhaps] $1,000 or $1,500, apart from [his] passport, credit cards, and jewelry from his wife. One can attack him and rob him, or we can enter his hotel room, kill him, and rob him.[19]

In 2005, a voluminous treatise written by al-Suri, entitled "Call to Global Islamic Resistance," leaked onto the internet. As al-Suri explained, the book "was written to teach those who seek to comply with the obligation of jihad and to fight our enemies, the infidels, and their allies, the apostates and hypocrites."[20] In 2005, around the first anniversary of the 3/11 attacks, he posted a letter online in which he defended "the right of those who committed these attacks to fight against Spain."[21] Between March and May 2005, the Pakistani authorities located and arrested al-Suri in the city of Karachi and handed him over to the US authorities. The United States later rendered him to Syria, his native country. In December 2011, according to several reputable sources, al-Suri secured his freedom from a Syrian prison.[22]

Chej Saleh, the other founder of the al-Qaeda cell in Spain, left Madrid in October 1995, about four months after Abu Musab al-Suri departed for London. The authorities tapped Saleh's phone in September of that year.[23] He relocated to Peshawar, where Osama bin Laden initially had established the headquarters of his organization in Pakistan. Bin Laden's organization, which operated under the cover of a so-called Afghan Services Bureau (Maktab al-Khidamat; MAK), actually had served as a facility for receiving and registering foreign jihadists since 1984.[24] From here, Saleh dedicated himself to receiving and facilitating the movement of young Muslims from around the world who were interested in receiving training at the al-Qaeda camps in Afghanistan. He served in this position until 2001, right before the US military intervention dismantled these camps following 9/11.

In Peshawar, Saleh was under the command of Abu Zubaydah, who managed the affairs of al-Qaeda in Pakistan.[25] Born in Saudi Arabia in 1971, but with Palestinian ancestors, Abu Zubaydah's real name was Zayn al Abidin Muhammed. As al-Qaeda's manager in Pakistan, Abu Zubaydah acted as the liaison for the charitable Islamic entities that provided al-Qaeda with financial resources, managed the relationships with other jihadist organizations or Islamist parties throughout Asia, and ran a training camp near the Afghan town of Khost.[26] He also had direct access to Osama bin Laden, and served as his intermediary with Djamel Beghal, then the most notorious member of al-Qaeda residing in France. Beghal's detention in the United Arab Emirates on his return from Afghanistan in July 2001 had disrupted the preparations for a series of attacks in Paris.[27] In Spain, Beghal had hoped to meet with an al-Qaeda representative who would be capable of transmitting him funds to finance these attacks.[28]

The authorities detained Chej Saleh in Pakistan sometime in 1999 or 2000. Once released, he remained in the Afghan city of Jalalabad until the overthrow of the Taliban in late 2001.[29] Pakistani police arrested Abu Zubaydah on March 28, 2002, in a building in Faisalabad that was being used by the jihadist organization Lashkar-e-Taiba (Army of the Pure; LeT), an organization related to al-Qaeda.[30] LeT had emerged in 1993 as an armed spin-off group from an extremist movement created in Lahore sometime before. Despite its relationship with al-Qaeda, LeT was sponsored by the Pakistani intelligence services and used primarily against Indian citizens and interests. The house in which Abu Zubaydah was staying had been protecting al-Qaeda members and their families in Faisalabad who were fleeing the American bombing of their facilities in Afghanistan. During this time, Abu Zubaydah had been preparing to send suicide bombers to attack Western targets.

When Abu Musab al-Suri and Chej Saleh left Madrid in 1995, Abu Dahdah took over the cell they established.[31] (From here on, all references to the cell will speak of it as Abu Dahdah's cell.) Abu Dahdah had been born in the Syrian city of Aleppo on October 28, 1963, and had arrived in Spain in 1986 and acquired Spanish nationality by the time he was thirty. Even though he was married and had five young children, by 1998, numerous police records described him as "the man of Osama bin Laden's organization."[32] The Central Unit for External Intelligence (Unidad Central de Información Exterior, UCIE), the special division within the CNP's General Commissariat for Intelligence (Comisaría General de Información; CGI) for combating international terrorism, first tapped Abu Dahdah's phone in October 1995, and succeeded in extending the wiretap order throughout the next six years.[33]

"All land stolen from Palestine to Al-Andalus"

Abu Dahdah and his associates engaged in activities aimed at mobilizing human and material resources for terrorist ends. In addition to proselytizing on behalf of al-Qaeda and other jihadist organizations, the main members of the cell recruited adherents in and outside of Madrid. They held frequent, exclusive, and clandestine meetings in places of worship like the Al Huda oratory in the Lavapiés neighborhood in central Madrid, at commercial establishments, and at homes owned by cell members. At times, they held meetings at outdoor sites along the Alberche River, southwest of Madrid, likely to reduce their exposure to surveillance. In those meetings, the group shared the written ideas of Osama bin Laden, Ayman al-Zawahiri, and Abdullah Azzam.

In the writings of these three men, the founding members of al-Qaeda, there are direct and indirect references to Spain that go beyond the manifestations of anti-Western rhetoric typical of ideologues of the global jihad. In this regard, Azzam, the mentor of Osama bin Laden, was the most conspicuous. Azzam died in somewhat mysterious circumstances in November 1989, after a bomb exploded in his vehicle while he was driving on a road near Peshawar in Pakistan.[34] Shortly before his death, around the time the Soviets announced their plans to withdraw from Afghanistan in 1987, he published an influential pamphlet on the religious imperative of jihad. The pamphlet, translated into English as "News of Victory," includes paragraphs like the following:

> This obligation should not end with victory in Afghanistan, and jihad will remain an individual obligation until all other lands that were Muslim return to us and Islam reigns in them again. Before us lie Palestine, Bukhara, Lebanon, Chad, Eritrea, Somalia, the Philippines, Burma, Southern Yemen, Tashkent, and Al-Andalus.[35]

Azzam, one of the ideologues whose influence on the members of the 3/11 network was noticeable, spoke of "Al-Andalus" as if were a real land under occupation. Al-Andalus was the Arabic name for the territory in the Iberian Peninsula that had been under Islamic domination between the eighth and fifteenth century. Its shape varied, but at its height it extended over much of what is now Spain and Portugal. For the ideologues of Salafist-jihadism, Al-Andalus is a present reality that compels them to target Spain relentlessly; for them, the territory is a lost space that they hope to retake by force.

This perception explains Osama bin Laden's frequent references to Al-Andalus throughout his leadership of al-Qaeda until his death at the hands of a US Navy SEAL team in Abbottabad, Pakistan, in May 2011. As early as 1994, in an open letter to the religious authorities of Saudi Arabia, bin Laden publicly appealed for jihad in order to recover "all land stolen from Palestine to Al-Andalus and other Islamic lands that were lost due to the treachery of the rulers and the weakness of the Muslims."[36] On October 7, 2001, less than a month after the September 11 attacks, bin Laden released a message through the Qatari television channel Al-Jazeera in which he spoke of "the tragedy of Al-Andalus."

In December 2001, Ayman al-Zawahiri published his well-known "Knights under the Prophet's Banner," where he asserted that jihadists around the world are called to set up a force "eager to avenge the blood of martyrs, crying mothers, deprivation of orphans, the suffering of the prisoners and the wounds of torture in the lands of Islam, from East Turkestan to Al-Andalus."[37] In July 2006, al-Zawahiri himself issued a statement in which he clarified the meaning of the concept of "jihad in the path of Allah," and referred to "a jihad aimed to liberate Palestine, all of Palestine, and any territory that was Muslim, from Al-Andalus to Iraq."[38] In February 2007, almost a month before the third anniversary of the Madrid bombings, al-Zawahiri referred to the evolution of jihadist groups and organizations in the countries of the Maghreb, and encouraged al-Qaeda members and leaders, "Allah grant you the favor of stepping with your pure feet soon on the usurped Al-Andalus."[39]

A last and later example of the many hostile references to Spain inherent in the jihadists' consideration of Al-Andalus as an Islamic country under occupation is dated April 2009, slightly over five years after the 3/11 attacks. Abu Yahya al-Libi, then al-Qaeda's third-in-command, appeared in a video that was shared on various jihadi websites. In the video, al-Libi stated that in addition to Palestine:

> The jihad in Afghanistan, Iraq, Somalia, Chechnya, Al-Andalus, East Turkestan, and the occupied lands of Muslims, all of them, are legitimate and must be supported with money, arms, and [one's] body.
>
> American occupiers, Spanish, Russian, and others in these occupied countries are warriors. Shedding their blood and seizing their wealth is legitimate. And it is licit for Muslims to kill their men, taking over their money and destroying their installations within the territory.[40]

The reconquering of the territory formerly under Islamic rule in the Iberian Peninsula, which in this last statement justifies any criminal actions against non-Muslims who live there, has therefore appeared on the agenda of Salafist-jihadism since at least the mid-1980s. Because Al-Andalus is regarded as land that has been usurped by infidels, the jihadists approve acts of defensive jihad until a new Islamic authority emerges.[41] As this volume's account of the 3/11 bombings will show, consonant with these Salafist-jihadist notions, the members of the local cell that prepared and executed the 3/11 attacks spoke of themselves as the "brigade found in Al-Andalus" and as "the Al-Andalus battalion."[42]

Interestingly, only one of the above-mentioned eighteen individuals who were charged with and convicted of belonging to Abu Dahdah's cell was born in Spain. This man, José Luis Galán, had converted to Islam around 1991 and adopted the name Yusuf Galán. As a member of the cell, Galán had attended a training camp in Indonesia before the authorities arrested him in November 2001. In his home in Madrid, the authorities recovered a pistol, a carbine, a repeating rifle, ammunition, swords, and machetes.[43] Despite this and other evidence, Galán voiced a different opinion in a December 2011 interview hosted on www.webislam.com, a website for Spanish and Spanish-speaking Muslims. In the interview, which took place after he had served the sentence imposed by the National Court, Galán is presented as someone that the Spanish authorities had convicted of "a (supposed) [sic] crime" of belonging to a terrorist organization.[44] He then declared, "I am a criminal because that is what judges and the police decided," adding that "my crime is to believe in *laa ilaha il-la Al-lah* (there is no god but Allah)."[45]

"Prevent the very possible commission of attacks that may develop in our country"

In addition to proselytizing, members of Abu Dahdah's cell engaged in terrorist financing. Throughout the mid- to late 1990s, they relied on diverse means to raise money.[46] For example, they benefited from voluntary donations to their leader from Arab businessmen, some of whom had considerable personal fortunes, who shared their same Salafist-jihadist ideology. They also took up charitable collections among Muslim merchants in Madrid neighborhoods that were home to significant numbers of immigrants, such as Lavapiés, asking for their support to help Muslims affected by the ongoing conflicts in Bosnia and Chechnya. In addition, they made fraudulent use of credit cards, usually acquired by third parties who had stolen them, to make purchases in commercial establishments owned by cell members.

Abu Dahdah delivered a portion of the funds to the previously mentioned Abu Qatada in London. As the leader of al-Qaeda in Spain, Abu Dahdah made around twenty trips between Madrid and London for this purpose from 1995 to 2000, staying in Abu Qatada's own home during his visits.[47] Abu Dahdah also assisted the leaders of the Tunisian Combatant Group, including Tarek Maaroufi (who was residing in Belgium at the time) and Seifallah ben Hassine, when they were immersed in North African jihadist networks active in Western European countries.[48] The cell used another part of the money to maintain infrastructure to support jihadist organizations in the Middle East, South Asia, and Southeast Asia. This money also was used to help jihadists in Spain who were not members of the Abu Dahdah cell, such as by allowing them to rest from armed conflicts like Chechnya, pay for any needed special care, or at the very least stay hidden for a time. (One such individual who was helped in this way was Salaheddin Benyaich, known as Abu Mughen, whose connections to the 3/11 network will be discussed in greater detail in forthcoming chapters.)[49]

Abu Dahdah also financed trips of individuals who had been recruited in Spain so that they could attend terrorist training camps abroad, first in Bosnia, then in Indonesia, and finally in Afghanistan.[50] In Bosnia, the destination was the town of Zenica; in Indonesia, it was the island of Sulawesi near Borneo; and in Afghanistan, it was the Al-Faruq and Martyr Abu Yahya camps. Incidentally, Jasem Mahboule, a member of Abu Dahdah's cell and a Bosnia veteran who was in one of these Afghanistan training camps for a second stint, hurriedly returned to Spain in 1998 after receiving notice that the local Madrid government had granted him an apartment and that he needed to sign papers in front of a notary.[51] Mahboule's example shows how jihadists were able to settle in Spain, even when they were under surveillance, and how they found ways to exploit both the absence of administrative controls in certain areas and the poor information exchange between public institutions at various levels of government in those days.

Since at least 1997, UCIE reports sent to the corresponding National Court investigative magistrate who had authorized the wiretaps on members of Abu Dahdah's cell had specified that the objective of the police investigation for which the wiretaps had been requested was to "prevent the possible commission of attacks that could develop in our country."[52] Perhaps unsurprisingly, while searching the homes of Mahboule and two others who later would also be convicted of belonging to Abu Dahdah's cell, Najib Chaib Mohamed and Hassan al Hussein, the Spanish authorities found documents that detailed how to make explosives.

On June 23, 1998, the UCIE requested that the Central Investigative Judge No. 5 of the National Court order the arrest of six individuals linked to Abu Dahdah's cell. The arrests were intended to prevent the expiration of charges for a series of crimes that these individuals had committed while the authorities continued the investigations into their terrorist activities. After the al-Qaeda attacks in Kenya and Tanzania that August, the police delayed the arrests, fearing that similar attacks could take in Western countries and that the planned arrests might alert Abu Dahdah and his associates of the ongoing investigation.[53] The Spanish authorities would not dismantle the cell and imprison many of its members until the start of Operation Dátil in November 2001.

These UCIE investigations in the late 1990s were particularly important because, in addition, they revealed Abu Dahdah's connection to Mohamed Bahaiah, a key intermediary between al-Qaeda's senior leadership and its representatives on European territory. Although he lived in Turkey, Bahaiah (who also was known as Abu Khaled) frequently traveled to Granada and Madrid, always staying at the home of Abu Dahdah. Bahaiah had been married to a Spanish woman, which allowed him to obtain Spanish residency even though the two of them had divorced. Later, he married the sister of Mohamed Galeb Kalaje Zouaydi, a close associate of Abu Dahdah. In June 1999, aware that the Turkish police were searching for him, Bahaiah finally fled to Afghanistan, but not before informing Abu Dahdah of his departure.[54]

Abu Dahdah and his associate Zouaydi were also in close contact with a Syrian-born businessman, Mamoun Darkazanli, a major al-Qaeda financier living in Germany. Darkazanli often traveled to the Maghreb, Middle East, South Asia, North America, and Europe, and he visited Spain repeatedly between April 1997 and July 2001. The Spanish National Court accused Darkazanli of having strong ties to Abu Dahdah's cell, but even though Darkazanli had been arrested and imprisoned in Germany in October 2004 at the request of the Spanish authorities, the German Constitutional Court finally refused his extradition in June 2005.[55] The Spanish authorities requested his extradition again in February 2006, but the German federal attorney general again denied their request five months later because he did not believe that the Spanish authorities had provided sufficient evidence. This happened despite the fact that the German federal attorney general admitted in writing that Darkazanli had been an al-Qaeda partner and was involved in al-Qaeda business activities from 1993 to 1998.

The German attorney general further argued that Darkazanli had "acted as the sole example of an organization that exists only outside the Federal Republic of Germany," which under the then existing German law was not punishable unless the accused had been associated with at least two other individuals. He continued by paradoxically noting that instead of finding evidence of Darkazanli's involvement in terrorist activities, he understood that "since the mid-1990s, [Darkazanli] maintained friendly and business relationships with people who belonged to the al-Qaeda cell" in Spain.[56] Owing to this gap in bilateral counterterrorist cooperation, Darkazanli had continued to live in Hamburg, though he was unable to continue his commercial ventures because his businesses had been included in a list of entities sanctioned by the European Union for their links to Osama bin Laden and al-Qaeda.[57] However, he received noncontributory unemployment benefits, and became an imam at the Hamburg mosque that later would be frequented by the 9/11 hijackers. (The German authorities eventually would close the mosque in August 2010, claiming that the site spread an antidemocratic ideology and fomented jihadist recruitment.)

What Precipitated Operation Dátil?

After the September 11 attacks, the American and German intelligence services, among others, asserted that since the 1990s, Abu Dahdah, as leader of the Spanish al-Qaeda cell, had ties to Mohamed Atta, the Egyptian who had led the hijacking of one of the two planes that had struck the World Trade Center. Atta had shared an apartment in Hamburg with two other cell members, Ramzi Binalshibh and Said Bahaji, the former a Yemeni national and the latter a German of Moroccan descent. Inside the Hamburg apartment, authorities found a planner that Bahaji had left behind, which included Abu Dahdah's phone number in Madrid. Abu Dahdah had advance knowledge of al-Qaeda's plans to attack the United States and received updates regarding their preparations.[58]

Atta traveled twice to Spain in 2001. The first trip, about which little information exists, was aboard Iberia Flight 6122 from Miami to Madrid in January. The second trip, also from Miami, occurred in July, during which Atta met with Binalshibh and another individual who was not positively identified. Binalshibh had been denied an entry visa to the United States and could not serve as one of the 9/11 suicide bombers; instead, he acted as administrator and liaison for the rest from Europe.[59] Atta arrived in Madrid on July 8, and stayed in room 109 of the Hotel Diana Cazadora. The next day, Binalshibh took Aero Lloyd Flight 1408 from Hamburg to Reus, in Tarragona province in northeastern Spain. (Before these events, he communicated his movements to Marwan al-Shehhi, who would help prepare the attacks on 9/11 and later serve as one of the hijackers.)[60] During their discussions, Atta and Binalshibh stayed in nearby towns on the Tarragona coast, the former at the Hostal Residencia Montsant in Salou and the latter at the Hotel Mónica in Cambrils. Before Atta and Binalshibh returned to the United States and Germany on July 16 and 19, respectively, they finalized the details for the September 11 attacks.[61]

The presence of Abu Dahdah's associates in these locations and days, in addition to their telephone contacts during the same period, convinced the Spanish police that some of them—likely Amer Azizi in particular—had facilitated the meeting. One other possible meeting attendee was the Algerian Mohamed Belfatmi, an al-Qaeda member who had entered Spain illegally in 1999 but had obtained residency for "exceptional reasons" and lived in Pineda-Vilaseca, another Tarragona coastal town close to Cambrils. Between May and July, Belfatmi regularly phoned Abu Dahdah and Azizi.[62] He kept contact with another associate of Abu Dahdah, the Moroccan Driss Chebli. Days before 9/11, Belfatmi fled to Istanbul, and on September 3, he and Said Bahaji—Mohammed Atta's former Hamburg roommate, who was fleeing from Germany—jointly boarded Turkish Airlines Flight 1056, bound for Karachi. In Karachi, the two spent the night in the Embassy Hotel before leaving the next day and disappearing into Quetta, near the border with Afghanistan.[63]

Ramzi Binalshibh was the one who communicated the order to evacuate Europe and move to Pakistan, after confirming with Atta that September 11 had been the date chosen to attack New York and Washington.[64] Binalshibh fled through Spain. Six days before 9/11, he arrived in Madrid on a flight from Dusseldorf. He slept two nights in a hotel on Carretas Street, and on September 7 he flew to Pakistan via Dubai, using a forged Saudi passport obtained in Spain from an Algerian collaborator of al-Qaeda who was living in Torrevieja, in Alicante province.[65] Binalshibh was personally responsible for informing bin Laden in Afghanistan of the date chosen for the attacks;[66] he was arrested in Karachi in September 2002.[67]

The evidence that there were close connections between the Hamburg cell responsible for 9/11 and Abu Dahdah's cell in Madrid led the Spanish authorities to order that Abu Dahdah's cell be dismantled, nearly seven years after the CNP's counterterrorist services detected its presence in Spain and started wiretapping its leaders' communications. Operation Dátil began in November 2001. All of the members of the nucleus of the cell, including its leader Abu Dahdah, were arrested, except for Amer Azizi, who was in Iran at the time. Most of the other members of the cell were also apprehended—but not all.

2

From Abu Dahdah's Cell to the 3/11 Network

Four years before 3/11, Abu Dahdah's cell—the al-Qaeda cell established in Spain in 1994—had consolidated itself. Indeed, before the September 11 attacks, Madrid, along with other important European cities such as London, Hamburg, and Milan, had become a focal point in Western Europe for al-Qaeda, which at the time still had its base in Afghanistan. The members of the al-Qaeda cell in Spain had extensive links to countries besides Afghanistan, including nations inside and outside Western Europe. It was precisely around 1999 or 2000 when five individuals, all of whom would play a key role in the evolution of the 3/11 network, joined Abu Dahdah's cell.

Four of these cell members—Mustafa Maymouni, Driss Chebli, Said Berraj, and Jamal Zougam—were Moroccan. The fifth, Serhane ben Abdelmajid Fakhet, was nicknamed "El Tunecino" ("the Tunisian") because of his country of origin. Spanish authorities were not able, under the then-existing antiterrorist legislation, to apprehend these individuals either during the beginning of Operation Dátil in November 2001 or during its second phase in 2002. The five of them, with a few others, thus made a transition from their brief experience in Abu Dahdah's cell to their decisive participation in the configuration of the 3/11 terrorist network, especially in Madrid. A few months after the authorities dismantled al-Qaeda's Spanish cell, Maymouni and Chebli initiated and began to develop the jihadist mobilization that would create the 3/11 network. Chapter 7 will discuss Maymouni and Chebli and their activities; this chapter focuses on the actions of their three comrades: Fakhet, Berraj, and Zougam.

In addition to their contributions to the jihadist mobilization initiated by Maymouni and Chebli, these three men participated in the preparation and execution of the Madrid bombings. Fakhet was one of the seven 3/11 suspects who thwarted the Spanish police's attempt to arrest them by blowing themselves up in an apartment in the city of Leganés in Madrid's metropolitan area, on April 3, 2004. Berraj escaped Spain after the 3/11 attacks and evaded arrest. Zougam, for his part, was arrested and convicted as a material author of the attacks. Their cases, as well as those of Maymoni and Chebli, demonstrate above all the continuity between Abu Dahdah's cell—or, more precisely, its remnants following Operation Dátil—and the 3/11 network.

Serhane ben Abdelmajid Fakhet: "A person imbued in jihad"

On March 11, 2004, Serhane ben Abdelmajid Fakhet was thirty-five years old and was married. He committed suicide along with the other terrorists in the Leganés apartment on April 3, four days after authorities released an international warrant for his arrest.[1] Fakhet had first arrived in Spain in 1990, having received a scholarship from the Agencia Española de Cooperación Internacional (Spanish Agency for International Cooperation; AECI), the Spanish government's international aid organization, to complete a PhD in economics at the Universidad Autónoma de Madrid. In 1998, however, AECI denied Fakhet's request to further renew his scholarship. The loss of this scholarship perhaps contributed somehow to Fakhet's jihadist radicalization, but the real influence most likely came from the Centro Cultural Islámico (Islamic Cultural Center)— popularly known as the "M-30 Mosque" for its location near Madrid's M-30 motorway—where he had worked as an assistant accountant since 1994.

By the latter half of 1998, Fakhet had extensive jihadist connections. One particular connection was Ahmed Brahim, an important and well-off Algerian member of al-Qaeda who had a business trading sporting boats in Palma de Mallorca. Brahim also engaged in illicit activities alongside his commercial ties. The Guardia Civil (Civil Guard), Spain's other national security law enforcement agency alongside the CNP, arrested Brahim early in the day on April 14, 2002, in the Sant Joan Despí municipality near Barcelona, where he had moved the year before. He was accused of belonging to a terrorist organization. The sentence issued by the National Court stated that through his extensive ties with important al-Qaeda figures, Brahim intended to disseminate jihadist propaganda in French over the internet.[2] When authorities searched his home, they found twelve computers used for that purpose. Documents found on Brahim's computers contained phrases illustrative of the intended propaganda: "Islam imposes itself by force," "a Muslim cannot receive death for assassinating a non-Muslim," and "jihad guarantees paradise."[3]

One of the more notable al-Qaeda members whom Brahim knew was Mamdouh Mahmud Salim, also known as Abu Hajer al-Iraqi. In the late 1990s, Salim was one of the five members of the Majlis Shura, the al-Qaeda advisory council. He had helped establish al-Qaeda in 1988, and he spread religious edicts with his religious credentials, initiated funding programs, and sought ways of integrating modern technology into al-Qaeda's communications.[4] In May 1998, Brahim had met with Salim in Palma de Mallorca. Brahim used his company, Nora Yachting S.L., to facilitate Salim's travel along with two others, one of whom was close to Osama bin Laden's personal secretary.[5] Salim was detained in Germany in September 1998, and was extradited to the United States and prosecuted for his involvement in planning the attacks on the US embassies in Nairobi and Dar es Salaam earlier that year. At present, he is serving a life sentence in a maximum-security federal penitentiary in Colorado.

In those years, Brahim also kept closely in touch with prominent jihadist ideologues in the Arabian Peninsula, including Abdulmajid al-Zindani and Salman al-Ouda.[6] At the time of his connections with Brahim, Zindani was around seventy years old. Born in Yemen, Zindani had been Osama bin Laden's mentor in the 1980s when they were fighting alongside each other in Afghanistan. In 2009, the Spanish newspaper *ABC* interviewed Zindani in Yemen, where he resided and continued to draw important attention because of his political and religious roles in spite of his extremist views. When asked about Islam and about Osama bin Laden, Zindani said:

> Our obligation is to extend the word of the prophet to the rest of the world, and if necessary, give our life for Allah. For that reason, at times, assassination is a just cause. Regardless of the lies from the West, the master bin Laden is only putting these words into practice.[7]

Asked in that same interview about Spain, Zindani formulated the question in relation to Al-Andalus, situating it ideologically with Salafist-jihadist interpretations that echoed al-Qaeda's own ideology:

In the past, Al-Andalus was a fundamental piece of our history, and for that reason we should recover it, whatever the cost, from the infidels.[8]

Salman al-Ouda was the other key ideological figure with whom Brahim remained in contact. Born in Saudi Arabia in 1955, Ouda became one of the most important Islamist ideologues of the late twentieth century. He combined the traditional Salafist strain of Saudi Arabia, Wahhabism, with the political Islamism that originated in Egypt.[9] His aphorisms and writings attracted the youth of his home country because of his critical take on the Saudi regime, while situating the Islamist debate in a global context extending beyond the Arabian Peninsula. Saudi authorities detained him in 1994, and following his release in 1999, he continued his propaganda activities. The alignment of Ouda's ideas with the global jihadi struggle became explicit once Osama bin Laden returned to Afghanistan in 1996 and cited Ouda in his "Declaration of Jihad against the Americans That Occupy the Land of the Two Holy Places," alluding to Mecca and Medina.[10]

During their acquaintance, Serhane ben Abdelmajid Fakhet and Ahmed Brahim communicated primarily by telephone. In November 1998, for example, the latter called the former four times.[11] However, they also met in person in Madrid at the M-30 Mosque.[12] They appear to have forged strong personal relationships with one another, as demonstrated by the fact that Brahim's wife and daughter used to spend time in Fakhet's home in Madrid.[13] There is no concrete evidence to indicate how and why Fakhet became more connected with Abu Dahdah's cell, but fact is that by the spring of 2000, Fakhet was among Dahdah's associates. He attended the cell's meetings, and showed his support for the ideas expressed by both Abu Dahdah and Amer Azizi, the two most respected members of the group.[14]

Before joining Abu Dahdah's cell, Fakhet had immersed himself in a Tablighi Jamaat congregation based in Madrid.[15] Tablighi Jamaat is one of the largest missionary Muslim movements worldwide, whose purpose is to reinvigorate the Islamic identity of its followers by advocating the return to orthodox principles of the religion. This orthodoxy requires strict practice, even though it may seem alien when compared with the Western society where its members reside. The organization accommodates itself pragmatically to different contexts, but its adepts ultimately hope to install and expand Islamic dominion.[16] Various individuals implicated in terrorist activities in Western Europe, including members of the 3/11 network and those involved in the London Underground and bus bombings of July 7, 2005, have belonged to

Tablighi Jamaat.[17] This milieu, along with Fakhet's relationships with Brahim and other radicals, may have helped to radicalize him further.

By 2000, Fakhet followed strict Islamist principles, admonishing individuals of Maghrebi origins for listening to music (which is forbidden as sinful, according to rigorous Salafism) or for working in a café where alcoholic beverages were served. He openly justified burglary against non-Muslims and considered that a good Muslim would be "[he] that practices jihad."[18] Further, he shared photocopies of lectures by bin Laden, and before 9/11, he reproached the imam of the M-30 Mosque for not speaking of violent jihad in his prayers and sermons.[19] Throughout 2001, Fakhet attended numerous meetings held by Abu Dahdah's followers, including some in Fakhet's own home, where they watched videos on Chechnya, Palestine, and other conflicts involving Muslims.[20] In this manner, he developed ties with other members who recently had joined Abu Dahdah, including Mustafa Maymouni, Driss Chebli, and Said Berraj.

In November 2001, Operation Dátil abruptly suspended the late integration of these new Maghrebi members into Abu Dahdah's group. Fakhet avoided arrest, although he expected that he would be a suspect in the investigation. According to one of the three individuals he lived with at the time, some "months after the arrest of Abu Dahdah's group," Fakhet told them to stay calm, even at night, "[because] surely the police would come for him, because they had arrested a friend of his in Barcelona."[21] He was referencing the arrest of Najib Chaib Mohamed, who also had avoided arrest in November but whom the authorities finally apprehended on January 2, 2002, in Hospitalet de Llobregat, just outside of Barcelona.[22] The police did not go looking for Fakhet, but later court documents noted that "Serhane cut his hair, his beard, and significantly changed his physical appearance" in anticipation of his expected arrest.[23]

Shortly after the disassembly of Abu Dahdah's cell, and with a large portion of its members in prison, Fakhet distanced himself temporarily from other cell members at large. However, this did not imply that he had abandoned his extremist attitudes and behavior. By the end of 2001, he had established links with Rabei Osman Es Sayed Ahmed, also known as Mohamed al-Masri, an itinerant Egyptian jihadist recently arrived in Madrid. (Al-Masri's role in the network will be discussed in more detail in chapter 5.)[24] In March 2002, Fakhet began again visiting other individuals associated with Abu Dahdah, primarily Maymouni and Chebli. On May 29, 2002, the UCIE—which had received information about this activity—sought authorization to tap Fakhet's telephone. The wiretaps showed that between June and October 2002, Fakhet conversed with both Maymouni and Chebli, as well as Said Berraj and others, including Mohamed Afalah, Allekma Lamari, and Fouad el Morabit Amghar. (Allekema Lamari's incorporation into the 3/11 network is the focus of chapter 3. Mohamed Afalah's connections are detailed in chapter 4, and Morabit Amghar will receive further attention in chapter 5.) Through these individuals, he also communicated with Mohamed Larbi ben Sellam and Jamal Zougam, two men who were joining the local group that became the 3/11 network. Showing his situational awareness, Fakhet frequently changed his telephone number and used prepaid phone cards as a security measure, which made it difficult for the police to monitor his contacts.[25]

Fakhet's fellow Madrid cell members were particularly aware of his commitment to the cause of jihad. Despite their extensive ties and common backgrounds as coreligionists and members of the same jihadist cell, Mustafa Maymouni noted in his declarations to the Moroccan police in April 2004 that "Serhane was a person imbued in jihad."[26] In the summer of 2003, Fakhet was serving as the local head of the 3/11 network—he had come into this position by accident, for reasons that will be explained—and had been tasked with incorporating the final component of the operation, a band of common criminals who had been radicalized with similar Salafist-jihadist tenets. It was then that he told some of his close relations about the preparations for an attack in Madrid, and suggested that they should abandon the city because, as he put it, something "rather strong" was to occur.[27]

At the time, Fakhet was occupied with preparations for renting a rural property at Morata de Tajuña, in the municipality of Chinchón, south of Madrid, which would serve as the operational base for the 3/11 terrorists. Mustafa Maymouni had first used the rural property in March 2002, but he formalized the lease in October of that year, and then renewed it again in January 2004, taking advantage of Fakhet's employment at the real estate company Arconsa.[28] He designated Fakhet as the leaseholder, and Fakhet himself was located in the property in February 2004, the month prior to the attacks. During this time, Fakhet expressed an unusual interest in recovering money and settling debts.[29]

One particularly interesting fact about this property in Morata de Tajuña, the operational base for the Madrid train bombers, further illustrates the continuity between the Abu Dahdah cell and the 3/11 network. The rural property first used by Maymouni and then leased by Fakhet actually belonged to Mohamed Needl Acaid, who had been arrested in November 2001 during

Operation Dátil. Although he was in jail during the time that Maymouni, Fakhet, and the others were occupying the property, he had registered the property in his wife's name.[30] In 2005, the National Court convicted Acaid for belonging to Abu Dahdah's al-Qaeda cell.[31]

The investigations inside Fakhet's home after 3/11 revealed previously unknown vestiges of his jihadist militancy. For instance, one item the authorities found was a photocopy of a passport belonging to a Bulgarian by the name of Toni Radev Milenov.[32] Milenov had lived in Madrid in 2002 and had returned to Bulgaria by bus on March 3, 2004, eight days before the attacks. The Bulgarian authorities had investigated Milanov—who also was known as "Anas the Turk"—years before because of his propaganda activities among the Muslim population of Turkish origin in the country. Following a request by Spanish authorities, the Bulgarian police arrested Milanov on April 9, 2004. In his home in Sofia, police found two notebooks. One contained Spanish-language explanations for making bombs, complete with illustrations. The other described the El Atazar dam in the Lozoya valley north of Madrid, and showed how its hydraulic system worked. Milanov later admitted that Fakhet had given him the notebook that contained the instructions for making explosives.[33]

Said Berraj: A Terrorist Trained by Al-Qaeda in Afghanistan

Said Berraj was one of the individuals whom Fakhet encountered frequently at the meetings held by Abu Dahdah in 2001, before the cell was dismembered. During the arrests in November 2001, the Spanish authorities did not detain either Berraj or Fakhet, which allowed them to maintain their relationship throughout 2002 and 2003. In fact, they stayed in close contact until March 2004, as both incorporated themselves in the burgeoning 3/11 network in its initial stages. However, Berraj was no ordinary network member; he was one of the few members who had jihadist training, including specialized experience in the manufacture and use of explosives like those used on the commuter trains on March 11.

In the fall of 2000, Abu Dahdah had sent the newly recruited Berraj to an al-Qaeda training camp in Afghanistan. Berraj's itinerary included a stop in Istanbul, where authorities arrested and held him temporarily, along with three other Moroccans who were traveling to the same destination. One of the three Moroccans who were detained with Berraj was the already several times mentioned Amer Azizi, a prominent member of Abu Dahdah's cell as well. The other two were Salaheddin Benyaich (also known as Abu Mughen) and Lahcen Ikassrien. Ikassrien was traveling on a fake passport with the name of Mohamed Haddad, another Moroccan individual they all knew from their same social circles in Madrid. Ikassrien was captured about one year later by US forces in 2001 in Afghanistan, where another al-Qaeda detainee stated he was until then part of an artillery group commanded by Abd al Hadi al-Iraqi, a senior al-Qaeda member and leader of the Arab front lines. Ikassrien was sent to Guantánamo and subsequently transferred to Spain on July 2005.[34] (Ikassrien's more recent whereabouts are discussed in chapter 10). After the Turkish authorities released Berraj, who was carrying a visa to enter Iran, he completed his journey and reached Afghanistan. At the time, Afghanistan was still under Taliban rule, and the Taliban leadership allowed al-Qaeda and a number of related organizations to maintain indoctrination and terrorist training infrastructure. Berraj returned from Afghanistan in February 2001.

In December 2002, Spain's National Court requested an international letter rogatory from Turkey's judicial authorities to establish better evidence of Berraj's membership in Abu Dahdah's cell. This evidence was necessary, given the state of Spanish antiterrorist legislation and judicial knowledge of jihadist terrorism in Spain at the time. The Turkish documents confirmed that Berraj had been one of the individuals detained in Istanbul in 2000, a fact that would allow the Spanish government to detain him for questioning. Yet the Turkish documents, which were then considered necessary for further action in Spain, did not reach the National Court until almost a year after they had been solicited. They were sent by the Interpol offices in Ankara and the corresponding interior attaché, and arrived at the UCIE premises in Madrid on March 10, 2004—one day before the 3/11 attacks.[35] Berraj had abandoned his home in Madrid two days prior. At thirty-one years of age, he intended to participate in the Madrid bombings. Before he did so, he took his wife and daughter to the home of one of his wife's family members in Málaga, in southern Spain.

As early as 2002, Berraj had collaborated not only with Fakhet but also with Mustafa Maymouni and Driss Chebli, as well as with Mohamed Afalah, Larbi ben Sellam, and other individuals, such as Abdelmajid Bouchar (who will be discussed more extensively in chapter 4), who became part of the 3/11 network. Berraj, who had attended high school at the Spanish Institute in Tangier, had developed a keen interest in Spain's Islamic past during his radicalization process. Among his belongings, authorities found a photocopied textbook on the history of Al-Andalus.[36] Days before the Madrid train

28

bombings, he left his job, claiming that he had to attend his sister's funeral in Morocco. In truth, Berraj had no sister and never went to Morocco.

The CGI had wiretapped Berraj's phone since January 2004, and the tap was still active on the day of the Madrid attacks.[37] This wiretap was part of the UCIE's continued investigation into Abu Dahdah's cell and its members, and it reveals, once more, the continuity between the cell dismantled in November 2001 and those who carried out the attacks in March 2004. The surveillance on Berraj's phone also helped the authorities locate the apartment building in Leganés where some members of the network found refuge after the attacks.

Ten days after 3/11, a senior police officer investigating suspected members of Abu Dahdah's cell for the trial which was about to start noted that in a list of suspects' telephone numbers compiled by the UCIE, the last three digits of one of the listed numbers appeared to be related to the wiretapped phone used by Berraj; it varied by only twelve numbers. This finding signified that Berraj might have bought his phone in the same location as the wiretapped phone, and that the wiretapped phone might have been bought by a person connected with Berraj. A thorough analysis of the incoming and outgoing calls on Berraj's phone, combined with the tracing of a SIM card activated under the same base transceiver station in Morata de Tajuña as the SIM card found in one of the backpack bombs that did not detonate during the attacks, revealed that at the end of March 2004, Berraj had received a phone call from a manager of the rural property that Serhane ben Abdelmajid Fakhet had rented the month before. The manager had called from San Cristóbal de los Ángeles, a neighborhood in the southern outskirts of Madrid. During police questioning, the manager who had called Berraj stated that men of North African descent had rented an apartment in the Carmen Martín Gaite Street in Leganés, and he provided the police with the Foreigner Identification Number of the person who had rented the apartment. The police found that the number belonged to Mohamed Belhadj, another individual who was involved in the 3/11 network.[38] (Chapter 4 will discuss Mohamed Belhadj, and his connections to the 3/11 network, in greater detail.)

Early in the afternoon on April 3, Spanish authorities began to confirm the details of the Leganés hideout. They were about to locate the apartment that the 3/11 terrorists had rented. A few hours later, just as the police were about to raid the apartment, seven of the conspirators who had been hiding in the apartment caused an explosion that resulted in all their deaths. A police officer, a member of the Special Operations Group (Grupo Especial de Operaciones; GEO), was also killed in the explosion. He became fatality number 192 of the

3/11 network. Said Berraj, however, was not among those who committed suicide in the Leganés apartment. He managed to escape Spain, even though an international warrant for his arrest had been active since March 30, 2004.[39] (Chapter 13 will discuss how Berraj escaped, where he went, and what happened to him.)

Jamal Zougam: "Great friend and follower of Abu Dahdah"

When Said Berraj traveled to his native Tangier, he met frequently with Jamal Zougam, another Moroccan who also knew Abu Dahdah. Berraj and Zougam had been living in the same neighborhood in Tangier before immigrating to Spain, and they knew each other well. Zougam arrived in Spain in 1989. At the time of the 2004 attacks, he was thirty years old and married. He had a previous criminal record in Spain for assault, but he was also a business associate of a cell phone store in Madrid's Lavapiés neighborhood. He was arrested on March 13, 2004, and was tried and convicted for participating in the March 11 attacks, found guilty of belonging to a terrorist organization and carrying out terrorist killings.[40]

After the Madrid attacks, Zougam's brother defined him as a religious person; a coworker, going a bit further, noted that Zougam only went out "with other people that liked to talk about religion," whom he defined, moreover, as "strange people."[41] Zougam's radicalization may have begun in 1997, or even before that, when he started attending the same Tablighi Jamaat congregation as Serhane ben Abdelmajid Fakhet. In Zougam's case, though what drove him to Abu Dahdah's cell likely was his relationship, from a young age, with a jihadist with an extensive international background: Salaheddin Benyaich, already mentioned in this chapter, who went by the alias Abu Mughen. Zougam and Abu Mughen had regularly attended jihadist meetings in Madrid since 1998.[42]

Abu Mughen also was one of the three individuals who had traveled with Said Berraj to Afghanistan in 2000, and had been arrested and interrogated by the Turkish police. He moved to Spain after participating alongside some local jihadists in the conflicts in Chechnya and Bosnia, where he was gravely injured. In the Chechen conflict, which started in the early 1990s and extended throughout the northern Caucasus, the Russian army fought homegrown Islamist insurgents aligned with the global jihad movement. Jihadists from other countries, including Abu Mughen, often joined the ranks of the local insurgents. Members of Abu Dahdah's Madrid cell hosted

Abu Mughen because he needed surgery to treat the injuries he had received in Chechnya. By 1998, Jamal Zougam was participating in jihadist meetings with Abu Mughen in a Lavapiés oratory. Indeed, they sometimes met in Zougam's own home.[43]

In declarations that he made after he was arrested in Morocco in June 2003, Abu Mughen provided examples of the ideas that he might have used to radicalize Zougam. In his testimony to Moroccan authorities on August 8, 2003, he admitted that during his time in Spain, he kept close ties with Zougam, and that he went to the United Kingdom through Portugal, using a fake British passport, due to suspicions that security services were monitoring him.[44] On June 6, 2004, a National Court magistrate interviewed Abu Mughen in a Moroccan penitentiary. Abu Mughen expressed his hope that the community of believers would continue to fight together "underneath the flag of the Prophet," and after defining the objective of jihad, he introduced an allusion to Spain inherent to the Salafist-jihadist ideology: "make war against the infidelity of the entire world, including Al-Andalus, Palestine, and Iraq, and establish an Islamic regime."[45]

Already in 2000, French authorities, through an international letter rogatory, requested official registry information on Zougam's apartment and his cell phone shop in Madrid's Lavapiés quarter. After fulfilling this request in June 2001, and under recurrent pressure from the antiterrorism courts in Paris, the Spanish police found links between Jamal Zougam and Abu Dahdah. Among Zougam's belongings were notes about Abu Dahdah and other notable members of his cell (in particular, Amer Azizi), as well as abundant jihadist propaganda.[46] Nonetheless, in his declaration before the National Court magistrate who was preparing the court procedures for the 3/11 attacks, Zougam affirmed that he only knew Abu Dahdah "because he was a person who was in the neighborhood."[47]

In the summer of 2001, an interesting connection developed between Zougam's business in Lavapiés and two individuals who at the time were considered to be key members in Spain of the Moroccan Islamic Combatant Group (MICG).[48] These individuals, two brothers named Mohamed and Kamal Chatbi, were both residents of the small town of Autol in the La Rioja region of northern Spain. They contacted a Moroccan named Mohamed, who later hosted the brothers in his home in Madrid. This Mohamed was the user of the telephone number 696 627 355—a number associated with Jawal Mundo Telecom, a business on Tribulete Street in Lavapiés. Zougam ran this business with his half-brother, Mohamed Chaoui. (In November 2002, the

Moroccan authorities detained the Chatbi brothers, and by January 2003, the UCIE had requested and obtained authorization to wiretap two numbers related to Jawal Mundo Telecom.)[49]

In August 2001, Zougam traveled to Morocco. He remained in touch with Abu Dahdah until his return, which suggests that he made the trip on an order from the latter.[50] Returning to Madrid, Zougam told Abu Dahdah, among other things, that he had prayed at the mosque where the imam Mohamed Fizazi preached, and spoke of maintaining a relationship with him from that point forward.[51] At the time, Fizazi was considered the principal ideologue of Salafist-jihadism in Morocco, an ideology he disseminated from the pulpit in the Tchar Bendibane neighborhood in Tangier.[52] Fizazi had acquired his radical vision, substantially different from the Islamic traditions that are customary in Morocco, in Saudi Arabia. His opinions did not impede his initial return to Morocco to act as an imam, but when he spoke out against the Moroccan regime, calling it corrupt and promoting jihad, the Moroccan government reacted and arrested him in 2003.

The prosecuting attorneys of the National Court held no doubts that Zougam was a "great friend and follower of Abu Dahdah."[53] Likewise, the CGI's experts in international terrorism noted that Zougam's communications with Abu Dahdah revealed the two men's "extensive relationship and complicity."[54] Despite the items found in his home, his extensive ties with Abu Dahdah, and the UCIE experts' belief in his complicity with the cell's activities, Zougam managed to avoid arrest during Operation Dátil. After the disarticulation of the cell in November 2001, he kept in contact with other jihadists. Importantly, in early 2002, he connected Abu Mughen with another member of the cell, Mustafa Maymouni, a fact which shows that he had maintained ties with the latter.[55]

Throughout 2002, in the Villaverde district in Madrid, Zougam attended religious celebrations and meetings with individuals who shared his own commitment to Salafist-jihadism. He also attended similar meetings in 2003 in a hair salon in Lavapiés and other establishments in that area of Madrid. In this way, he stayed in contact with Mustafa Maymouni, Said Berraj, Driss Chebli, and Serhane ben Abdelmajid Fakhet.[56] Zougam became part of the 3/11 network and contributed decisively to the mobilization of resources for the operational nucleus. In addition, he was directly implicated in the actual execution of the Madrid attacks, a point that indicates the importance of Fakhet's visit to Zougam's business so that they could communicate face-to-face weeks before the bombings.[57]

The bombs used on the trains in Madrid were triggered by cell phone alarms, and materials recovered from undetonated bombs provided further evidence linking Zougam to the bombings. A prepaid phone card from Amena (a Spanish mobile network operator) with the telephone number 652 282 963 was found in an undetonated bomb in El Pozo train stop and was deactivated by the police. This prepaid card originated from Zougam's cell phone business. It belonged to a lot of thirty prepaid phone cards, a good portion of which were used to activate the bombs or were used as phone cards by those involved in the 3/11 attacks.[58] At the time of his arrest on March 13, Zougam had a mobile phone whose SIM card originated in the same lot as the ones used by the bombers. However, Zougam's phone number was not the one that the authorities had tapped, a further proof of the security measures he adopted in his communications. Like Fakhet, Zougam and the other bombers had used various cell phone numbers and multiple prepaid phone cards in a preemptive manner to prevent the police from effectively monitoring their communications.

In a hearing before the Spanish Parliament's investigative commission for the Madrid bombings on July 7, 2004, the then head of the UCIE explained the reason why, two days after the attacks, the Arabic and Islamic affairs services of his police force assumed control over the investigation:

> There is a determinant element, and that is when it is confirmed that one of the prepaid cards was sold in a cell phone shop in Lavapiés. That is when I realized that we were on the right track.[59]

Authorities detained Jamal Zougam at 4:40 p.m. on March 13, 2004, two hours after his connection with the phone cards was discovered.[60] Until his sentencing by the National Court in October 2007, Zougam was held in the Alicante II penitentiary. Between 2003 and 2006, he organized various incidents of "insubordination" in the prison, "gravely rendering unusable dependencies" and making "threats and attacks" toward prison employees.[61]

"Practically crystal clear" (*Blanco y en botella prácticamente*)

During the aforementioned parliamentary hearing, the head of the UCIE pointed out that the prepaid phone card was only one part of the Spanish authorities' information in the 3/11 investigation:

More than the card, it is the previous work over the years that we developed. Once we know the place, we automatically know roughly who could be implicated and, if they tell us that someone is named X, the other Y, and another Z, their proper names: it is practically crystal clear [*blanco y en botella prácticamente*].[62]

That translated the expression "practically crystal clear" alludes to the multiple deeds and connections that demonstrate the continuity between the Abu Dahdah cell and the 3/11 network—or rather, the continuity between the remnants of the cell that had been broken up in November 2001 and important members of the 3/11 network. More concretely, three of the cell members who had evaded arrest for one reason or another during Operation Dátil formed a critical part of the group of terrorists that carried out the Madrid train bombings: Fakhet, Berraj, and Zougam.

These connections implicate more than just these three individuals associated with Abu Dahdah before 9/11. They also involve two more associates of Abu Dahdah—Mustafa Maymouni and Driss Chebli—who would participate in the formation of the 3/11 network. To further emphasize the continuity between Abu Dahdah's associates and 3/11, it is important to reiterate a most relevant fact mentioned previously. The rural property at Morata de Tajuña in Chinchón, used as an operational base by the terrorists, belonged to another individual who had joined Abu Dahdah's cell in 1995, whom the Spanish authorities had arrested during Operation Dátil, and who was being held in prison during the Madrid attacks: Mohamed Needl Acaid.

With these details in mind, it is important to ask whether Abu Dahdah himself, in jail awaiting trial before the National Court, was aware of the preparations to plant bombs on the commuter trains on March 11, 2004. In this respect, the records show that Fakhet stayed in frequent contact with Abu Dahdah's wife and children while Abu Dahdah was in prison. There is also evidence that Walid Altarakji al-Masri, a close friend of Fakhet who also served as an intermediary in the leasing of the rural property at Morata de Tajuña and who had known Abu Dahdah at least since 1995, visited the cell's former leader regularly in the Soto del Real penitentiary north of Madrid. Between June 2003 and March 2004, al-Masri visited Abu Dahdah fourteen times. His last visit took place five days before the 3/11 attacks.[63]

3

"He swore that the Spanish would pay dearly for his detention": Allekema Lamari and Algerians in the 3/11 Network

Allekema Lamari was born in Algiers in July 1965. He was thirty-eight years old when he died alongside six other terrorists of the 3/11 network on April 3, 2004, when they committed suicide after the police surrounded their Leganés apartment. He had not been a member of Abu Dahdah's cell, but he had been connected indirectly with the group. He originally had belonged to the Armed Islamic Group, the Algerian jihadist organization that was formed in 1992 and would become affiliated with al-Qaeda.[1] Soon after its formation, the GIA expanded its presence throughout Western Europe. In 1996, it formed a cell in Valencia and the nearby town of Torrent, where Lamari operated, but Spain's National Police Corps dismantled this cell in April 1997 as part of a counterterrorism sweep called Operation Apreciate. It was the first jihadist cell ever dismantled in Spain, some four years before the dismantling of Abu Dahdah's cell.

Apart from Lamari (who on occasion used the nickname "Yassin"), the authorities arrested five other GIA cell members during Operation Apreciate, including the cell's two leaders, Abdelkrim Bensmail and Nouredinne Salim Abdoumalou. Some of the members had traveled to Spain from Algeria to create the cell; others were recruited from the immigrant Algerian population in Spain. In 2001, a National Court tribunal convicted the GIA cell members of belonging to an armed group, among other terrorist crimes.[2] The authorities detained a last Algerian member of the same cell in 2002 and sentenced him for the same crimes in 2003.[3] Together, the GIA cell in Valencia dedicated itself to recruitment, falsification of documents, and terrorist financing. They also trained in the use of firearms in a camp near Picassaent, also in the vicinity of Valencia. It is a very real possibility that the GIA cell members had considered attacking Spain either before or after returning to Algeria.[4]

At the time of his arrest, Lamari held a permit to live and work in Spain, but had no known occupation. The authorities wiretapped his phone between March and April of 1997.[5] Although Lamari received a fourteen-year prison sentence in 2001, he was unexpectedly and provisionally released in late June 2002 because of a legal technicality. According to Spanish law, he had spent the maximum allowed time in prison without having his Supreme Court appeal resolved. By the time that Lamari left prison, the Spanish authorities had acted against Abu Dahdah's cell. However, until their imprisonment, the GIA cell leaders Abdelkrim Bensmail and Nouredinne Salim Abdoumalou had had ties with Abu Dahdah.[6] Like Abu Dahdah, Abdoumalou in particular had links with important al-Qaeda leaders in Afghanistan and throughout Europe.[7] These existing ties between the al-Qaeda cell and the GIA cell in Spain allowed Lamari to make contact with Mustafa Maymouni, Driss Chebli, and Serhane ben Abdelmajid Fakhet—three key members of Abu Dahdah's cell who had eluded capture in November 2001.

By the fall of 2002, Lamari had well-established links with individuals of the burgeoning 3/11 network, such as Mohamed Afalah (whose connections to the network, as already indicated, will be discussed in more detail in chapter 4, focusing on the component from the Moroccan Islamic Combatant Group).[8] Evidence shows that as early as 2003, Lamari traveled between Valencia and Madrid.[9] Because of the relationships he had developed in prison before his release, it was not difficult for him to ingratiate himself among Algerian jihadists in Spain who were already operating through the Salafist Group for Preaching and Combat (Groupe Salafiste pour la Prédication et le Combat, GSPC). This organization, a successor of the GIA, had emerged in 1998 with Osama bin Laden's approval.[10] All those in Spain who previously had been affiliated with the GIA aligned themselves with the GSPC. In 2002, even though the Supreme Court judges had confirmed the sentence handed down by the National Court in 2001 and ordered Lamari to return to prison, he was able to use his connections to remain at large, join the 3/11 network, and thus continue his jihadist activities.

Lamari's ease in integrating himself into the 3/11 network was not merely a product of these interpersonal relations. The incipient terrorist network's efforts to achieve an operational capacity gave him the opportunity to take revenge against Spain and the Spaniards, a goal in which had been encouraged by imprisoned GIA cell leader Abdelkrim Bensmail. When Lamari left prison in 2001, he was picked up by a Syrian friend of his who was living in Valencia. This man, when questioned by the police four months after the Madrid train bombings, noted that Lamari had been fixated on avenging the dismantling of his GIA cell and the imprisonment of its leaders and the rest of its members.[11] On March 27, 2004, sixteen days after the 3/11 attacks, Lamari made a last call from Madrid to his Syrian friend. On this occasion, Lamari—who was aware of the fact that the police were searching for him—ended the conversation swearing that "they would not capture [him] alive," and told his friend that "they would see each other in heaven."[12] A week later, he died in Leganés in act of suicide terrorism.

"A violent action by him is imminent": Pre-3/11 Intelligence Documents on Lamari

To understand Lamari's personality and mindset, it is necessary to read document C/15697, written by the National Intelligence Center and dated November 6, 2003, about four months before the 3/11 bombings. This CNI document attributed worrisome behavior to Lamari and noted that trustworthy sources suggested that Lamari was preparing and intending to carry out terrorist acts in Spain soon. It also placed Lamari in Madrid, where by then the 3/11 network had formed. The document, translated into English from the Spanish original, reads as follows:

SUBJECT: ACTIVITIES OF ALLEKEMA LAMARI

According to a reliable source, whose reliability is considered moderately high, it is known that the Algerian citizen Allekema Lamari—detained in Valencia in April 1997 during Operation "Africa" [code-named Operation Apreciate by the National Police Corps] and accused of belonging to an armed group (GIA), and set free on June 29, 2002— made five (5) money transfers between October 17 and 20 [2003] of €150 each to the following individuals, all of whom are serving sentences in Spanish prisons for the crime of belonging to an armed gang:

Nourredine Salim Abdoumalou

Bachir Belhakem

Abdelkrim Bensmail

Mohamed Amine Akli

Soubi Khouni

The source claims that the fact that Allekema made transfers for these individuals and made it known to him suggests this could be a farewell message, because he [Allekema] intends to leave Spain or because a violent action by him is imminent. On the other hand, it is not considered normal that Allekema would give so much money as a favor to prisoners, given his precarious economic situation.

The money transfers were deposited in a post office near the Plaza de Colón or Plaza de Alonso Martínez, or more precisely on Génova Street in Madrid.

This source happens to be the same one who communicated to us in the middle of September [2003] that some Algerian elements intended to attack Spain, perhaps by causing a forest fire over a profitable target of great dimensions (an option apparently discarded for various reasons) or an action against some building using a vehicle driven by a "martyr." In this case, the source pointed out Allekema Lamari as one of the organizers and possible executor of these actions.

To emphasize the importance of finding Allekema, it is known that sometime in the middle of October, he made two telephone calls, one from the number 913 378 8124 (corresponding to the mobile phone shop "Multicom Net" located on Capitán Blanco Argibay Street, 47, Madrid) and another from the number 914 708 731 (corresponding to the bar located on the Estébanez Calderón Street, 7, Madrid). Further, since his release from the Alama (Pontevedra) prison in June 2002, he seems to have established his residence in the Tudela area (Navarre).

This information is communicated because of the danger posed by Allekema's attitudes and activities.

Date written: 11/06/2003[13]

On December 17, 2003, about a month after this CNI document was prepared, the Directorate General of Police electronic data bank had registered a request from the French authorities that urged that Lamari be referred for "specific control."[14] This request came following investigations in France concerning Lamari's relationship with terrorist groups and organizations whose members had moved to France, showing the relevance of his activities outside of Spain. The end date for this request was the middle of December 2004—but nine months before that date would expire, the Madrid bombings would have occurred, and Lamari would have been one of its executors.

Another CNI document, C/5301, dated March 15, 2004—just four days after the Madrid attacks—notes that Spanish intelligence knew beforehand that Lamari intended to seek revenge against Spain, following his release from prison, for his arrest and that of other members of his GIA cell. The document notes that Lamari had spoken about committing acts of terror and that he had the technical capacity to do so. It also emphasizes that Lamari had considerable knowledge of both Alcalá de Henares and Madrid, the two locations connected by the trains targeted by the 3/11 network. The document reads as follows:

SUBJECT: TERRORIST ACTIVITY INDICATORS

The principal line of investigation of our service indicates that the 3/11 attacks are attributable to a local group of people, with a rudimentary organization, that respond to the ideological orientation of *International Jihad*, radicalized in countries near Spain, consisting mainly of North Africans.

Along this line, one of the names cited as a possible planner and/or executor of the attacks of 3/11 in Madrid is Allekema Lamari @ (i.e., also known as) "Yacine" or "Yassine," (D.O.B. 07/10/1965). This individual was arrested in Spain in 1997 and was jailed for belonging to the Algerian GIA. He spent six years in prison (two in Alcalá-Meco) and was released in June 2002. Currently, a search-and-capture warrant is out for him so he can fulfill his sentence of more than 14 years for terrorist activity.

He may be able to use a Spanish passport, real but with a substitute photograph, with the name of Khaled Ali Ghadban Alhassan, D.O.B. 03/25/1962. He generally employs different names depending on the city (Mohamed in Madrid, Yacine/Yassine in Valencia).

It is known that one of Lamari's associates is known as Abdulnabi Chdadi, brother of the imprisoned Saif Chdadi, who might be associated with one of those detained this past Saturday in relation to the attacks in Madrid. This operative line is being investigated by this center.

Lamari was released from prison in June 2002 and, according to our sources, he swore that the Spanish would pay dearly for his detention. Indeed, he declared that he would commit some act with "explosives or derailing." Allekema knows very well the Spanish cities of Valencia, Tudela, Madrid, and Alcalá de Henares. He adopts extreme security measures with his contacts, he does not use cell phones, and he periodically makes money transfers to imprisoned members of his network. He financed himself with armed burglaries. Right now, he is under search and capture, as he has finally been convicted for his activities in 1997.

It is considered that Lamari has sufficient leadership, degree of fanaticism, motivation, and technical capacity to prepare, in all of its details, attacks like those that occurred on 3/11. (On him and his intensions, as well as his photograph, an informative was remitted to the Secretary of Security for the State and the Commissariat General of Information of the CNP on 11/06/2003.)

The information that indicates Allekema Lamari's participation comes from internal human sources, of medium-high confidence, from within and from outside of Spain, and are being intensely investigated by our service. Right now, this constitutes one of the principal lines of investigation.

As consequence of the previous, it is estimated that, in the short term, it is likely the execution of [further] indiscriminate attacks in places with large concentrations of people. As the most likely place, the sources have cited the city of Valencia, coinciding with the celebration of *Falles* [a traditional celebration in honor of Saint Joseph, held in Valencia in mid-March] 2004.

As such, the location and detention of Allekema Lamari are considered of maximum priority and urgency.

Date written: 03/15/2004[15]

This book does not corroborate the conjectures formulated by the CNI in this document written four days after 3/11, whether in attributing the attack to a group of domestically based North Africans organized along rudimentary lines and only inspired by international jihad or in identifying the individual (namely, Allekema Lamari) considered most relevant in planning the attack. The second half of this book, however, will show how the local cell that became a large portion of the 3/11 network benefited from important international leadership, organizational, and strategic connections. Indeed, the man who initially took the decision to attack Spain was living well outside Spanish borders at the time.

Lamari's Resentment toward Spain

Another CNI document, C/9997, dated May 18, 2004, two months after the 3/11 attacks, connected Lamari with Moroccan jihadists who were living in Spain and plotting an attack on Spanish territory. Among these associated Moroccans were the aforementioned Abu Mughen, a close associate of Abu Dahdah's cell and Jamal Zougam in particular. This document also indicated how Driss Chebli, who had evaded arrest in November 2001, had sought out Lamari in September 2002 to integrate him into the 3/11 network—showing a mobilization from the top down rather than from the bottom up. It demonstrates also the intense animosity that Lamari felt toward Spain.

SUBJECT: TERRORIST ATTACKS IN MADRID. ALLEKEMA LAMARI

1. Summary

As a continuation of the note C/15697/06.1.2003, the CNI considers that the Algerian individual Allekema Lamari, 39 years old and with a profession of technical architect, could be one of those responsible for the planning of the March 11 attacks in Madrid. It is suspected that he could be the seventh individual who committed suicide in the explosion that occurred on April 3 in a flat in Leganés.

2. Analysis

In 1996 and 1997, a group of fanatic Arabic Islamists formed in Valencia. Among its members were Salaheddin Benyaich @ Abu Mughen; Allekema Lamari @ Mohamed @ Abdesalam; Saad Hussaine @ The Chemist; and Driss al-Atialah.

This group emerged with the goal of "awakening" the Islamist sentiment in Morocco, and its medium-term objective was to prepare attacks

41

from Spain that it would execute in Morocco, in particular in Casablanca and Fez. For that, Salaheddin Benyaich, as the most relevant member of the group, established first in Valencia and later in Madrid his logistic bases to travel to Afghanistan, London, Bosnia, and Turkey. He also traveled to Morocco for the purpose of recruiting youths to take to training camps in Afghanistan. For that reason, he was the person directing the formation, indoctrination, and training of the members of [the] group.

In 1996, while Abu Mughen lived with Allekema Lamari in Valencia, there was a failed plot in Morocco. This act, along with Saad Hussaine's detention for possessing false documents and his subsequent exit from Spain, as well as the detention in April 1997 of a group of Muslims belonging to the "Armed Islamic Group" (GIA), to which Allekema Lamari belonged, led to this group ceasing its activities on Spanish territory.

Allekema Lamari was convicted in [June] 2001 [and sentenced] to 14 years of prison, but after having completed 6 years since his detention and pending an appeal, he left the prison in A Lama (Pontevedra) in June 2002. During his release, he was housed by Abdelkrim Beghdali in [the latter's] home in Tavernes de la Valldigna (Valencia).

In September of that year, two Moroccan residents of Madrid, Abdulghani Chedadi and Driss Chebli, went searching for Lamari in Valencia with the intention of having him move to Madrid and form part of a radical Islamist group composed mainly of Moroccans, which included, besides those mentioned, Mohamed Afalah, Abdelmajid Bouchar, and Mohamed Bouharrat.

After his release from prison, Allekema Lamari, already stern and religious, presented a more fanatical profile. He showed himself solitary, cautious, ideologically uncontrollable, and dangerous. In his activities, he strengthened his security measures and ceased using cell phones to communicate. The radicalization of his character and his life clandestinely came about from his conviction that he was part of a trap by the National Police Corps that led to his detention in Picassent in 1997 during Operation "Africa."

This radicalization and resentment toward Spain have created, since his release, his sole objective, as he made clear to his closest associates, to carry out domestic acts of terrorism of various dimensions, with the purpose of causing the highest number of victims possible. He also commented on the possibility of making good on his threat to carry out a derailment of trains or provoke a great fire.

His strong volition and determination in this sense were confirmed once it was known that Allekema Lamari had had the opportunity to abandon Spain five months ago, using fraudulent documents, an opportunity he turned down, claiming that his existence had only one objective, and that he would not cease in his desire and that he would never return to prison.

From the data available concerning the movements and activities of this individual, it is known that he had no paying job. He obtained money from robberies and muggings of individuals in the drug world, where he was assured that he would not be accused. He made various money transfers to five imprisoned Algerians, detained with him in 1997 (Bachir Belhakem, Soubi Khouni, Nourredine Salim Abdoumalou, Mohamed Amine Akli, and Abdeklarim Benesmail). These transfers were interpreted by people among his associates as a farewell message.

After the explosion in the apartment in Leganés on April 3, 2004, various objects found there pegged Mohamed Afalah, Abdelmajid Bouchar, and Mohamed Bouharrat as part of the group that committed the March 11 attacks in Madrid.

There were also two videotapes found, recorded probably on March 27, where three people appeared. The person sitting in the middle recited a lecture of a Quranic verse following the threat to commit [further] acts of terrorism in Spain conditioned on the withdrawal of Spanish forces from Iraq and Afghanistan before April 4.

Due to the height, width, tone of voice, expressions, and emphasis used by the lecture in the [video], the person sitting in the middle of the image of the video has been identified, with high probability, as Allekema Lamari.

3. Conclusions

It is considered of great interest to identify the seventh suicide in Leganés and rule out the possibility that it could be Allekema Lamari, given that sufficient existing indicators suggest that possibility. If this is not the case, it is certain that Allekema Lamari possesses the volition, determination, and coldness, excusing himself with religious motivations, to continue with his particular revenge against the Spanish population and its interests by executing [further] terrorist acts.

Date written: 05/18/2004[16]

Surprisingly, none of these CNI documents mentions that Lamari lived with individuals linked to the GSPC in the town of Gandia, in Valencia, sometime between November 2002 and May 2003. The GSPC cell that hosted Lamari reconstituted itself in Spain in 2002 after a previous cell was dismantled by the CNP in September 2001.[17] A police informant who entered this cell later provided information, as a protected witness, concerning Lamari's whereabouts and other noteworthy revelations about the articulation of jihadi terrorism in Spain, especially concerning Algerians, as well as about the 3/11 plot.[18]

"Fewer enemies of Allah and more victors of Paradise"

Lamari was not the only Algerian jihadist in the 3/11 network. Daoud Ouhnane, born on February 4, 1970, in Mohammadia, also joined the group through other individuals who also gathered in Lavapiés. After the suicide explosion in Leganés on April 3, 2004, Ouhnane rapidly fled Spain. Nonetheless, in the flat where Lamari and six others immolated themselves, the authorities found fingerprints belonging to another Algerian, one whom the State Security Forces and Corps (Fuerzas y Cuerpos de Seguridad del Estado, FCSE) and the CNI considered to be an important member of the GSPC cell in Spain. In addition to maintaining contact with the head of the Valencia GIA cell to which Lamari had belonged that had been dismantled in 1997, Abu Dahdah had maintained links with an individual who acted as intermediary between the GSPC cell established in Spain and the organization's base in Algeria.[19]

In relation to the attacks in Madrid, the above-mentioned police informant heard important members of this Spanish GSPC cell proclaim that "any strike against the Christians was a victory, no matter the manner or the casualties sustained, because every time that this occurred there were fewer enemies of Allah and more victors of Paradise."[20] About four months after the 3/11 attacks, one of the GSPC cell leaders told the informant that among those implicated was "a Mokthar, of Algerian nationality, who was an expert in computers," and that after the attacks, "he hid in Pamplona, fleeing afterward to Italy."[21] This Mokthar, according to what the GSPC leader told the informant in July 2004, "had been traveling to Madrid for six months to study the places where there were the most people and which would cause the most victims with an attack."[22] Mokthar—which could have been his real name or a nickname—was also known among his coreligionists as Abu Hafj. The GSPC cell leader also affirmed in front of the witness that "those who were really responsible" for the 3/11 attacks "had been trained in Afghanistan and Pakistan" and that "they were safe."[23] In accordance with all of the information that the witness provided to his contacts in the CGI, the more notable members of this GSPC cell "swore that they would commit further attacks in Spain."[24] Shortly after, in October and November of 2004, the CGI's Operation Nova was able to prevent a suicide terrorist attack in Madrid, this time against the National Court.[25] Among those implicated and convicted for this attempt were individuals associated with this GSPC cell.

Abderrahmane Tahiri, known as Mohamed Achraf, acted as the operating agent for the imprisoned author of the planned GSPC plot against the National Court. Mohamed Achraf had a criminal record in Spain, having spent time in prison for counterfeiting money and documents and for armed robbery. Held in various jails between 1999 and 2002, he helped radicalize numerous individuals in prison, mostly petty criminals of North African descent. After serving his sentence, he moved to Switzerland, where he sought refuge as a stateless person. In June 2004, he returned to Spain to carry out the planned National Court attacks in Madrid. He led a cell composed mainly of former convicts, some who had been Salafist-jihadist adepts before their stint in prison and others who had been socialized in this ideology of violence during their incarceration.

Mohamed Achraf laid out his terror intentions in a letter written in March 2001, which he sent to Saif Afif, a coreligionist who would be convicted in Spain in 2008 in the same criminal proceedings in which Achraf himself was convicted. In that letter, Achraf outlined his intentions as well as those of acolytes—including the message's recipient, with whom he hoped he could reunite once they were released from prison:

> I announce some good news. I have formed a group, which includes all the brothers that I spoke to you about. They are like my brothers and I know them well; they are preparing to die in the name of Allah at whatever [moment]. Just wait until they leave [prison], if Allah wants, so that work can begin, and you, if Allah wants, will be with us, inside of our group. This is our duty: think, plan, prepare because after our exit, if Allah wants, we will begin work immediately. We just need to execute [it]. We ask Allah [for] success.[26]

4

The Moroccan Islamic Combatant Group and Its Involvement in the 3/11 Network

In addition to the individuals who previously were linked directly or indirectly with Abu Dahdah's cell, the growing 3/11 network incorporated elements of the Moroccan Islamic Combatant Group (MICG), another jihadist terrorist organization affiliated with al-Qaeda. Youssef Belhadj, a Moroccan who was twenty-seven years old when the Madrid bombings were carried out, served as the linking node of this component. He was arrested in Belgium in February 2005, and following the bombing trials the National Court in Spain sentenced him to twelve years in prison for belonging to a terrorist organization.[1] Another MICG member, Hassan el Haski (also known as Abu Hamza), who was born in Guelmim in southwestern Morocco on August 5, 1963, received fifteen years in prison for the same crime. Haski received the stronger sentence because he had acted as the MICG's effective leader in connection with the 3/11 attacks.[2]

With the approval of Youssef Belhadj, other Moroccans residing in Madrid—namely Mohamed Afalah, Mohamed Belhadj, and Abdelmajid Bouchar—joined the 3/11 network. These last three fled Spain after seven of their comrades committed suicide in Leganés. However, of the three of them, only Mohamed Afalah was able to avoid arrest. The Syrian authorities arrested Mohamed Belhadj and later extradited him to his home country of Morocco, where he was sentenced to eight years in prison for his involvement in the Madrid bombings.[3] Serbian security forces detained Abdelmajid Bouchar and delivered him to Spain, where he was sentenced to eighteen years in prison for belonging to a terrorist organization and for the possession of explosives.[4] Before turning to the features and vicissitudes of those who formed the MICG component of the 3/11 network, it is necessary to briefly explain the origins and evolution of this North African jihadist entity.

The MICG, Tarek ben Ziyad, and al-Qaeda

The MICG emerged at the end of the 1990s around a group of Moroccans who had fought against the Soviets in Afghanistan, alongside other Islamist fighters such as Osama bin Laden.[5] In early 2000, the leaders of the incipient organization, Mohamed Guerbouzi and Noureddine Nafia, met in London with the influential Salafi cleric Abu Qatada to get his opinion on the possible legitimacy of the MICG. Abu Qatada—already mentioned in chapter 1—granted his approval for their venture, and stressed the importance of good infrastructure and vision, adding that it was permissible to carry out attacks against Morocco.[6] Before the MICG's consolidation as a separate organization, many Moroccans had joined the Libyan Islamic Fighting Group (LIFG), another North African jihadist organization that had a greater presence in Afghanistan.[7] The LIFG had installations on Afghan soil designed to receive and train terrorist candidates from countries in the Maghreb or from the diasporas of Maghrebi origin in Western Europe. A number of individuals born in Morocco thus became LIFG members. Once the MICG formed, the heads of both organizations agreed that Moroccans who belonged to the LIFG could join the MICG and to coordinate their activities.[8]

As the MICG grew in size and developed the necessary internal organization, its leaders sought to collaborate with al-Qaeda in the so-called World Islamic Front for Jihad against Jews and Crusaders, the terrorist alliance managed and formally started by Osama bin Laden and Ayman al-Zawahiri in February 1998.[9] In July 2000, Noureddine Nafia, the then-leader of the MICG, met with al-Zawahiri in Afghanistan. Following this meeting, with the consent of the Taliban and the assistance of al-Qaeda trainers, the MICG established a reception center in Jalalabad and a training camp named Tarek ben Ziyad, after the eighth-century Muslim commander who conquered most of the Iberian Peninsula and established Islamic rule over Al-Andalus.[10] Ziyad's victory over the mainly Visigothic population of the Iberian Peninsula, at the head of an army of several thousand recently converted North African Berbers and a significant contingent of Arabs, had secured Islamic control of Al-Andalus for nearly 800 years. The significance of naming the camp after Tarek ben Ziyad, with his connections to Al-Andalus, emphasizes the strength of both images as common references for jihadi terrorists from the Maghreb.[11] Notably, the 3/11 terrorists included references to both Ziyad and Al-Andalus in a video recorded on March 27, 2004—two weeks after the bombings—which was recovered from the rubble of the destroyed apartment in Leganés. In the recording, the group referred to itself as "the brigade found in Al-Andalus" and warned that "[they] will continue [their] jihad until [achieving] martyrdom in the land of Tarek ben Ziyad."[12]

According to Noureddine Nafia's 2004 testimony, the MICG used its training camp in Jalabalad for religious indoctrination, falsification of documents, and training in the use of remotely detonated explosives, especially using cellphones in coordinated bombings.[13] MICG members in Afghanistan also attended al-Qaeda training camps such as Al-Faruq or the LIFG's Martyr Abu Yahya camp, where they learned how to use weapons and manufacture bombs.[14]

Although Zawahiri supported the MICG, the group's leaders waited until August 2001 to meet Osama bin Laden in Kandahar. During their reunion, assisted by Zawahiri, bin Laden insisted that Morocco become a base of the global jihad. Afterward, bin Laden gave permission for the MICG to use al-Qaeda–affiliated camps in Afghanistan and instructed that they meet with Mohamed Atef (also known as Abu Hafs al-Masri), who at the time was al-Qaeda's military chief.[15]

Attack against (the House of) Spain in Casablanca

MICG, along with the other al-Qaeda–affiliated organizations, lost its base of operations in Afghanistan following the US invasion in October 2001. Like all groups based in Afghanistan, MICG was forced to relocate and alter its strategy in the aftermath of the military intervention. For the MICG, this shift entailed focusing on Morocco as a target for the global jihad, following Osama bin Laden's instructions from August 2001. Within this new context, the MICG immersed itself in the environments from which its members and collaborators had originated. This decision had major implications for both Morocco and Spain. In Morocco, the MICG's new focus and location led directly to the May 16, 2003, attacks in Casablanca, in which fourteen terrorists carried out five simultaneous suicide attacks against five locations in the city, killing almost fifty people and injuring more than a hundred.

Until the 2003 attacks, Morocco had been affected only rarely by jihadist terrorism, despite its shared border with Algeria, a country that had long suffered from the violence committed first by the Armed Islamic Group and later by the Salafist Group for Preaching and Combat. Even nearby Tunisia had experienced jihadist terrorism: on April 11, 2002, the El Ghriba synagogue on the island of Djerba was attacked by an al-Qaeda suicide bomber who detonated a natural-gas tanker trunk that had been fitted with explosives. Although it was no secret that many Moroccans had moved to Afghanistan in the 1980s and had been trained in guerrilla combat techniques there, the general Moroccan population remained convinced that their country's political and social order inhibited opposition in the form of terrorism.[16] This, however, is not to say that Morocco had evaded terrorism entirely in its history. One earlier terrorist attack in particular is important from a Spanish perspective, even though it took place nine years before the 2003 Casablanca attacks.[17] On August 24, 1994, three French youths of Moroccan descent burst into the upscale Atlas Asni hotel in Marrakesh. They opened fire with automatic weapons, shooting indiscriminately at the tourists in the hotel, and killed two Spanish visitors. The youths, who were from Paris, had been radicalized by a Moroccan expatriate who had spent time in Afghanistan.[18] Likewise, elements of the 2002 Djerba attack were related to Spain. The Djerba bombing had left twenty-one dead, mostly German tourists visiting the synagogue. Khalid Sheikh Mohammed, the mastermind of 9/11, had organized the attack with the help of a German convert who was close to Osama bin Laden. Funding for the Ghriba synagogue suicide bomber's fuel tanker, which had been filled with 5,000 liters of liquid natural gas, came from a Pakistani resident living in Logroño, Spain. The National Court later prosecuted and convicted the funder for his role in the Djerba attack.[19] This connection provides further evidence of the established presence of individuals related to the global jihad in Spain before 3/11.[20]

The Casablanca attacks also showed that Spain was a literal and figurative objective of jihadist violence. One of the main targets chosen by the planners of attacks evoked Spain, as they chose the Casa de España (House of Spain) restaurant, which was a part of Casablanca's Centro Cultural Español (Spanish Cultural Center).[21] Most of those who were killed in the attacks in the restaurant and the other targeted locations were Moroccan, but four of the victims were Spanish. It is possible that the decision to target the Casa de España stemmed from the Moroccan Salafists' view of the restaurant and its uses as sinful, or the fact that the women who visited the restaurant dressed in Western fashion, contrary to the strict requirements of radical Islamist groups such as Takfir wal

Hijra.[22] It seems reasonable to interpret this act of terrorism as an act of particular significance, perhaps as both an attack on Spain and an omen of 3/11.

Following the attacks in Casablanca, Spain's National Court opened a judicial proceeding that later proved essential in reconstructing how the 3/11 network developed throughout 2002, under the leadership of Mustafa Maymouni.[23] This court documentation provides information on why the node of the MICG component introduced into the 3/11 network was based in Brussels, owing to the MICG's loss of infrastructure in Afghanistan and later to the Moroccan's government strong response to the Casablanca attacks. Police investigations within and outside Morocco revealed the role that the Brussels-based MICG had played in planning and executing the Casablanca attacks. Because most MICG members resided outside of Morocco, they had to recruit individuals who were living in Morocco at the time. The individuals recruited came from an extremist group called Assirat al Moustakin (Straight Path),[24] an entity that belonged to the heterogeneous Salafist-jihadist community in Morocco. This community took the MICG as its model.[25] The group had been recruited by Abdelatif Mourafik, also known as Malek al-Andalusi (who is discussed extensively in chapters 9 and 10), and it had dozens of individuals available for carrying out the attacks in and around Casablanca.

In the months following the May 16, 2003, bombings in Casablanca, the Moroccan police carried out a major internal sweep that resulted in an extraordinary number of arrests. They arrested many individuals who were directly or indirectly related to the attacks, as well as many others who were not connected to the attacks but whom the authorities believed were involved in jihadist groups and organizations. Further, the Moroccan authorities sent arrest warrants and extradition requests for various MICG leaders and members who were known to reside in Western European countries, and who in some cases had even acquired citizenship. These arrests further weakened the MICG, which was still recovering from the relatively recent loss of its bases in Afghanistan. In a report dated January 2004—less than six weeks before the Madrid bombings—Europol, the European Union law enforcement agency, stated that "the Moroccan Islamic Combatant Group (MICG) is weakened in the interior of Morocco, but still maintains logistic and financial cells within Europe."[26] At the time, MICG structures remained confined to Belgium and France, though it also had members in other countries such as the United Kingdom and Spain. The MICG introduced itself into the 3/11 network from its Belgian cell with support from its French counterparts. It is no coincidence that the Belgian authorities dismantled the MICG cell there on March 19,

2004, eight days after the attacks in Madrid. Just two weeks later, immediately after the suicide bombing in Leganés, a French counterterrorist operation broke up the MICG cells in France on April 4 and 5.

Was the Date for the Madrid Bombings Set in Molenbeek?

Youssef Belhadj, the MICG node in the 3/11 network, belonged to the Belgian MICG cell. In March 2004, at the time of the Madrid bombings, his compatriot Hassan el Haski was serving as one of the MICG's principal leaders in Europe, where it had remained active despite the organization's substantial losses in Morocco. Between 2003 and 2004, Haski had been involved in a dispute with Abelkader Hakimi over the leadership of the MICG in Europe, trying to determine who would succeed Nafia, who at the time was in prison in Morocco. This dispute notwithstanding, Haski and Hakimi were close associates. When the Belgian police acted decisively against the MICG cell in Belgium, in Hakimi's home they found a passport that belonged to Haski and had been issued in Las Palmas de Gran Canaria in 2002.[27]

Haski had lived in Damascus, and had spent time in Afghanistan and in Lanzarote in the Canary Islands in 2002 before settling in Belgium. He returned to the Canaries to hide during the aftermath of 3/11 and the ensuing reaction against the MICG in Belgium and France. He had to do so in a hurry after French security forces detained his coreligionists in Mantes-la-Jolie in the Parisian suburbs.[28] Surprisingly, given his police record, Haski received Spanish residency on October 3, 2004.[29] The Spanish authorities located him in Lanzarote and captured him, along with three other supposed MICG members, on December 17, 2004. Owing to declarations made by those who had been detained in April of that year, it had become known that Haski was well aware of the plans to attack Madrid, that he personally knew at least one of the terrorists who had carried out the attacks, and that he had gone into hiding in the days before and after the bombings.[30]

A member of the French MICG cell explained to the police and judicial entities in France how Haski had hid in the days before 3/11:

> He was nervous and wanted a place to hide. It was then that he decided to rent an apartment to hide in. He thought—or, rather, I want to say, he knew that something was going to occur in the coming days, and was very nervous and alert. He paid special attention so that they wouldn't

locate him. After the attacks, when journalists said that [the perpetrators of the Madrid bombings] were Islamists, I immediately understood that my organization [MICG] was responsible, and that Hassan had had advance knowledge of what they were going to do.[31]

The same individual also spoke about the conversations he had with Haski before and after the Madrid attacks, saying that "if, before the attacks, he was extremely nervous, then he calmed down after they occurred."[32] He added that "he [Haski] told me that he knew Jamal Zougam," connecting Haski with one of the 3/11 network members directly involved in the train bombings. Haski also told another MICG contact that he was "proud" of what had happened in Madrid.[33]

For his part, Youssef Belhadj, the MICG node in the 3/11 network, was caught in the Belgian operation that unraveled his organization. The Belgian authorities initially let him go free, even though he had been implicated in terrorist activity. They detained him again on February 1, 2005, once they had acquired sufficient evidence linking him to 3/11. They could prove that in the two years prior to the attack, Belhadj had traveled from Belgium to Madrid to meet with associates in the local MICG cell.[34] His last trip to Madrid had occurred in February 2004, and he had stayed there until March 3. On that day, he had taken flight TV 861 from Madrid to Brussels.[35] After the Belgian police detained him for the second and last time in his dormitory in Molenbeek-Saint-Jean, a municipality close to Brussels, they found two cell phones. The one he used regularly operated with a prepaid card with the number 0485731886. This card had been purchased, with false identification, on October 19, 2003. The date that Youssef Belhadj had provided for his birthday was March 11, a date unrelated to him or any of his relations.[36] This is the first known occasion where an individual related to the 3/11 network left a written record of when they intended to attack. In addition to the false date, Youssef Belhadj gave 1921 as his year of birth, which likely was a subtle reference to the following text from Quran surah 21, verses 39 and 40:

> If those who disbelieved but knew the time when they will not avert the Fire from their faces or from their backs and they will not be aided. Rather, it will come to them unexpectedly and bewilder them, and they will not be able to repel it, nor will they be reprieved.[37]

This critical piece of information indicates that the March 11 date was recorded in writing in Molenbeek as early as October 19, 2003. It is the first of various documents linked to members of the 3/11 network that mention beforehand the date of the planned attacks. However, it does not necessarily mean that the exact date of the bombings was decided in that municipality close to Brussels. Some other person may have transmitted the information to Youssef Belhadj, perhaps because of his membership and position relative to the 3/11 terrorist cell. Nonetheless, Molenbeek is the first known place where the date of the bombings was documented in advance.

Surreptitiously recording the date of an attack is a common practice for terrorists of various ideologies. This was the case of Timothy McVeigh, the leader of an antigovernment white supremacist group in the United States, who detonated a truck bomb outside the Alfred P. Murrah Federal Building in Oklahoma on April 19, 1995. The attack, the largest act of domestic terrorism in the United States at the time, left 168 dead and around 500 wounded. Months before, as a security measure, McVeigh had obtained a fake driver's license. Apart from giving a fake name on it, he claimed that his birthdate was April 19, as a signal of his intent.[38]

Two other facts demonstrate the relevance of Molenbeek-related documents from October 19, 2003, that are connected with the Madrid bombing: a statement by Osama bin Laden, and the information from the second telephone belonging to Youssef Belhadj. In a message sent to Al-Jazeera on October 18, 2003, bin Laden mentioned Spain as a country deserving of reprisal.[39] It is plausible that this message was an anticipated signal for Belhadj and other senior members of the 3/11 network. It has additional importance in light of the fact that Belhadj supposedly maintained links with both al-Qaeda and the MICG.[40] With regard to Youssef Belhadj's second cell phone—purchased shortly afterward—he once again provided false date-of-birth information for the prepaid card. This time, he claimed that his birthdate was May 16.[41] This was the date on which the Casablanca attacks had been carried out earlier that same year. It is practically impossible to claim that this choice of dates was a mere coincidence, given the established role that the MICG had played in the Casablanca attacks and its active participation in the 3/11 network.

"Although he did not work, he handled money": Other Moroccans in the 3/11 Network

Besides Hassan el Haski and Youssef Belhadj, at least three other MICG members, based in Madrid, joined the incipient terrorist network. Belhadj frequently encountered these three Moroccans during his repeated trips to Madrid from Brussels, although they occasionally met in Belgium. These individuals were Mohamed Belhadj, Mohamed Afalah, and Abdelmajid Bouchar. Afalah was the one who ordered Mohamed Belhadj to rent the Leganés apartment that the operative members of the cell intended to use. For their part, Mohamed Afalah and Abdelmajid Bouchar had a long-standing relationship that had begun before the 3/11 network started to take shape; they had known each other even before they began their jihadist radicalization process during their time in Spain. These two Moroccans, under the influence of Youssef Belhadj, were part of the MICG component incorporated into the terrorist network that prepared and executed the attacks in Madrid.

Mohamed Belhadj was born October 15, 1977, in Douar Mnoud in northeastern Morocco. He was twenty-six on March 11, 2004, and had lived in Spain for about four years before the attacks. He was the one who, early in March, leased the apartment in Leganés where seven of the implicated terrorists would immolate themselves.[42] After he learned of the attacks and the destruction of the Leganés apartment, he fled with Afalah to Belgium. Interestingly enough, during his stay in Belgium, he received enough financial assistance from someone in Spain to support himself for a year. The Belgian authorities identified Mohamed Belhadj twice, first in June 2004 and then at the airport in Brussels in April 2005, but he still managed to flee to Syria, where he was arrested and extradited to Morocco in May 2009. The Spanish judicial authorities had issued an arrest warrant for Mohamed Belhadj, but Morocco does not extradite its own nationals. Instead, a Rabat court tried and convicted him in January 2010 for his involvement in the Madrid bombings.

Mohamed Afalah was born in the town of Ighmiran in northern Morocco on January 25, 1976; he was twenty-eight years old in March 2004. Abdelmajid Bouchar, born in Ait Lahcen Oualla on January 9, 1983, was twenty-one. Both Afalah and Bouchar had met Youssef Belhadj in late 2000, when the latter, along with his brother Mimoun Belhadj, visited a sick relative in Spain and stayed at the home of another brother who was living in Leganés. It was during their regular visits to an Islamic place of worship in Leganés that Youssef Belhadj and Mimoun Belhadj forged a relationship with Afalah and Bouchar, whom they progressively impregnated with jihadist ideas.[43] From that point forward until a few days before the massacre on the commuter trains, Youssef Belhadj traveled frequently to Madrid, where he continued radicalizing Afalah and Bouchar, incorporating them into the MICG component introduced into the 3/11 network.

Throughout 2002, when the network began developing, Afalah started attending meetings hosted by Mustafa Maymouni, Driss Chebli, and Serhane ben Abdelmajid Fakhet, with whom he maintained regular telephone contact at least between June and October of that year.[44] At the end of 2003, he also formed ties with the Algerian Allekema Lamari (the former GIA member discussed in the previous chapter).[45] One of Afalah's brothers, also a resident of Madrid, would later provide Spanish police with important information about Afalah's activities, such as the fact that his relatives found it strange that he had abandoned the family home before 3/11, and that "although he did not work, he handled money," instead of asking for it, as he did habitually.[46] In other words, Afalah had professionalized his involvement in jihadist terrorist activities—a not uncommon finding among those who have been condemned for terrorist activities in Spain since at least the mid-1990s.

Afalah escaped Madrid around 10:00 or 10:30 p.m. on April 3, 2004, as soon as he heard about the events in Leganés. That night, using a Volkswagen Golf owned by his brother, he fled with Mohamed Belhadj and drove to Barcelona, where they left the car parked.[47] Both men traveled to Belgium, from where Afalah managed to travel to Turkey a few months later. However, the Turkish authorities arrested him in Istanbul and held him in a detention center for undocumented immigrants. Afalah managed to escape by bribing one of the detention center's guards, using financial help that he received from Spain. He finally crossed into Syria and entered Iraq in April 2005.[48] (Chapter 13 will discuss Mohamed Afalah's intentions in Iraq.)

Abdelmajid Bouchar, a Moroccan friend of Afalah and a frequent attendee of the meetings held by Youssef Belhadj during his repeated trips to Madrid, also joined the 3/11 network. On occasion—at least once in 2003—he himself went to Molenbeek to meet with Youssef Belhadj.[49] On April 3, 2004, Bouchar delivered provisions to the cell members hiding in the Leganés apartment, and warned them about the police before he ran away from the building. Wandering through the nearby neighborhood of Getafe, he looked furiously for Afalah,[50] but soon learned that Afalah had already fled the city.[51] Bouchar also fled Spain, and was arrested in Serbia on June 23, 2005, as an undocumented traveler aboard a train traveling between Subotica and Belgrade. He claimed that he was Iraqi, perhaps hoping that the Serbian police would send him there, but the authorities positively identified him and extradited him to Spain in September of that year. While awaiting his trial before the National Court, Bouchar hoped to comply strictly with the obligations of his creed, and became a leader among other Muslims in prison with him, earning their respect.[52]

5

"They moved together while I moved on my own": Mohamed al-Masri in Egypt, Spain, and Italy

When the Madrid bombings occurred in March 2004, an important member of the 3/11 network found himself in Milan. This person had important connections to Abu Dahdah's cell as well as to individuals linked to the Moroccan Islamic Combatant Group inside and outside of Europe. He frequently traveled throughout southern Europe, acting as something of an itinerant inciter and facilitator of jihadism. The man in question is Rabei Osman es Sayed Ahmed, better known by his nicknames Mohamed al-Masri or Mohamed the Egyptian, in allusion to his country of origin. The available records are not clear on whether he was born in Gharbia or Alazizya Samnoud, but it is certain that he was born on July 22, 1971, and he was thirty-two years old when the Madrid bombings took place.

Al-Masri had arrived in Spain around October 2001, after having spent time in France and Italy. He was fleeing from Germany to avoid being deported by the German authorities, as he had arrived there illegally in June 1999. In an effort to delay the deportation process, he sought political asylum, falsely claiming that he was a Palestinian who had been born in a refugee camp. While the German authorities tried to resolve his file, they placed him in the Lebach interment center for asylum seekers in western Germany. During his time at Lebach, Al-Masri persisted in providing false identification to the authorities, and took it upon himself to act as an imam and agitate with other Muslim inmates. He fled from Lebach on August 29, 2001, and from that point on, until he was arrested in Milan for his involvement in 3/11 on June 7, 2004, he traveled, always irregularly, throughout Spain, France, and Italy.[1]

In these three countries, operating on the outskirts of Paris, Milan, and especially Madrid, al-Masri served as a radicalizing agent for young Muslims, indoctrinating them into Salafist jihadism and mobilizing them on behalf of al-Qaeda. In addition, he helped to provide false documents for individuals linked to jihadist organizations. He did more than this, though. From 2003, he actively recruited suicide bombers for Tawhid wal-Jihad, a militant jihadist organization that had been forced to leave its base in Herat, Afghanistan and relocate to northern Iraq in late 2001 or early 2002, as well as for Ansar al-Islam (known as Ansar al-Sunna temporarily since 2003), another jihadist entity based in the Iraqi Kurdistan that fought against the US forces in Iraq following the 2003 invasion. These activities, including his irregular movements across Western Europe and recruiter of suicide bombers, were consonant with his previous life.

Connections with Other Jihadists

In the 1990s, Mohamed al-Masri belonged to the Egyptian Islamic Jihad, a terrorist organization that had formed at the end of the 1970s and reconfigured itself in the 1990s under the leadership of Ayman al-Zawahiri.[2] In spite of its jihadist orientation, the group's main objective was the overthrow of the existing regime in Egypt. Its members succeeded in assassinating Egyptian president Anwar Sadat in October 1981; Egyptian security forces dismantled the group shortly thereafter. This disruption, combined with the need to secure resources to maintain the group's organization inside the country, stimulated the Egyptian Islamic Jihad to internationalize its strategy, and in 1998 it aligned itself with al-Qaeda.[3] In June 2001, the group finally merged with al-Qaeda, and Ayman al-Zawahiri became al-Qaeda's second-in-command. After Osama bin Laden's death in May 2011, al-Zawahiri assumed leadership of the organization.

During his time in Egypt, al-Masri completed three years of military service and later served an additional two years in the army, this time as a volunteer in a brigade specializing in explosives and headquartered in Port Said.[4] He also studied electronics at a level equivalent to professional training.[5] This made him, along with Said Berraj, another 3/11 network member who was familiar with explosives and electronics. Evidence suggests that because of his jihadist militancy, the Egyptian government sent him to the maximum-security Abu Zaa Abal prison, which held individuals who were suspected of or had been convicted of being involved in terrorism.[6] Following his release from prison, al-Masri entered Europe, though before his arrival he passed through Afghanistan, Syria, and Jordan, where he immersed himself in terrorist activities conducted by jihadist organizations.[7]

Once in Spain, he never found formal employment. Instead, he proselytized at Islamic worship sites around Madrid, including the Abu Bakr Mosque, which was an unwelcoming place for him and his associates because of their extremist views.[8] Al-Masri's radicalization activities attracted the attention of the Spanish authorities, and in January 2002, the police began to investigate him, keeping his phone under surveillance until May 22, 2003.[9] The National Court judge reviewing his case considered the evidence insufficient, under the antiterrorist legislation then existing in the country, to detain al-Masri or any of the individuals he met with, even though the UCIE considered him "an individual who was a danger to the security of whatever country he resided in."[10] Paradoxically, al-Masri received a temporary roots-based residency permit: a permit that is granted to immigrants who have resided in Spain from a particular date and can demonstrate established ties to the country.[11]

From the outset of his time in Spain, al-Masri surrounded himself with individuals who were linked to the former al-Qaeda cell in Spain that had been dismantled in November 2001. These individuals included Mustafa Maymouni, Driss Chebli, and Serhane ben Abdelmajid Fakhet, all of whom were primary members in the development of the new jihadist cell that would evolve into the 3/11 network. Al-Masri also knew Mohamed Afalah, a member of the new network's MICG component. He even aided the group by recruiting a Moroccan named Fouad el Morabit Amghar, who had been born in Nador on September 3, 1975, and who was twenty-eight years old when the Madrid bombings took place.[12] Morabit Amghar had arrived in Spain in 1999 to study aeronautical engineering in the Polytechnic University of Madrid, but he only attended three academic courses.[13] Instead, he started to collaborate with al-Masri in his proselytizing activities, and eventually he brought the latter into contact with Fakhet, whom Morabit Amghar had met early on during his time in Spain.

Another important person linked to Mohamed al-Masri was Mohamed Larbi ben Sellam. Sellam acted as al-Masri's liaison to the emerging cell led by Mustafa Maymouni. Sellam was born in Tangier on June 10, 1977, and arrived in Spain as an economic immigrant in 2000. He would be twenty-six years old on 3/11. Sellam participated in the propagation and preaching of the Salafist-jihadist ideology and justifications for the terrorism related to al-Qaeda that al-Masri was developing in Madrid. Through Larbi ben Sellam, al-Masri shared videotapes of various ideologues, above all Abu Qatada—whose writings were an important doctrinal reference for all the members of the 3/11 network—and Abu Oulaid al-Ansari.[14] Larbi ben Sellam acted as an intermediary for al-Masri with Madrid imams whom al-Masri believed in and adhered to, and he complemented al-Masri's strict and bellicose interpretation of Islam.[15] Whether or not al-Masri had instructed him to do so, Larbi ben Sellam was very conscientious in the security measures he used when attending meetings centered on jihad, showing the importance that these meetings had for him. Evidence shows that during these encounters, Larbi ben Sellam expressed his desire to extend his practices beyond active combat zones like Afghanistan, hoping to take them to Morocco and Spain.[16] In the spring of 2003, Larbi ben Sellam returned to Morocco to open a business and to get married, yet he kept his residency permit in Spain. He returned there in January 2004. In his own words, he felt that his activities were being more heavily monitored in Morocco than in Spain.[17] For his role in the Madrid bombings, the Spanish authorities sentenced him to twelve years in prison.[18]

Mohamed al-Masri's Movements in Milan

Mohamed al-Masri left Spain on February 27, 2003, and moved first to France before settling in Milan. He did not make this decision randomly; since the 1990s, an important jihadist scene had been established in Milan. In 1989, Egyptian immigrants had created the Islamic Cultural Institute in Milan. The institute had a worship site, and within five years it had become one of the most active jihadist centers in Western Europe. A considerable number of the institute's regular and visiting attendees and associates were involved in terrorist activities.[19] In 1994, the Italian authorities established that the Islamic Cultural Institute's imam was the leader of the Gamaat Islamiya, an Egyptian Islamist movement regarded as a terrorist organization, and that he had turned the institute into a base of operations for the movement.[20] Italian police raided the mosque in June 1995 and arrested a number of individuals associated with it, but the institute continued to function as a meeting place for North

African jihadists, and it helped send hundreds of Muslim youths recruited in Europe to al-Qaeda training camps in Afghanistan. In 2001, shortly before September 11, an Egyptian named Mahmoud Abdelkader es Sayed relocated to Milan. This man, a close associate of Ayman al-Zawahiri, had foreknowledge of the pending plot to attack the United States. He based his decision to move to Milan in part because of his long-standing connections with the Egyptian Islamic Jihad, as well as from instructions from al-Qaeda to revitalize the Egyptian jihadist community in northern Italy.[21] His presence demonstrated the importance of Milan for individuals like Mohamed al-Masri, who regarded it as a center for jihadist mobilization in Europe.

From Italy, Mohamed al-Masri maintained his contacts with Spain, traveling there occasionally. Between 2003 and 2004, he operated within a network that was tasked with sending jihadists from Madrid and Bilbao to Iraq by way of Milan. Al-Masri stayed in Madrid between December 2003 and the end of January 2004. It is known that he received a text message in his cell phone operating with a Spanish prepaid SIM card, welcoming him back to Italy, on February 1, 2004.[22] He again traveled to Madrid in early March, and left for Milan again a few days before 3/11. On April 17, 2004, he tried contacting Morabit Amghar at the Spanish telephone number 62706065; however, by this point, the Spanish police had already arrested Amghar for his supposed implication in the Madrid bombing.[23] When the authorities arrested Morabit Amghar, they found the Italian phone number 3391492264 scribbled down on a piece of paper. They informed their Italian counterparts immediately, and when the Italian authorities began their investigations at the end of March 2004 they traced the number to Mohamed al-Masri. They discovered him living in a building on Via Cadore alongside three other Egyptians. They wiretapped his phone, scoped out his home from the outside, and in May they started monitoring the conversations he held inside his home with microphones as well as his internet activities on his personal computer.[24] The surveillance furnished the Italian police and public security forces with unequivocal evidence of al-Masri's jihadist character and activities.

Mohamed al-Masri frequently used the internet to send and receive email and to access jihadist websites. He typically downloaded writings from Abdullah Azzam, Osama bin Laden, and Abu Qatada, among other documents. He also managed content produced by diverse jihadist organizations, including al-Qaeda, Ansar al-Sunna, and Tawhid wal-Jihad. He watched jihadist videos and downloaded documents on explosives. He also used sophisticated information technology software that, for example, allowed him to connect a personal computer to cell phones, erasing traces of the origins of the text messages he sent. Despite the abundant information collected by the Italian police, following his arrest he denied knowing how to use a computer.[25]

Al-Masri also used numerous prepaid cards and distinct cell phones that he switched out frequently. He also frequented shops that provided low-cost telephone and internet services, places often used by immigrants who needed to make international calls. According to the counterterrorist section of Milan's General Investigations and Special Operations Division (Divisione Investigazioni Generali e Operazioni Speciali; DIGOS), al-Masri adopted these measures to "make himself impermeable to observation."[26] On his cell phones, he often contacted the Saudi jihadist ideologue Salman el Ouda, a friend of Serhane ben Abdelmajid Fakhet's early jihadist connection in Spain, Ahmed Brahim.[27] He also communicated frequently with Ayub Usama Saddiq Ali, an internationally wanted fugitive who had been convicted of homicide in Egypt but had been granted political asylum by the German authorities in 1996. Like al-Masri, Ali had previously belonged to the Egyptian Islamic Jihad.[28]

Al-Masri conducted his activities with care. Apart from visiting the mentioned shops that provide low-cost telephone and internet services, he left his apartment only to attend the Viale Jenner and Via Quaranta mosques, both of which were known in Milan for housing wanted suspects from surrounding towns. Further, much as in his time in Spain, al-Masri did not seem to have formal employment—no record of it exists—although he occasionally did some painting. In April 2004, he received €2450 through *hawala*, a centuries-old system of transmitting money without a real transfer of funds, from a cell phone shop in the Raval district of Barcelona. Three Pakistanis residing in Barcelona sent him the money. In 2007, the authorities convicted all three for collaborating with a terrorist organization after they were shown to have transferred significant amounts of money to jihadists in Pakistan, including prominent al-Qaeda member Abu Talha.[29]

"The operation in Madrid was ours"

Al-Masri's telephone security measures notwithstanding, the Italian authorities discovered the first piece of evidence linking him to 3/11 when he tried contacting Fouad el Morabit Amghar.[30] On April 19, the Italian police intercepted a conversation from inside al-Masri's apartment where he admitted his participation in the Madrid bombings. In the conversation, al-Masri was speaking with Yahya Mawad, a twenty-year-old Egyptian who had been indoctrinated with radical Salafist ideas and whom al-Masri was trying to convince to become a martyr. Al-Masri told his acolyte that to "sacrifice oneself in the name of Allah, there is only one solution: integrate into Al-Qaeda."[31] Later, he told Mawad about a couple of individuals he knew who had committed suicide attacks, as well as others that could not, and then said:

I do not [hide from you] that the thread for the operation in Madrid was mine. Understand? The trains . . . they were all my group. I was not with them the day of the operation, but on the fourth day, I [contacted them] and [learned] all the details. They moved together while I moved on my own.

The program was of a high level. Indeed, I was prepared to become a martyr, but certain circumstances impeded it. Everything is in the hand of Allah. This operation required many lessons and much patience over two-and-a-half years.[32]

Another piece of evidence against al-Masri appeared on May 24, 2004, during a conversation he had with Mourad Chabarou, a Moroccan residing in Belgium whom al-Masri had met in Madrid in 2002. Al-Masri asked Chabarou, "Did you hear what happened there. . . . I don't want to say the country?" Chabarou said that he had, and al-Masri asked, "[Do] you know the entire group?" After Chabarou inquired, "What happened to the youths there?," al-Masri responded, "The youths, our friends, were behind the problems there," mentioning "Serhane and the friends, and the rest!" When Chabarou insisted, "What happened to them then?," Al-Masri responded, "They have gone with Allah, yes, all with Allah."[33] Belgian police would later arrest Chabarou in Brussels on June 8 during their operations against the MICG.

On June 1, the Italian police recorded another conversation inside al-Masri's apartment. This time, as he was addressing a disciple on his vision for the observance of religious precepts, he also spoke about Muslim territories that were experiencing conflict, and said:

I do not want to hide anything; the operation in Madrid was ours.[34]

On the night of June 7, six days after the recorded conversation, the Italian police detained both Mohamed al-Masri and Yahya Mawad. They held them in the national police's facilities in the Questura in Milan, in which the authorities had placed listening devices. The audio recordings showed that al-Masri was visibly confused and surprised by his capture in the early hours of the morning. While instructing his acolyte on what to say, he commented, "Listen, Yahya, my movements are like lines, like rails, neither to the left nor right, always silent."[35] Hours later, he said, "They want me in Spain." Minutes later, he added, "I was in Spain on the third month, but I went and returned."[36] The third month is March, referring specifically to March 2004. This admission correlates with the testimony of a witness in the 3/11 investigations that identified al-Masri as one of the individuals who visited the terrorists' base of operation in Morata de Tajuña on March 6 and 7.[37] This was the place where they prepared the explosives used in the attacks. Similarly, the collected proof shows that al-Masri knew of the impending attacks. On February 4, five weeks before 3/11, al-Masri activated an email address, kishk-mohammed@yahoo.com, and provided March 11 as his date of birth.[38] When the Spanish National Court judge directing the Madrid bombing investigations asked Mohamed al-Masri about this coincidence, he gave excuses, claiming that someone else living in his apartment had opened the account and that he did not remember the username or identity used for it.[39]

Inside his Milan apartment, Italian police discovered, among various documents related to actors and ideologues within the global jihad, a sheet of paper with Arabic on it containing an important connotation. Translated into English, the text says:

March 11 of 2004

Martyr

Honey[40]

The date obviously corresponds to 3/11. "Martyr" is a reference that evokes suicide terrorism because the terrorist will die, or is willing to die, as consequence of an act of jihad. "Honey" is a term commonly used by al-Qaeda and other organizations to refer to explosive substances. In a Spanish police investigation into the MICG predating 3/11, one of the individuals apprehended claimed that his boss had given him a sheet of paper with terminology to use when talking on the phone. The sheet included the word "honey"; its real significance was to refer to a bomb or explosive artifact.[41]

On November 6, 2006, a Milanese court sentenced Mohamed al-Masri to ten years in prison, following an investigation that implicated him in three roles: acting as an organizer for the terrorists who carried out 3/11 and the Leganés suicide attack, recruiting suicide terrorists, and coordinating terrorist cells in at least three European countries.[42] The Milan appeals court reduced his sentence to eight years. On appeal, the court argued that Italy was not the proper place to judge al-Masri for what had happened in Madrid, although it accepted the evidence presented by the Italian police that showed "serious evidence of his implication in the organization where that offense originated."[43]

6
Common Delinquents Turned into Jihadists: The Final Component of the 3/11 Network

The final component of the 3/11 network was a gang of common delinquents-turned-jihadists who joined the emerging terrorist structure created by the remaining elements of Abu Dahdah's cell and the European component of the Moroccan Islamic Combatant Group. This crucial piece centered on some ten Moroccans who were residing in Spain. Before joining the network, they had trafficked drugs, committed home burglaries, fenced stolen goods, and falsified documents. Most had criminal records; some had spent extensive stints in Spanish, Moroccan, and French prisons. This cast of delinquents joined the conspiracy to prepare and execute the attacks on the commuter trains because of their loyalty to the gang's linchpin, a man named Jamal Ahmidan, also known as "El Chino" ("The Chinese").

Ahmidan proved decisive in radicalizing his group and recruiting them into the burgeoning 3/11 network. He was one of the seven terrorists who immolated themselves in the Leganés apartment on April 3. Three other members of his band died with him that day: Rachid Oulad Akcha, Mohamed Oulad Akcha, and Abdenabi Kounjaa. Four days earlier, the Spanish police had released a national and international search-and-arrest order for them and other members of the 3/11 network.[1] Police captured several other members of the delinquent group, including Hamid Ahmidan (a cousin of Jamal's),

Othman el Ganoui, and Rachid Aglif, and later would convict them of belonging to a terrorist group.[2] Hicham Ahmidan, another cousin of Jamal's and Hamid's, avoided arrest in Spain, but Moroccan police were able to detain him at the end of March 2004 and later convicted him for his role in the Madrid bombings.[3]

"Chosen by Allah to benefit his people": Jamal Ahmidan's Radicalization

Jamal Ahmidan did not sleep at home on the night of March 10, 2004.[4] At thirty-three years old, he intended to participate fully in the attacks planned for the following morning. Born in Morocco's northern port city of Tétouan on October 28, 1970, he had been engaged in drug trafficking and the fencing of stolen vehicles since at least 1990. In 1992, Spanish police arrested him for drug trafficking, and for three years he was incarcerated in Madrid's Valdemoro prison.[5] He later married a native Spanish woman, and had a son who was born in Spain in 1995. The Spanish authorities arrested him at least nine more times between 1996 and 2000 for narcotics sales and the use of fake documents corresponding to ten different identities. In 1998, the French police also arrested him for a brief period.

These arrests finally saw Ahmidan end up in the Foreigner Internment Center at Moratalaz in Madrid under the name "Said Tlidni." Months after 3/11, authorities confirmed that Said Tlidini's real identity was Jamal Ahmidan.[6] The director of the Moratalaz internment center later recalled Ahmidan's forceful personality, in particular how he exercised leadership over other interred Muslims, on whom he imposed himself during conflicts and whom he led during the common prayer.[7] During a long conversation with Ahmidan (known at the time as Said Tlidni), who was awaiting deportation from Spain, the director remembered him stating that he had millions coming from drugs, but that he "had been chosen by Allah to benefit his people," and that since he lacked "the fear of death" he was "more or less invincible."[8] Ahmidan also spoke of his grand dream to go to Israel "to kill Jews," and warned that he would create problems in the internment center if he were to be bothered during his "high mission."[9]

Jamal Ahmidan escaped from the Moratalaz internment center on April 16, 2000, using a canister of tear gas against a police officer. The next day, he called the center's director at around 4:00 p.m., and insulted him and the chief of security, referring to the latter as the "great Satan" that "represented the cru-saders." He also challenged the director to find him, claiming that his escape was embarrassing to the state security forces. He harassed the director and the chief a further five times in as many days.[10] After his escape, Ahmidan moved to Morocco, but shortly thereafter the Moroccan authorities arrested him on murder charges. He entered the prison in Tétouan in December 2000 as a common criminal and remained there until June 17, 2003. There is no record explaining why the Moroccan authorities released him from prison, whether because of a lack of evidence to convict him or because Ahmidan had received some outside help to secure his release by means of a bribe.[11] During his time in prison, Ahmidan modified his attitudes and behaviors. He adopted, with an unnerving intensity, the attitudes and beliefs of Salafist-jihadism.

Ahmidan was familiar with the Islamic creed. In the latter half of the 1990s, he donated large sums of money derived from narcotics to the Estrecho and M-30 mosques in Madrid.[12] During Ramadan in 1999, according to an individual who "drank, smoked, and was a pleasure seeker" like Ahmidan had been until that time,[13] Ahmidan adopted a more religious behavior and expressed his desire to go to Afghanistan or Chechnya after watching jihadist videos. This makes it likely that his radicalization had begun during the brief period he spent in prison in France the year before, or shortly after, when he visited an Islamic worship site in Amsterdam.[14] The position as preacher he assumed before other imprisoned Muslims in the Moratalaz internment center and his conversations with the center's director demonstrated not only that Ahmidan viewed himself as a Muslim, but also that his radicalization began toward the end of the 1990s—in other words, it predated both 9/11 and the 2003 Iraq war.

Jamal Ahmidan is a case study showing how prisons and detainment centers for foreigners can be conductive environments for radicalizing individuals toward jihad, or at the very least for encouraging this process among criminals from social environments where the Islamic creed is hegemonic and stems from family tradition.[15] For these characteristics to evolve, the criminal must interact with other inmates who have been convicted of participating in jihadist ter-rorist activities, or with other radicalized individuals, such as extremist imams, who visit prisoners and indoctrinate them in rigid, bellicose visions of Islam.[16] No matter how it happens, the exposure to a doctrinaire or propagandist proves pivotal. In this sense, it is noteworthy that during Ahmidan's stint in prison in Tétouan, he was reluctant to consider other strains of Islam, like the Justice and Charity movement, a conservative Islamist movement that rejects violent action. Rather, he was drawn to Morocco's version of Salafist-jihadism and the ideas of the radical preacher Mohamed Fizazi, for many years the main proponent of this Islamist strain in Morocco.[17] (In terms of the connections between radical doctrine and jihadist action, is also noteworthy that Jamal Zougam—the owner of the Lavapiés cell phone shop connected with the devices used in the Madrid bombings—had visited Fizazi in the summer of 2001, while Ahmidan was in prison.) In 2003, the Moroccan government arrested Fizazi, accusing him of participating in the Casablanca attacks that had taken place in May. Months before his arrest, shortly after the commencement of the war in Iraq, Fizazi abused his position as an officially sanctioned religious authority by speaking out to justify attacks like those that would occur on March 11, 2004. According to Fizazi, "The death of those that remain silent and ally themselves with the United States of America is licit, [and] authorized."[18]

Although the Spanish government had denied Jamal Ahmidan's residency request in 2000, he returned to Spain in July 2003 to continue his criminal activities. During this period, he adopted the attitudes and beliefs espoused by Spanish jihadists like Abu Musab al-Suri, Serhane ben Abdelmajid Fakhet, Mohamed al-Masri, and Mohamed Larbi ben Sellam that justified criminal acts against non-Muslims. Once in Spain, Ahmidan reunited quickly with his former criminal gang to inculcate them with his newly adopted religious fervor. He also wanted to meet other individuals who shared his beliefs. This was not difficult, as he had met Serhane ben Abdelmajid Fakhet through friends. Indeed, both men had first met in 1996.[19] It was through Fakhet that Ahmidan inserted himself and members of the criminal group into the 3/11 network. Evidence suggests that Fakhet, now the leader of the local cell within the 3/11 network, agreed that Ahmidan should assume responsibility for various operative facets related to preparing and executing the attack on the commuter trains. To this end, Ahmidan recruited several individuals from his criminal band, and also mobilized others to form the final component of the 3/11 network.

Recruited for Their Loyalty to "El Chino": Brothers, Cousins, and Local Friends

Jamal Ahmidan began his mobilization efforts in Spain by contacting two brothers, Rachid and Mohamed Oulad Akcha. Like Ahmidan, the brothers had been born in Tétouan: Rachid on January 27, 1971, and Mohamed on December 17, 1975. They were thirty-three and twenty-eight years old, respectively, when the bombs exploded in Madrid.[20] Rachid Oulad Akcha had arrived in Spain in 1995, enrolling in Granada University's School of Technical Architecture. The authorities arrested him in February 1998 on narcotics charges and kept him in prison until August 2003. He benefited from Spain's "third-degree" regime—an open correctional model that allows prisoners freedom of outside movement during the day on the condition that they return to the prison at night—from at least 2002.[21] From the outset of his internment, he presented himself as a friend of Jamal Ahmidan.[22] His coworkers at a construction firm that produced partition walls (his place of employment starting in January 2003) considered Rachid a person of profound religious convictions, but "a little extremist."[23] Six days before the Madrid bombings, he left his post and said that he would return in two weeks.[24] He did not return.

Rachid's brother, Mohamed Oulad Akcha, arrived in Spain in 2001, and followed an irregular lifestyle. He worked as carpenter around Madrid. Rachid and Mohamed also had an older brother, Khalid Oulad Akcha, who was in the Topas penitentiary in Salamanca in western Spain on the day that his younger brothers immolated themselves in Leganés. Khalid had been in prison since 2001, and had a penal record dating back to 1995, when the Spanish authorities had arrested him for armed burglaries, falsification of documents, and aggravated fighting. He also belonged to Jamal Ahmidan's gang, and he had been in contact with his brothers before and after 3/11.[25] Ahmidan had no difficulty recruiting Khalid's younger brothers, as they had established ties with Abu Dahdah's cell during Ahmidan's prison stint in Morocco.[26]

Through his work connections, Rachid Oulad Akcha also recruited a friend for the 3/11 network. This individual, Abdenabi Kounjaa, was born in Taourirt, in northeastern Morocco, in 1975. Toward the end of 2002, Kounjaa, in the company of Mohamed Oulad Akcha and others like Said Berraj, had attended meetings held by Larbi ben Sellam that were designed to affirm an individual's adherence to Salafist-jihadism. Kounjaa would meet Sellam after finishing work in the market in the Madrid neighborhood of Chamberí.[27] Indeed, when he was not proselytizing, Sellam occasionally worked at places where members of Ahmidan's group also worked. For his part, Kounjaa brought in another Moroccan from his workplace, Saed el Harrak. El Harrak, born in Beni Gorfet on April 10, 1973, had arrived in Spain in 1996. He was thirty years old when the Madrid bombings took place.

From his gang, Ahmidan also recruited his two cousins, Hamid Ahmidan and Hicham Ahmidan. Hicham was born in Tétouan on June 8, 1979, and was twenty-four years old on March 11. He had a long criminal record in

Spain; between 1996 and 2000, he had been arrested a dozen times, with a few additional arrests outside Spain. His criminal activities included narcotics sales and sales of stolen vehicles. He went back to Morocco four or five days before the March attacks, and repeatedly called his cousin Hamid to ask how things were progressing.[28] Hamid Ahmidan was born in Tétouan on November 20, 1970, and was thirty-three years old on March 11. Jamal Ahmidan tasked both of his cousins with collaborative roles in the 3/11 project.

Around the same time, Jamal Ahmidan netted another Moroccan in his preparations for the attack. This man, called Othman el Gnaoui, was born in Tétouan on April 25, 1975. He was nearly twenty-nine on March 11. He had worked regularly as a mason in Morocco, but found only irregular employment when he arrived in Spain in 2001. He had been in prison at the Valdemoro penitentiary, which was where he met Rachid Aglif, another member of Jamal Ahmidan's group. Aglif was born in Khourigba on November 19, 1979, and was twenty-four on March 11. Aglif and Ahmidan had become friends through Ahmidan's regular visits to a butcher shop owned by Aglif's father. Ahmidan also was able to insert Aglif into the 3/11 network, and contacted him to this end toward the end of August 2003.[29]

These links between all these men derived directly from their criminal activities associated with Jamal Ahmidan's band, and later from their adoption of a similar rigid and bellicose conception of Islam. Because of their frequent encounters, even those who initially did not share Ahmidan's extremist beliefs before June 2003—such as the Oulad Akcha brothers or Kounjaa—soon adopted them. For example, el Gnaoui began to mention his religious beliefs when talking on the phone, stating that he no longer consumed alcoholic beverages.[30] In a conversation on February 9, 2004, he told the person he was speaking to that he followed orders from Ahmidan, prayed every day, went to bed early, and never went out at night.[31] While el Gnaoui was in jail awaiting trial, the Spanish authorities sanctioned him for "aggressions," and noted that he engaged in "hunger strikes." They also stated that some other members of Ahmidan's group who were awaiting trial, such as Ahmidan's cousin Hamid, showed an observance "rooted" in Islam; in other cases, such as Rachid Aglif and Saeed el Harrak, the group members "were not [known] for their attachment to Islam."[32]

"Revenge is an obligation": Preparing for the 3/11 Attacks

Key among the responsibilities assigned to Jamal Ahmidan for carrying out the Madrid bombings was securing the necessary infrastructure and logistics to guarantee success in the attacks. Ahmidan also assumed responsibility for financing the attacks with drug trafficking, and for using his underworld connections to acquire the explosives and other elements to build the bombs that would be placed on the commuter trains. Ahmidan and others in his group were adequately prepared for these tasks, because their criminal career inside Spain had brought them into contact with explosives dealers and document falsifiers.

With regard to the infrastructure preparations, Ahmidan and Serhane ben Abdelmajid Fakhet signed a lease on the rural property in Morata de Tajuña, in Chinchón, that the 3/11 network would use as a base of operation starting two months before the attacks.[33] Abdenabi Kounjaa and Rachid Oulad Akcha were the ones who rented the house in Albolote, a town very near the emblematic city of Granada, on March 6, five days before the attacks.[34] The gang's underworld experience helped them make it more difficult for the Spanish authorities to trace their work; they used fake documents when they leased both the Chinchón property and the house in Andalucía. In contrast, Mohamed Belhadj, who had joined the 3/11 network through the MICG, used his real personal information when he rented the flat in Leganés, a fact that ultimately helped the Spanish investigation.

Members of Ahmidan's group charged themselves with preparing the rural Chinchón property for various uses. Among these uses were hosting the meetings of members of their criminal gang component, arranging meetings between main members of these and other components of the 3/11 network, setting up meeting dates with the explosives dealers, stockpiling the explosives in secure places, and assembling the bombs used in the attacks. When Jamal Ahmidan was not present, Hamid Ahmidan and Othman el Gnaoui made sure to do these preparatory tasks themselves, as they were well aware of the purpose of their activities.[35]

Apart from acquiring the necessary infrastructure, Ahmidan tasked the Algerian Nasreddine Bousbaa with falsifying documents, and other individuals from his own gang with acquiring vehicles. The gang members did not lack vehicles among themselves—the Ahmidan cousins and the Oulad Akcha brothers, for instance, had cars of their own—but they wanted fake license plates, a requirement ordered by Hicham Ahmidan.[36] On February 28, 2004, the gang stole a Renault Kangoo van, which they would use to travel to the Alcalá de Henares train station—the starting point of the attacks. Later, the authorities would find biological forensic evidence inside the van, and were able to connect it with both Kounjaa and Daoud Ouhnane, as well as with another gang member, a Moroccan named Rifaat Anouar Asrih, who was twenty-three years old when he committed suicide in the Leganés apartment explosion. On March 29, 2004, the gang also stole at gunpoint a Citroën C3 in Fuenlabrada, southwest of Madrid; Jamal Ahmidan, along with Kounjaa and Mohamed Oulad Akcha, was found to have used this vehicle.[37] Along with these vehicles, which were stolen shortly before and after the attacks, the gang stole a Skoda Fabia on September 17, 2003, in the coastal city of Benidorm. Mohamed Afalah and Allekema Lamari, 3/11 network members linked to Abu Dahdadh's cell and the MICG, used this vehicle.[38] The Spanish authorities located the Fabia on June 15, 2004, a few meters away from where they found the Renault Kangoo van in Alcalá de Henares.

The police investigation recovered more than simply biological evidence from the stolen cars; the Kangoo and the Fabia in particular contained materials pertaining to the terrorists' jihadist ideology. Inside the Kangoo, which the authorities discovered the same day of the train bombings, they found a plastic bag with remnants of the same type of Goma-2 Eco dynamite used in the attacks, detonators, and a cassette with a recording of the third surah of the Quran, which details the battle that Islam wages against its adversaries.[39] Another cassette, found in the Fabia, contained songs and psalms in Arabic that extolled jihad. The audio recordings also included admonitions stating that "the victory is for Islam and the Quran is its flag" and that "if some day I die like a martyr, I will be like a minaret."[40] Interestingly, songs recorded on the cassette found in this second vehicle also explicitly stress the idea that "revenge is an obligation."

"If we don't see each other on earth, we'll see each other in heaven, you'll see": Financing and Launching the 3/11 Attacks

The gang of delinquents in the 3/11 network acquired all the necessary funding, the material substances, and other necessary items for the plot to work. Estimates place the total direct cost of the preparing and executing the attacks at around €105,000, not taking into account all other costs that the network incurred since the beginning of its formation. After the execution of the attacks, the terrorists had an estimated €1.5 million in reserve.[41] These amounts come from an appraisal of the value of the narcotics that the Spanish authorities recovered from people who were linked members of the 3/11 network.[42] It is also highly likely that different members of the cell contributed their own money. The authorities know, for example, that network members who were not part of Ahmidan's group—including Said Berraj, Abdenabi Kounjaa, Daoud Ouhnane, and Abdelmajid Bouchar—withdrew most of their money from banks sometime between the middle of 2003 and March 2004, even though they had received cash income, in amounts between €300 and €3,000, on the same day or the day after draining their accounts.[43] In addition, when searching the remains of the destroyed Leganés apartment, the authorities found bundles of cash with dozens of banknote denominations, ranging from €500 at the highest down through €200, €100, €50, €20, and €10.[44] This financial information demonstrates that starting in September 2003, two months after arriving in Spain, joining the 3/11 network, and receiving from Serhane ben Abdelmajid Fakhet the responsibility for creating the network's operational nucleus, Jamal Ahmidan began the money transfers that would enable the gang to use drug sales to finance the purchase of explosives.

Rachid Aglif, a member of Ahmidan's band, was a key point of contact for the acquisition of the explosives; he knew another Moroccan named Rafa Zouhier, who also was involved in the criminal world. Zouhier had met Antonio Toro, an explosives trafficker, while both men were serving time in Villabona prison, and together they acted as intermediaries between Jamal Ahmidan and the dynamite supplier Jose Emilio Suárez, a former worker at the Caolines de Merilles quarry in Asturias, in northern Spain. Starting in September 2003, Ahmidan, typically accompanied by Aglif and the Oulad Akcha brothers, met with the Spanish explosives dealers.[45] Their shared criminal history permitted a group of common delinquents, originating mainly from Morocco and converted into jihadists, to meet with their Spanish counterparts, who were motivated not by ideology but by money.[46] For the criminals of the 3/11 network, their driving motivation involved fulfilling their understanding of the imperatives of their interpretation of jihad in the bloodiest way possible.

Between December 2003 and January 2004, Jamal Ahmidan, Mohamed Oulad Akcha, and Abdenabi Kounjaa traveled to Asturias to coordinate the acquisition of the explosives. Early in 2004, Jose Emilio Suárez, one of the Spanish explosives dealers implicated in the attacks, had sent three bags with samples of the dynamite and detonators to Madrid. On the morning of February 29, eleven days before the attacks, Ahmidan, Oulad Akcha, and Kounjaa extracted the explosives—specifically, Goma-2 Eco dynamite—from the Caolines de Merilles quarry, some twenty kilometers outside of the town of Tineo. The gang conveyed the dynamite from the quarry to Madrid in a black Volkswagen Golf with fake license plates.[47] On that same day, while Ahmidan was driving from Asturias to Madrid in a car stocked with explosives, two agents from the Guardia Civil stopped him. The car had fake license plates, and Ahmidan provided the authorities with fake documents bearing the name Youssef ben Salah. Surprisingly, Ahmidan received only a fine. He paid it in cash, and as a result was able to arrive at his destination without further complications. Their final destination was the rural property in Morata de Tajuña where Othman el Gnaoui, following orders from Jamal Ahmidan, had been told to hide explosives in a cabin on the property.

Samples recovered from the March 11 and April 3 explosions indicated that the terrorists had used the same explosives in both instances.[48] Further, the detonators had come from the same quarry.[49] Other items used to manufacture the bombs, such as the cell phones, the prepaid phone cards, and the containers used to transport the bombs to the train stations, came from individuals (like cell phone shop owner Jamal Zougam) who belonged to the two other components of the 3/11 network. Around the middle of February 2004, or perhaps earlier, members of the operational nucleus started constructing the bombs, preparing them for the explosives that would arrive at the end of February. The final products of their efforts were seen with tragic effect on the morning of March 11.[50]

Overall, the individuals of the criminal gang who were loyal to Jamal Ahmidan constituted one of the key components of the 3/11 network, but they should not be taken for the network as a whole. The Madrid bombing network cannot be reduced to a bunch of delinquents radicalized more or less rapidly in the tenets of Salafist-jihadism. Similarly, although the plot against the commuter trains had been conceived long before Jamal Ahmidan's criminal band was incorporated into the network, he and his associates were fundamental in carrying out the attack with the desired reach and lethality envisioned by the original planners. Moreover, the criminal group did not join the network simply to finance and develop the infrastructure necessary for the attack. They did so because they were willing to implicate themselves directly in the practice of terrorism, something that they accomplished in a bloody and deadly manner. For them, as much as for the others, this was a matter of jihad. Indeed, on April 3, 2004, four of these common-criminals-turned-jihadists, alongside three other members of the 3/11 network in Leganés, opted to commit a suicide attack rather than face prison. Jamal Ahmidan implicitly shared his intentions with Suárez, the former quarry employee who served as the network's explosives dealer. Suárez took Ahmidan and his associates at their word that they would use the bombs to "rob jewelry stores and vans"—and yet he had reason to doubt their story.[51] He would later tell the Spanish police that Ahmidan had claimed that Muslims "had the most powerful army in the world, that bin Laden did well, and that it was good to place explosives and kill."[52] Further, on March 4—seven days before the attacks—Jamal Ahmidan called Suárez and told him goodbye with these words: "If we don't see each other on earth, we'll see each other in heaven, you'll see."[53]

7

How the 3/11 Terrorist Network Formed

The jihadists involved in the March 11 attacks, as the first chapters of this book have shown, came from three different components. The first emerged from the remnants of the Abu Dahdah cell that the Spanish authorities disbanded during Operation Dátil in November 2001. The second formed around the Moroccan Islamic Combatant Group structure already present in Western Europe, especially in Belgium. The final component originated from a band of common criminals who adopted a violent conception of the Islamic creed and involved themselves in the terrorist activities of the 3/11 network. Their overlap notwithstanding, each component retained its own distinct character. They established ties through informal relationships and the activities carried out by each of their corresponding nodes. Although the remnants of Abu Dahdah's disbanded cell had three individuals who successively coordinated its efforts, the key MICG and criminal gang nodes remained constant in the form of Yousself Belhadj and Jamal Ahmidan, respectively. These three components grew in a progressive manner over the period of a year and a half—even attracting individuals who did not necessarily fit neatly into the structure of any of these three components—to form the 3/11 network.

In general, these individuals, apart from sharing the basic content of their Salafist-jihadist ideology, resided in Spain or traveled there during the formation of the network. Many helped prepare and execute the massacre on the commuter trains; some may have played a meaningful role in both stages. The authorities arrested and convicted some of them, both inside and outside of Spain; others perished in the Leganés apartment group suicide; and several escaped capture entirely. Moreover, it is likely that some other participants in the Madrid train bombings have not been identified, and continue to evade justice.

From March 2002 to August 2003: The 3/11 Network under Mustafa Maymouni

The 3/11 network first began to develop in March 2002, two years before the attacks, and was fully formed by August 2003, six months before the attacks. In other words, its inception dates to five years after the Spanish authorities made an initial attempt to dismantle the country's first jihadist cell (June 1997), six months after the al-Qaeda attacks on New York and Washington (September 11, 2001), and four months after the United States and its coalition partners intervened in Afghanistan and, above all, Spanish police launched Operation Dátil against radical Islamists such as Abu Dahdah (November 2001). More important, the 3/11 network formation predates the 2003 Iraq war by more than a year, the Casablanca bombings by fifteen months, and the announcement of the March 14, 2004, Spanish general elections by twenty months.

After Abu Dahdah's cell was dismantled, Mustafa Maymouni took the local initiative in creating the new jihadist faction in Madrid that would evolve into the 3/11 network. Maymouni, a Moroccan, had become Abu Dahdah's acolyte in 2000. Abu Dahdah, in turn, had encouraged Maymouni to attend an al-Qaeda training camp in Afghanistan. Maymouni attempted to travel to Afghanistan in October 2000 but was unsuccessful, and he later evaded arrest during Operation Dátil, briefly hiding in Morocco. In March 2002, he returned to Spain and started to reestablish links among those of Abu Dahdah's followers who also had avoided arrest. Maymouni's goal was to create a new jihadist cell in Madrid, with aspirations to carry out an attack on Spanish soil.

This initiative centered on the remnants of Abu Dahdah's followers, and to do so Maymouni connected with two individuals he already knew. The first, Driss Chebli, was a Moroccan who had arrived in Spain in the early 1990s and had first met Maymouni at some point in the latter half of the decade. The second, Serhane ben Abdelmajid Fakhet, had met Maymouni sometime before 2001 on the grounds of Madrid's M-30 Mosque.[1] When Maymouni returned to Madrid in March 2002, he roomed temporarily in a house with Fakhet and Chebli. This property, located in the neighborhood of San Cristóbal de los Ángeles in the southern outskirts of Madrid, belonged to Abdelkrim el Ouazzani, a native of Casablanca born in 1969. Abdelkrim's cousin, Mohamed el Ouazzani, who had been born in Taza, Morocco, in 1981, lived there also.[2]

Abdelkrim el Ouazzani allowed Maymouni, Chebli, and Fakhet to use his home for meetings, where they discussed jihadist mobilization and radicalization of Muslims, especially Moroccan Muslim immigrants. Mohamed, Abdelkrim el Ouazzani's cousin, went so far as to join the growing network. The authorities would arrest both Abdelkrim and Mohamed el Ouazzani a few months after 3/11, in October and December 2004, respectively. Three years later, Abdelkrim would be convicted of collaborating with a terrorist group and Mohamed would be convicted of the more serious offense of being a member of a terrorist group.[3]

The el Ouazzani cousins' home, in this respect, was the incubator for the new jihadist cell in Madrid that would become the 3/11 network.[4] In addition to sheltering Maymouni, Chebli, and Fakhet, it became the scene of conspiratorial meetings attended by Mohamed Afalah, the network's point of contact for the Moroccan Islamic Combatant Group structure in Belgium. Allekema Lamari, the former member of the defunct Armed Islamic Group of Algeria—who had been released from prison in 2002, even though he had received a prolonged sentence for his membership in the GIA—also attended these meetings.[5] Along with these encounters in San Cristóbal were others that took place in different sites throughout Madrid and its outskirts. These meetings attracted other young men who would join the network, including Said Berraj, whom Maymouni had met through Driss Chebli in late 2001.[6] Berraj previously had belonged to Abu Dahdah's cell, and like Maymouni he had avoided arrest during Operation Dátil. Other network participants, such as Abdelmajid Bouchar, were Moroccan immigrants who were being radicalized—in Bouchar's case, under the influence of Mohamed Afalah.

Unexpected Changes to the Ringleaders: Driss Chebli and Serhane ben Abdelmajid Fakhet

Even as the 3/11 network was starting to develop, the UCIE was monitoring its members' activities, relying on an informant who attended the meetings that were led by Maymouni with the assistance of Chebli and Fakhet.[7]

From June to October 2002, the authorities tapped Fakhet's phone, and the recorded conversations revealed his close relations not only with Maymouni and Chebli but also with the aforementioned Mohamed Afalah, Said Berraj, and Allekema Lamari. Fouad el Morabit Amghar also joined the group, a connection made possible by his relationship with Mohamed Larbi ben Sellam, who was an active member of meetings run by Maymouni, and Rabei Osman Sayed Ahmed, better known as Mohamed al-Masri.[8] Al-Masri, who had arrived in Madrid in late 2001, left Spain for Italy in February 2003 and concentrated his activity in Milan. His followers incorporated themselves into the Madrid-based terrorist network.

This jihadist accretion continued and attracted new members such as Jamal Zougam, whose cell phone shop in Lavapiés would supply much-needed equipment for the network, and Youssef Belhadj, Mohamed Belhadj, and Rifaat Anouar Asrih, who were connected to the MICG. Another new member was Mohamed Bouharrat, who had been born in Tangier and was twenty-five years old on March 11, 2004. The Spanish courts would later convict Bouharrat of membership in a terrorist organization.[9] Over time, two of the three different components of the nascent 3/11 network—one from the dismantled Abu Dahdah cell, and the other linked to the MICG's European structure—would continue to develop their connections. On October 28, 2002, Mustafa Maymouni took the network's preparations a step further and rented property in Morata de Tajuña. This space would serve as an operational base for the 3/11 network, providing working and meeting space for the local cell members and for those who were the operational nucleus of the 3/11 network.[10]

In late 2002, however, Maymouni suspended the activities of the emerging jihadist network, as he and his associates feared that someone present at their gatherings was providing information to the police.[11] As indicated earlier, these suspicions were not without truth; one of those attending the meetings, a Moroccan immigrant, had been maintaining telephone contact with the UCIE, and by September or October 2002 he had expressed his willingness to cooperate with the CGI's experts in international terrorism. The informant reported that individuals professing jihadist ideas had invited him to their meetings, but in exchange for his information he demanded financial compensation and assistance when the time approached to renew his residency permit in Spain.

Meanwhile, Maymouni, having been in Kenitra and Tangier in February and April 2003, made another trip from Spain to Morocco in May of that year. His stay coincided with the suicide bombings in Casablanca on May

16. During the vast counterterrorist operation that immediately followed the Casablanca bombings, Moroccan security forces arrested Maymouni and charged him with terrorism offenses that eventually led to his conviction in his own country. As such, the Spanish authorities convicted him in absentia, suspending the case that came before the judicial proceeding in the National Court, since the Casablanca attacks had killed four Spanish citizens.

Following Maymouni's arrest in Morocco, Chebli assumed local direction of the jihadist network. He too had the dedication to prepare and execute terrorist acts in Spain, but a month later, in June 2003, the Spanish authorities arrested him during the third phase of Operation Dátil, accusing him of having been involved in Abu Dahdah's dismantled cell. With Maymouni imprisoned in Morocco and Chebli imprisoned in Spain, Serhane ben Abdelmajid Fakhet took charge of the local cell and continued its preparations for the attacks on the commuter trains. By that point, Fakhet and Maymouni had strengthened their ties of mutual loyalty, and had even become brothers-in-law following Fakhet's marriage to one of Maymouni's sisters.[12]

After becoming the latest unexpected local head of the 3/11 cell, Fakhet insisted on fulfilling the obligation of jihad for believers of Islam, and in attacking Spain.[13] In the summer of 2003, during the clandestine meetings held by the group, individuals associated with the band of common criminals led by Jamal Ahmidan joined the network. Among these new recruits were Mohamed and Rachid Oulad Akcha and Abdenabi Kounjaa. Jamal Ahmidan in particular was a promising recruit, having left a Moroccan prison and returned to Spain with the firm intention of influencing his previous circle of followers in Madrid and contacting other like-minded individuals. He had no difficulty in approaching Fakhet. Thus, by August 2003, the 3/11 network was complete.

Young Male Immigrants—Brothers, Cousins, Friends, or Neighbors

Although the number of jihadists who were related in one form or another to the 3/11 network might actually be larger, it is possible to substantiate enough evidence on at least twenty-five of its members. All of them were free when the Madrid attacks took place (although an arrest warrant had been issued for Allekema Lamari). Fifteen of the twenty-five received some type of court sentence in legal proceedings that were opened following the Madrid bombings: eleven in Madrid, three in Rabat, and one in Milan. Seven died during the Leganés apartment suicide bombing, while three managed to flee and avoid capture. By analyzing the existing personal data on these twenty-five individuals, a broader picture of those who formed the 3/11 network can be developed.

First, the network was made entirely of men. This was typical among those who implicate themselves in terrorist activities under jihadist influence in the context of Western societies.[14] The oldest of these individuals was born in 1960 and the youngest was born in 1983. A large majority of the network members were born between 1970 and 1979, while half were born between 1975 and 1979. All but three of them were between the ages of twenty-one and thirty in 2004, and nearly half were between twenty-six and thirty. The range and distribution of ages are common for those involved in terrorist activities or attacks inside Spain and other parts of Western Europe.[15]

All of the members of the network were foreigners: twenty-one of the twenty-five were of Moroccan nationality, two were Algerian, one was Egyptian, and one was Tunisian. Their nationalities corresponded to the countries where they were born, meaning they all came from North Africa.[16] Given that the vast majority of Muslims living in Spain are from Morocco, the fact that nearly 85 percent of the 3/11 network members were Moroccan is not surprising. Only two of the network members were living outside of Spain when the bombings occurred in Madrid. Among those who were living in Spain, a few had come to pursue higher education and the rest were economic migrants. Almost all of them resided in Madrid and other nearby locations. About half of them had their administrative status resolved and were legal residents of Spain, while the other half were living illegally in Spanish territory. Around a third had criminal records in Spain before March 11, 2004; among those with criminal records, almost all had spent time in Spanish prisons.[17]

Their educational backgrounds and occupations were equally diverse. Although many had only a primary or secondary education, a few members had college experience. In general, their employment status was in line with the economic standing of the majority of first-generation immigrants in Spain, and for that matter in many other Western countries. Although some managed their own businesses, most performed unskilled labor. Indeed, some had professionalized their jihadist militancy and did not hold down a job to supplement their lifestyle.[18] Regarding their marital status, the number who were unmarried was comparable to those who were married; the latter usually had children. However, all of them understood the religious imperative of jihad and did not mind any of the consequences toward their families.

Notably, the members of the 3/11 network had not adopted their professed Salafist-jihadist ideology in the same places, at the same time, or by the same processes.[19] Most had been radicalized in Spain, but the extremism of their attitudes and beliefs increased in some cases during temporary stays outside of the country, especially in northern Morocco. For example, five of the seven Leganés suicide bombers—the Oulad Akcha brothers, Jamal Ahmidan, Abdenabi Kounjaa, and Rifaat Anouar Asrih—had adopted most of their extremist views after attending a mosque in Morocco that was associated with the Tablighi Jamaat movement. This mosque was located in the Jemma Mezuak district in the city of Tétouan, which had been the capital of the former Spanish protectorate in Morocco from 1912 to 1956.[20] Nonetheless, their process of radicalization culminated under influences present within Spain. Most of the radicalization occurred in places of Islamic worship, prisons, and (above all else) private homes; these were the environments that led to most of these individuals becoming involved in the 3/11 network. It is possible to divide the 3/11 network into three subgroups of around equal number based on when they became radicalized. About a third of them adopted Salafist-jihadist attitudes and beliefs in the 1990s, before 9/11. Another third did so after the September 11 attacks, but before the invasion of Iraq in early 2003. The remaining third were radicalized after the start of the conflict in Iraq.

The most senior and well-connected network members themselves encouraged radicalization among those who were newer to the group. This was the case for members in all three components of the network: Mustafa Maymouni, Mohamed al-Masri, Youssef Belhadj, Serhane ben Abdelmajid Fakhet, and Jamal Ahmidan intervened at various points to help radicalize those who would be involved in the preparation and execution of the attacks. Materials from jihadist doctrinaries such as Ibn Taymiyya, Abdullah Azzam, Abu Mohammed al-Maqdisi, Nasir bin Hamad al Fahd, Abdul Munim Mustafa Halima, Abu Qatada, Mohamed Fizazi, Osama bin Laden, and Ayman al Zawahiri were used for this purpose, and the authorities found writings and recordings from these key figures on computers that were available to and used by members of the 3/11 network.[21]

Previous kinship, friendship, and neighborhood ties not only facilitated the processes of jihadist radicalization, but also allowed the complete terrorist mobilization of the 3/11 network.[22] One-fifth of the members of the network had at least one family member within the network. Rachid Oulad Akcha and Mohamed Oulad Akcha were brothers. Jamal Ahmidan, Hamid Ahmidan, and Hicham Ahmidan were cousins. Place of birth and residence also played a critical role in shaping the network's connections: 40 percent of the individuals covered by this analysis had been born in or had resided in Tétouan or Tangier.

Those who had not known each other through family or neighborhood connections strengthened their friendships in places of worship or at work, as in the cases of Abdenabi Kounjaa and Saed el Harrak (who worked in the same Madrid neighborhood) and Mohamed Bouharrat and Abdelmajid Bouchar.

Returning to the beginning of the formation of the 3/11 network, a number of crucial questions remain. Was the decision to create a new jihadist cell in Madrid a personal initiative from Mustafa Maymouni, or was he following someone else's instructions? When Maymouni was arrested and jailed in Morocco in May 2003, did Driss Chebli follow the plans as they had been conceived by Maymouni and Fakhet, or did he receive guidance from another person? When Chebli himself was arrested and jailed in Spain in June 2003, did Fakhet limit himself to finishing the plan that he and his comrades had already developed, or was he acting in connection with a partner whose orders he fulfilled? If the local Madrid cell did not plan the train bombings solely on its own initiative, who did? Why was Spain chosen as the site of the attacks? The second part of this book answers these and other questions.

Part II

The Al-Qaeda Connection:
Revenge, Opportunity, and Strategy

8

"Transforming the tranquillity of the crusaders into a hell": Amer Azizi and the Al-Qaeda Link to 3/11

A further clue that gave credibility to the hypothesis that the 3/11 attacks were linked to al-Qaeda appeared weeks after an incident on December 1, 2005, in a location more than 6,500 kilometers away from Madrid. In the early hours of that day, a Hellfire air-to-surface missile struck a building in the small town of Haisori in northeastern Pakistan, killing five people. The missile had been launched from a Predator drone, a small unmanned aircraft used by American intelligence agencies to target al-Qaeda members in that area.[1]

The area of impact was close to Miranshah, the administrative capital of North Waziristan, one of the seven agencies or districts in Pakistan's Federally Administered Tribal Areas (FATA), a region adjacent to the Afghan border. The majority of al-Qaeda's leadership, as well as most of its members and those of other affiliated organizations, had relocated to the region and the nearby Khyber Pakhtunkhwa province from Afghanistan at the end of 2001 and beginning of 2002. This forced transfer occurred following the US invasion of Afghanistan in October 2001 and the ousting of the Taliban regime shortly thereafter.[2] Afterward, around the middle of 2004 and the beginning of 2005, al-Qaeda had further confined the majority of its activities and what remained of its infrastructure to North Waziristan because of the protection afforded to it by the Pakistani Taliban. At this point, the Pakistani Taliban operated mainly in the FATA and the Afghan border regions.[3] When the US-guided missile reached its target on December 1, 2005, one of the five people it killed was Hamza Rabia, the then chief of al-Qaeda's external operations and therefore the man responsible for all the terrorist plots that the organization had planned, mainly for Europe and North America. At the time of his death, analysts regarded him as one of the top individuals in al-Qaeda's hierarchy, next to Osama bin Laden and Ayman al-Zawahiri.

At the beginning of 2002, shortly after fleeing Afghanistan, bin Laden and al-Zawahiri had decided to divide al-Qaeda's operations. One side focused on internal operations, encompassing both Afghanistan and Pakistan. Abu Faraj al-Libi, a Libyan whose real name was Mustafa al-Uzayti, took over this sector. The other command focused on external operations, or the organization's worldwide terror plots. Khalid Sheikh Mohammed, the mastermind of 9/11, initially took charge of this sector, but after the Pakistani authorities arrested him in Rawalpindi in March 2003, Abu Faraj al-Libi took over from him. Hamza Rabia, however, became the effective director.[4] When the Pakistani authorities arrested al-Libi in May 2005, Rabia became the formal commander of al-Qaeda's international efforts.

How does this information relate to Spain and 3/11? What is the relationship between the drone strike in Haisori on December 1, 2005, and the Madrid train bombings? To begin, one of the four casualties, alongside Rabia, was a former important member of the Spanish al-Qaeda cell created in 1994: Amer Azizi. Azizi, whose name has been mentioned many times throughout the first part of this book, had been in Iran at the time of Operation Dátil in November 2001 and thus had escaped capture by the Spanish authorities. From Iran, he joined up with al-Qaeda's central organizational structures in Afghanistan and Pakistan, and would go on to become instrumental in the crafting of the plan to attack Spain.

"Bravo for Amer, who went to wage jihad in Afghanistan!": From an al-Qaeda cell in Spain to al-Qaeda's Central Organization in Pakistan

The US authorities confirmed Amer Azizi's identity sometime after his remains were found following the Haisori attack.[5] Azizi had various nicknames, including Othman el-Andalusi—another allusion to Spain and Al-Andalus—and occasionally, during his time in Spain, he went by the name Othman al-Farouk, after al-Qaeda's Al-Faruq training camp in Kandahar, Afghanistan, which Azizi had attended in 2001. Later, when he was living in Afghanistan and Pakistan, he adopted other nicknames, such as Yafar al-Maghrebi and Yafar Marrakeshi (both of which alluded to his Moroccan origins), or simply Yafar or Ilyas for short. Azizi's name also appeared as "Ilyas the Spanish," alongside that of Hamza Rabia, in a notebook of telephone numbers that belonged to an important al-Qaeda director of operations. This man, a British citizen of Pakistani origins, was arrested in 2006 and convicted in 2008 by a Manchester Crown Court.[6]

Amer Azizi was born in 1968 in Hedami, Morocco, some 70 kilometers southeast of Casablanca. According to his brother, Azizi had a difficult childhood, owing to his absent parents. His father died when he was six months old, and his mother gave him to one of her brothers, who was married but lacked children.[7] A childhood friend remembered Azizi as someone who drank "too much" beer, smoked hash, enjoyed reggae, and was considered "an open individual, open to Europe and the Europeans."[8] He immigrated to Spain at the end of the 1980s or beginning of the 1990s, and sometime after moving to Madrid he immersed himself in Islam, adopting an exclusive and rigorist view. In his home, this change did not occur unnoticed. In the words of his childhood friend, "he became a different Amer. He could not understand us. He would not stop saying 'this is a sin,' 'that is a sin.' We grew distant. The new Amer had become a complete stranger."[9] During his time in Madrid, Azizi met a native Spanish woman, Raquel Burgos, who converted to Islam and married him.

If one were to identify an experience in Spain that changed Azizi's perspective on Islam from the faith practiced in his native Morocco, it was his attendance at Tablighi Jamaat meetings. In this, he shared the experience of other individuals who would be attracted to Abu Dahdah's cell, including Serhane ben Abdelmajid Fakhet and Jamal Zougam. In that religious environment, Azizi attracted Abu Dahdah's attention, an acquaintanceship that further radicalized Azizi's beliefs and attitudes, until he joined Abu Dahdah's cell in 1995. Abu Dahdah immediately sent him to receive training in the use of arms and explosives in a training camp in Zenica, Bosnia.[10] By 2000, Azizi also had received training in Afghanistan in al-Qaeda's Al-Faruq camp and in the Libyan Islamic Fighting Group's Abu Yahya camp.[11]

Azizi's experience in these and perhaps other camps converted him into a revered member of Abu Dahdah's cell, and he became a trusted confidant of the leader.[12] Azizi stood out for his activities radicalizing and recruiting terrorists. He made jihadist proclamations in the meetings convened by Abu Dahdah and his followers, and at Islamic oratories in Madrid neighborhoods like Embajadores e Iglesia. On various occasions, he directly addressed the senior officials of notable Islamic institutions like the M-30 mosque, reproaching them for following what he considered an incorrect version of Islam because they were not sufficiently fundamentalist or bellicose.[13] In 2000, during a dispute with the directors of the mosque, he even assaulted one of them, a man who used a wheelchair.[14]

The effects of Azizi's jihadist mobilization efforts, mainly in Madrid, were evident both inside and outside of Spain. At the end of 2001, British soldiers who were participating in the US invasion of Afghanistan found al-Qaeda documents pertaining to Moroccans living in Spain who had or were meant to receive training in Afghanistan. The documents noted that the person who was sending these individuals to Afghanistan for training in the use of arms and explosives was Othman el-Andalusi, or Amer Azizi.[15] In November 2001, during Operation Dátil, Azizi was in Iran, sorting out business relating to the route taken by jihadists who had been recruited in Spain. At the time, the authorities in Tehran tolerated those activities.[16] Azizi's work in Iran allowed him to avoid arrest, making him one of the six members of Abu Dahdah's cell who remained free after Operation Dátil. In December 2001, Azizi managed to reach Pakistan.[17]

Once the Spanish authorities realized that Amer Azizi had escaped, they released a search-and-arrest warrant against him, charging him with belonging to a terrorist organization. Among the documents that police found in Azizi's home in Madrid were items written by him that defined jihad as "one of the most elevated actions that a Muslim can dedicate himself to."[18] In those same pages, he wrote that "to assure survival and expansion, the Islamic faith established jihad or holy war, and its objective is none other than subjecting the world to the world of Islam."[19] Among Azizi's belongings, Spanish police also found various videos with images of battles in Bosnia, Chechnya, Kashmir, and Palestine, as well as CDs with propaganda from the Taliban in Afghanistan and sermons and texts by jihadist ideologues like Abu Qatada.[20] Azizi certainly would have used all of these materials as instruments for proselytization and indoctrination when he was recruiting individuals to send to training camps in Afghanistan or Indonesia. The jihadist websites that Azizi visited and the contents that he downloaded from those sites served the same purpose.[21] However, the items that surprised the National Police Corps agents the most during their search were the axe and the huge black wooden truncheon they found in his home.[22] On September 17, 2003, the Central Investigative Court No. 5 of the National Court of Spain indicted Azizi on the charge of his connections with terrorist organizations. By this point, though, Azizi had become part of al-Qaeda's central organizational structure, which he joined after arriving in Pakistan to evade the ongoing police search in Spain.

Once inside al-Qaeda, at the beginning of 2002, Azizi took part in the military incursions that al-Qaeda led into Afghanistan. Above all, he participated in attacks against the International Security Assistance Force, to which the Spanish government had contributed troops as part of a provincial reconstruction team.[23] Azizi's activities were known in jihadi circles as well as other Islamic collectives around Madrid; in their discussions, they would comment that "the people say that he [Azizi] went to Afghanistan," or "rumor has it that he went to Afghanistan."[24] In meetings held in 2002 in an apartment in the Madrid neighborhood of Villaverde Bajo, attended by members of the incipient 3/11 network such as Mustafa Maymouni, Driss Chebli, and Serhane ben Abdelmajid Fakhet, the attendees praised Azizi, saying: "Bravo for Amer, who went to wage jihad in Afghanistan!"[25]

Owing to his contributions to the organization's efforts, Amer Azizi progressively ascended the ranks of al-Qaeda and assumed new tasks within the terrorist structure. As the Spanish authorities continued to investigate the components of Abu Dahdah's dismantled cell, a new indictment dated April 28, 2004—just over a month after the Madrid bombings—expanded the list of terrorism-related accusations against Azizi and enabled the authorities to fulfill the requirements for an international arrest and extradition warrant. In particular, the indictment contained evidence from emails that linked Azizi to an al-Qaeda facilitator who maintained ties with Khalid Sheikh Mohammed, the mastermind of 9/11.[26]

An Adjunct to al-Qaeda's External Operations Chief

Although Amer Azizi was killed by the US drone strike in December 2005, US intelligence did not make the information it had on his death, as well as his high-ranking position in al-Qaeda's hierarchy, available to the Spanish authorities until September 2006. At the time, the United States needed information from police specialists in Spain about whether Azizi had maintained contacts with other terrorists in Latin America, and US intelligence passed the following message to the Spanish internal security authorities:

We are pleased to advise your service that Amer Azizi, who was wanted by your government for his ties to Imad Eddin Barakat Yarkas [i.e., Abu Dahdah], was recently identified as Pakistan-based Al-Qa'ida operative Jafar al-Maghrebi aka Iyas. Jafar worked directly for Hamza Rabia, the former chief of Al-Qa'ida external operations. Both individuals were killed in December 2005.

This note does not mention the manner in which Rabia and Azizi died. This omission results from the fact that the use of Hellfire missiles launched from drones, although authorized by the White House and frequently discussed in the mainstream press, remained officially classified in those days.[27]

A month after sharing this information, US counterterrorism officials expressed more concern about the potential connections that Amer Azizi might have developed in other countries, especially in Latin America, where it would be possible to launch or support al-Qaeda attacks against the United States. For that reason, in October 2006, US intelligence asked the Spanish authorities once more for relevant information on this topic. Along with their petition for further information, they provided more information regarding Azizi's death:

We previously advised your service that Amir el-Azizi, who prior to 11 September 2001 was a member of Barakat Yarkas' [i.e., Abu Dahdah's] Spain-based Al-Qai'da cell, was killed in December 2005 in Pakistan. At the time of his death, el-Azizi was closely linked to then chief of Al-Qai'da external operations, Hamza Rabi'a (also killed in December 2005). In Pakistan, el-Azizi was known as Jafar al-Maghrebi aka Ilyas.

It is now our assessment that el-Azizi was intimately involved with Rabi'a in the planning of the global operations on many fronts. Prior to their deaths, we deem it plausible that el-Azizi may have recommended to Rabi'a the use of his (el-Azizi's) global contacts as potential participants in future operations. Thus, tracking historical contacts of el-Azizi might aid us in uncovering current plans, and our service is in the process of searching all past information about el-Azizi and his network of contacts with the hope of developing new leads to potential operatives of interest.

Inside al-Qaeda's central command, Azizi developed his activities alongside senior member Abd al-Hadi al-Iraqi, who was charged with conducting raids into Afghanistan.[28] He also associated himself with Mustafa Abul

Yazid (known by his nickname "Said al-Masri"), a veteran leader who was at the forefront of al-Qaeda's financial committee. Another important link was Khalid Habib; until his death, also by a drone strike, in 2008, Habib was regarded as one of the most capable al-Qaeda strategists in South Asia.[29] Azizi's rapid trajectory since 2002 suggests that he was an important and highly valued member of al-Qaeda, with enough experience and knowledge to act as a director of terrorist operations in Western countries in general and in Europe in particular. In this sense, it proves significant that a 2005 European Union report on al-Qaeda's leadership alludes to an unidentified Moroccan operative who was based in Afghanistan and Pakistan. The EU report considered this unidentified individual to be one of the main leaders of the organization, and noted that he "formerly acted as an intermediary between [al-Qaeda senior leader] Abu Faraj al-Libi and Western Europe, where he resided."[30]

Throughout 2006, four captured al-Qaeda operatives who were being held in US custody provided more information on Amer Azizi. Their information not only corroborated the available information concerning his escape from Spain and his integration into al-Qaeda, but also elaborated on the role that he had played in Afghanistan and Pakistan. They described a figure of great importance inside al-Qaeda who did not lack conceit. They also revealed that at the moment of his death alongside Hamza Rabia, Azizi and his chief were planning similar attacks to those of 3/11 and the 2005 London bombings in an unspecified city in the United States.

In September 2007, the United States shared more information with Spanish intelligence. Part of this information came from the al-Qaeda operatives they had detained (quoting a US government source):

We would like to inform you that information from three detainees in the past year have revealed that Amer Azizi (also known as Ja'far Marrakeshi, Ilyas, and Uthman), whom we understand you have investigated as possibly having a role in the bombings in Madrid in March 2004, is the same person as Ja'far al-Maghrebi, a confirmed Al-Qa'ida operative active in Afghanistan and Pakistan during 2001–2005, and killed in the late 2005. According to these detainees as well as a fourth detainee, Ja'far arrived in Afghanistan in about 2001, and by 2003 had become a paramilitary sub commander, involved in cross-border raids into Afghanistan from Al-Qa'ida safe haven in the Tribal Areas of Pakistan. One detainee even remarked that Ja'far in 2005 showed him articles from Spanish newspapers regarding the "manhunt" for an individual known as Amer Azizi, and Ja'far told the detainee that he was that person and they were not dealing with just a "normal guy." The detainee opined that Ja'far told him this to establish his terrorist credentials and standing with the detainee. Finally, two of the detainees stated that in 2005 Ja'far was a key assistant to Al-Qai'da external operations chief Hamza Rabi'a, and that Azizi was working with Rabi'a on a plot to send suicide bombers to the United States before the two were killed in an explosion in December 2005.

We hope that this information is helpful in your ongoing investigation of the perpetrators of the March 2004 attacks.

The US intelligence services are not the only valid source for information on Amer Azizi and his trajectory in Afghanistan and Pakistan since he evaded arrest in Spain in 2001. In 2009, an al-Qaeda chronicler named Abu Ubayda al-Maqdisi provided information that confirmed the reports shared by the United States with Spain. Al-Maqdisi wrote a concise but detailed homage to a man who had been an important member of Abu Dahdah's cell, and later an important figure in al-Qaeda's external operations until his death.

"Between majestic mountains began his journey, this son of Casablanca": An al-Qaeda Hagiography of Amer Azizi

Through important internet jihadi forums and websites, Tauhid Press disseminated a summary of Amer Azizi's life as part of series called "Martyrs of the Magreb al-Aqsa in the land of the Hindu Kush," dedicated to terrorists of Moroccan origins who died in Afghanistan and Pakistan. It published this brief biography in Arabic, and it includes significant traces of the activities that Azizi undertook in the heart of al-Qaeda, some of which coincided with the information known by US intelligence services. The following is an English translation of the contents of this biography:

Abu Yafar, the Preacher in the Path of Allah

Let Allah accept him as martyr.

How many lost individuals have found the path of truth through you?

How many of those in error have found the right path through the melody of your preaching?

How many incredulous individuals have exhaled the aroma of Islam and the fragrance of the faith with your sweet voice that proclaimed, "There is no other God but Allah and Mohammed is his prophet?"

Abu Yafar, whose name is Amer al-Azizi, was born in Casablanca. In his journey of coming and going in its alleyways, wide streets, and schools, he learned the secular sciences that prepared him to continue his studies in one of the universities of Morocco, where he specialized in translation. After spending some years in the hallways of that university, our martyr graduated with a degree in the Spanish language.

In spite of his leading a comfortable life, the idea of going to Spain took over his mind, and just as it happened to many of Morocco's children, with the hope of working in that land that once had sought protection under the Unity.

Amer prepared himself, gathered his things, and left his family and friends. Quickly, he began working in a mundane profession, losing his time vainly and rolling in the ignorance of Spain, until the Almighty wanted to show the True Way to this lost man.

On a blessed day, when he was dialoguing with a friend, who also was lost, this one began to insult Islam and taunted Muslims with indecent words. It was then that the flame of the religion of Allah lit itself in the most intimate part of Abu Yafar, and he began to defend Islam.

He returned home and began to ask himself the following questions: Am I really Muslim? How can I be Muslim if I am not dedicated to the teachings of Islam?

He had only begun to taste the return to faith, when he dedicated himself to the science of religion, becoming a preacher in the path of Allah, seeing himself pass through the mosques in Spain and its centers for preaching.

Among lost minds who found their way to Allah through his vocation is his Spanish wife, who quickly became a devoted wife who gave him three sons and shared with him the difficult journey of emigration and of jihad.

Impelled by the strength of that religion and by the invincible Muslim character, he journeyed to the land of combat and of martyrdom, Afghanistan, reuniting with those in charge of the training camps which he incorporated himself into and which he had the Quran and the sharia as company.

Only a few months had passed since his emigration when he gathered his things once more to return to Spain, a cause of his work, and with the desire to commit some jihadist action in those usurped lands.

Once inside Spain of the Cross, he began to prepare himself, along his compatriots in jihad, to attack targets of the crusaders but, shortly after, his secret was discovered and the Spanish intelligence services did not hesitate in detaining most of the jihadist cell, coinciding this deed with the blessed attacks in New York and Washington.

Before that bitter reality, our martyr, accompanied by his compatriot, the brother Bilal al-Magrebi, fled to Iran of the renegades and from there into Afghanistan.

As such, between majestic mountains began his journey, this son of Casablanca. He formed part of the first detachment that attacked the Christians after the sad invasion of Afghanistan. His role was not limited to military activity, and extended to the administrative environment, assuming responsibility for one of the military sections, in an administrative capacity. He excelled at this test, serving his brothers and guaranteeing their needs.

He had not been long at this work when the Emir placed his trust in him to establish an information team. This is where his qualities in the art of translation came to light, as he provided translations for numerous actions. After a few months, the emir general put him in charge of one the military sections, and in this way, the crusaders tasted the fury of the mujahedin, at the hands of him and his brothers.

Qualities and characteristics: noble, at the service of his brothers, translator of the highest quality, of great intelligence, filled with fervor for this religion.

Days passed quickly for our emir. After a long time in the frontlines of combat, he assumed the function of adjunct to the one in charge for exterior action, due to his singular mentality, his good management, and his ample horizons.

He began a new journey, focusing on foreign activities, as an instructor for the lions that came from afar with the purpose of transforming the tranquillity of the crusaders into a hell.

After much sacrifice, the Almighty permitted this wandering knight to incorporate himself into the caravan of the noble martyrs. As such, on a sad day, while our martyr was accompanied by his emir, the one responsible for external operations, in one of the secret refugee camps of the Unity, the traitors formed a conspiracy that ended with the life of a group of Mohammed's inheritors, and after the eyes of the apostates had verified the presence of the objective they sought in his hiding place, the traitorous tongues suggested to their bosses the necessity of bombing the hiding place where he was. A few minutes had passed when the crusaders fell like a whirlwind, with all their hate, on Abu Yafar and his brothers, transforming them into dust in that refuge.

And here, among the mounds of earth, the knight of Casablanca, who can be described as a brother of bravery, fell from his horse and became worthy that we should become echoes of his farewell.

Tauhid Press 1430–2009[31]

In addition to referring to other armed activities, his administrative activities, and the communications tasks that Amer Azizi carried out "between majestic mountains" in al-Qaeda's central organization, the document also confirms that when he died, he was assistant to the chief of external operations—namely, Hamza Rabia. As seen from Spain, where Azizi began his jihadist career as a member of Abu Dahdah's cell and where the Madrid train bombings occurred, there are other revelatory pieces. Of particular note is Azizi's role in helping to carry out external operations, and his part in instructing "the lions that came from afar with the purpose of transforming the tranquillity of the crusaders into a hell."

Was Spain Targeted by Azizi, on Behalf of al-Qaeda, Even Before 9/11?

Abu Ubayda al-Maqdisi's hagiography of Amer Azizi describes Azizi's work in training camps in Afghanistan in early 2001, suggesting that this "son of Casablanca" was tasked by al-Qaeda with perpetrating an attack in Spain before the September 11 attacks.[32] Al-Maqdisi writes that after a few months of "meeting with those who were in charge of the training camps which he incorporated himself into," Azizi returned to Spain "with the hope of carrying out some jihadist action in those usurped lands." This last phrase is a typical jihadist allusion to Al-Andalus, the medieval Islamic dominion over most of the Iberian Peninsula. Moreover, as the document explains, "once inside Spain of the Cross, [Azizi] began to prepare himself, in the company of other companions of the jihad, to attack targets of the crusaders."

Those intentions to attack in Spain would have dated to the summer of 2001. Several points provide clues to this line of reasoning. First, the summer of 2001 was when Azizi returned to Spain as a member of Abu Dahdah's cell. Second, as al-Maqdisi relates, Azizi's jihadist intentions would have been frustrated because "the Spanish intelligence services detained most of the members of that jihadist cell, something that coincided with the blessed attacks in New York and Washington." Even though this last point does not provide a precise date or name the specific Spanish security agency involved, it undoubtedly refers to the dismantling of Abu Dahdah's cell during Operation Dátil in November 2001. It may also be a subtle reference to the links between Abu Dahdah's cell in Madrid and the al-Qaeda cell in Hamburg, Germany, whose members were directly involved in preparing and executing the September 11 attacks. It is telling, too, that al-Maqdisi's account notes that the Spanish authorities detained "most" of the members of that jihadist cell in Spain—but not all.

Incidentally, it is interesting to note that Raquel Burgos, Amer Azizi's widow, married another man after Azizi's death: Said Bahaji.[33] Bahaji, a German citizen and the son of a Moroccan immigrant, lived with 9/11 hijacker Mohamed Atta and 9/11 coordinator Ramzi Binalshibh in Hamburg, and handled their affairs while they were abroad to ensure that their absence would not be noticed by the authorities.[34] On September 3, 2001, Bahaji had departed Hamburg for Afghanistan, via Istanbul and Karachi, and in Istanbul he boarded in the same place as the Algerian Mohamed Belfatmi, an al-Qaeda member who had resided in Spain and who was connected to both Abu Dahdah and Amer Azizi.[35] The information on this new marriage came from another source, the testimony of a German citizen of Syrian descent who had been integrated into al-Qaeda and who was captured by Pakistani troops in North Waziristan in June 2010. American officials interrogated this man and handed him over to the German authorities; currently, he is serving a prison sentence in Germany for his involvement in terrorist activity.[36] This source provided a number of revelations concerning the threat that al-Qaeda continued to pose to Western European societies in the decade after 9/11; in particular, he stated that he had been developing his activities alongside Said Bahaji in North Waziristan—the same place where Amer Azizi and Hamza Rabia were killed in early December 2005. Around 2012, it is possible that Said Bahaji was in charge of al-Sahab, the propaganda wing of al-Qaeda. In the fall of 2009, during an offensive against the Taliban and al-Qaeda in South Waziristan, the Pakistani army recovered two passports from the ruins of a demolished house. These passports belonged to Raquel Burgos and Said Bahaji.[37]

9
A Meeting in Karachi:
Making the Decision to Attack Spain

The terrorist mobilization process that culminated in the 2004 Madrid bombings did not begin in the Madrid neighborhood of Lavapiés, or among the Moroccan Islamic Combatant Group members on the periphery of Brussels. It began in December 2001 in the Pakistani city of Karachi. Karachi, an ethnically and linguistically diverse port city with more than 18 million inhabitants, is Pakistan's primary commercial and financial hub and home to its main airport. For more than two decades, numerous jihadist organizations have used Karachi as a refuge because it is home to hundreds of madrasas and Quranic schools that teach strict, extremist views of Islam.[1] Over the years, the Pakistani authorities have detained many al-Qaeda militants and militants linked to al-Qaeda affiliates, including some standout figures, in Karachi. Some of these individuals have planned and orchestrated terrorist attacks on other countries, while others have used Karachi as a staging ground to prepare attacks inside Pakistan.

Pakistan became the epicenter of global terrorism after the US invasion of Afghanistan in late 2001. The core of al-Qaeda and its related organizations left their former home and set up operations in the remote and often inaccessible northeastern part of Pakistan, where they could plan and prepare their attacks across the globe. Yet al-Qaeda and other jihadist organizations also found excellent refuge in metropolises like Karachi. Khalid Sheikh Mohammed, for example, relocated to Karachi in 2002, and from there he operated as chief of al-Qaeda's external operations until his arrest in March 2003. One of the cofounders of al-Qaeda's Spanish cell, Mustafa Setmarian Nasar (also known as Mustafa Musab al-Suri), who had left Spain for London in 1994 and then went to Afghanistan in 1996, also was detained by the Pakistani authorities in Karachi in April or May 2005. And Karachi was where, in December 2001, Amer Azizi colluded with another coreligionist of Moroccan descent, Abdelatif Mourafik, to make Spain suffer the full force of his jihadist retribution. Mourafik had arrived in Karachi after fleeing the American bombardment of al-Qaeda's and its affiliate organizations' Afghan infrastructure, and had intended to travel to Turkey via Iran.[2] The details of Azizi's and Mourafik's meeting appear in a highly revealing document from the US National Counterterrorism Center (NCTC), dated August 2008. This report, titled "The Case for Al Qai'da Links to the 2004 Madrid Bombing," compiled fundamental information from intelligence services around the world and included declarations from notable al-Qaeda members who had been detained in various countries since 2006. The information in this NCTC report is particularly critical when considering how the massacre on the Madrid commuter trains was planned and prepared.[3]

Amer Azizi and Abdelatif Mourafik: Building the Connections for the 3/11 Network

Abdelatif Mourafik, Azizi's fellow conspirator, was known as Malek al-Maghrebi, and at certain times as Malek el-Andalusi—yet another reference to his connections to jihadism in Spain. He had been born in Morocco, but he belonged to the Libyan Islamic Fighting Group, and had been radicalized and recruited in his home country in the latter half of the 1990s by another Moroccan named Karim el-Mejatti, a member of both the Moroccan Islamic Combatant Group and al-Qaeda. Mourafik had moved to Afghanistan in 2000 where he kept ties, both in Herat and in Kabul, with the Jordanian Ahmad Fadl Nazzal al-Khalayleh, better known as Abu Musab al-Zarqawi.[4] The relationship between Mourafik and Zarqawi highlights the transnational links of the members of the 3/11 network. With the acquiescence of al-Qaeda's senior leadership, Zarqawi and his group, Tawhid wal-Jihad, had aligned themselves with Ansar al-Islam, the emerging Sunni insurgent organization in northern Iraq, after having lost their base in Afghanistan at the end of 2001. Once relocated, Tawhid wal-Jihad cooperated from 2002 onward with Ansar al-Islam and al-Qaeda to design and develop terrorist activities in Western Europe, establishing cells based in the United Kingdom, France, Germany, and Italy. All of these cells had ties to Spain.[5]

Zarqawi and his cohorts were active in planning and preparing attacks, including some that had an unconventional character, such as the use of poisonous substances. To accomplish their group's joint projects, they sent a group of North African jihadists who originally had been based in the Pankisi Gorge in Georgia—an operational site frequently used by Islamist militants and Chechen rebels—into Europe. Counterterrorist operations conducted near Paris and London in December 2002 frustrated those plans.[6] Spain assisted these international operations through its own counterterrorism action, known as Operation Lago, developed by the National Police Corps in Catalonia in December 2002. During Operation Lago, the Spanish authorities detained thirteen individuals in Barcelona and the nearby city of Banyoles (Bañolas) who were linked to the Salafist Group for Preaching and Combat (GSPC) and had ties to the individuals detained in the Paris and London counterterrorist sweeps. In Barcelona and Banyoles, as well as in four other Catalan towns, the counterterrorism units recovered a considerable amount of flammable and toxic liquids that were capable of producing highly abrasive substances and could be incorporated into explosive devices.[7] Even though Operation Dátil had rounded up many individuals connected with al-Qaeda in Spain in late 2001, al-Qaeda and its affiliated networks had managed to maintain a presence in Spain, which would be reinforced in the months and years to come.

The December 2001 meeting in Karachi was not the first time that Azizi and Mourafik had found themselves working together. They initially had met in Afghanistan at the beginning of 2001 at the Martyr Abu Yahya camp, an indoctrination and training installation run by the LIFG, some 30 kilometers north of Kabul. The training camp's program emphasized terrorist tactics. Along with individuals recruited by the LIFG, mainly Libyans but also from other Maghreb countries, the camp hosted MICG recruits. At the end of the 1990s, the LIFG and the MICG had agreed to coordinate their activities, a decision that later would help enable the Madrid attacks. Leaders of both terrorist organizations would be implicated in the formation and development of the 3/11 network, and their decision to reorient and combine their operational activities directly affected the jihadist terrorist threat for Spain.

In spite of his al-Qaeda connections, when Amer Azizi decided to attack Spain in the wake of Operation Dátil, he did so not as an individual who was part of al-Qaeda's core organization, but rather as someone who recently had been cut off from the al-Qaeda cell to which he had belonged until November 2001. Therefore, Azizi's decision to orchestrate an act of terrorism in Spain does not reflect al-Qaeda's collective decision-making process; instead, it stemmed from the thinking of an individual who had belonged to a subordinate cell based in Spain and had extensive transnational connections. The initial decision of this "son of Casablanca" was made independent of the leaders of al-Qaeda, whom Azizi would lobby after he joined al-Qaeda central to approve his project for a major attack in Madrid.

"If they combat you, kill them until there is no persecution": Revenge as a Motivation

Although the biography of Amer Azizi reproduced in chapter 8 claimed that he had been considering an attack in Spain even before 9/11, it is plausible that the dismantling of Abu Dahdah's cell in November 2001 and the jailing of its leader and many of its members inspired a deep feeling of hatred that precipitated and exacerbated Azizi's jihadist desires. In this light, for Amer Azizi and his fellow conspirators, a desire for revenge on those who had thwarted their initial jihadist efforts would have been essential in the decision to attack in Spain and the early efforts to mobilize the 3/11 network. A few points corroborate this perspective. Azizi himself, a former member of the dismantled cell, played a key part in deciding to launch an attack in Spain and in securing al-Qaeda's approval for his efforts. Another former cell member, Mustafa Maymouni, took on the task of rebuilding a new and operationally decisive jihadist cell in Madrid from the remnants of the previous one. And three of Abu Dahdah's acolytes—Serhane ben Abdelmajid Fakhet, Said Berraj, and Jamal Zougam—played important roles in preparing and executing the commuter train bombings.

The importance of revenge—an emotional response, rather than one based on rational calculations—is often underestimated as a motivator for the execution of singular acts of terrorism. Nonetheless, studies of this phenomenon in its expressions as either left-wing or right-wing terrorism in Europe during the 1970s show that terror attacks often were committed with the intent of avenging the death or arrest of specific militants.[8] It therefore is important to appreciate that revenge—perceived by its instigators as a deliberate way to cause damage in retribution for a previous harm done—

can become an important impetus in the decision, at least initially, to plan an act of terror. This finding holds true, even in cases of indiscriminate attacks that are meant to harm the greatest number of targets, like those that occurred in Madrid in March 2004. Ultimately, the terrorist ideology stipulates the limits, if they exist, on the type or occasion of the attack or the nature of the victims.

In addition, in the case of 3/11, the desire for revenge extended beyond the personal feelings of Azizi and other members of Abu Dahdah's former cell. As discussed in chapter 3, Allekema Lamari, the Algerian militant who had been arrested as part of the dismantling of the Armed Islamic Group cell in Valencia in 1997 during Operation Apreciate, swore that Spain and the Spanish would "pay dearly" for his detention. According to evidence compiled by Spanish intelligence, Lamari failed to hide his "resentment toward Spain," declaring that once he left prison, his "only objective" was "to carry out terrorist attacks on national (Spanish) territory of enormous dimensions, with the purpose of causing the largest number of possible victims." One of the intelligence documents, written after the Madrid attacks and the Leganés suicide explosion, affirmed that if Lamari had not been one of those who had died in the Leganés apartment, he would have been dedicated to "continuing his particular revenge against the Spanish population and its interests with the execution of new terrorist attacks."[9]

In any case, this decision to attack Spain was not just about a desire for revenge on either Azizi's or Lamari's part. In his appearance before the Spanish parliament's 3/11 investigation commission on July 7, 2004, Mariano Rayón, the then head of the Central Unit for External Information—the CNP unit that specializes in investigating international terrorism—included these words in his response to a member of parliament:

> I believe that we have done—and I can verify this—more counterterror-
> ist operations than any of the other Western countries, which can count
> on more resources than us.[10]

Rayón added:

> Our unit is on permanent alert. It would be impossible otherwise to carry
> out as many operations as we have completed in the past few years.[11]

Responding to another question asked by a different member of parliament, he noted that between July 2002 and July 2004, the UCIE had launched seventeen operations against jihadist terrorism resulting in more than 150 arrests. He concluded, "It is practically impossible to do more."[12] Responding to a third member of the investigative commission, he insisted that "we have aborted various terrorist plots here and in other friendly countries in the European context."[13] Therefore, it is possible to suppose that a contributing motive for the jihadists formerly active in Spain—according to their version of reality, given their Salafist-jihadist ideology—is the sense that they were being persecuted by the Spanish authorities, and therefore they had become more hostile toward the country as a whole.

Whatever the predominating motivations, the initial decision to perpetrate a grand attack in Spain and to mobilize the necessary resources for the project that culminated so violently on four commuter trains heading toward Atocha station on March 11, 2004, originated with Amer Azizi in Karachi in 2001. Not coincidentally, even as Azizi was contemplating the possibilities for terrorist revenge against Spain and its citizens, the Spanish police, suspecting that he had fled the country, searched his flat in Madrid during Operation Dátil in November 2001. There they found, among other things, a piece of paper highlighted by "the son of Casablanca," whose language clearly evokes two verses from the second surah of the Quran. This text, marked by Azizi himself, expressly states his expected reaction to the counterterrorist operations—the persecutions—of the Spanish authorities:

"Combat in the path of Allah those that combat against you; kill them where you find them; if they combat you, kill them until there is no persecution and in its place the religion of Allah rises."[14]

Kill them, the Quranic verses proclaim, *until there is no persecution*—and Azizi, as well as Lamari and other individuals implicated in planning, preparing, and executing the Madrid attacks, felt that they had good reason to believe that they were being persecuted. The Spanish judicial authorities had released an international search-and-capture order for those who had been members of his cell. The Spanish state security forces, the Fuerzas y Cuerpos de Seguridad del Estado (FCSE) had acted against his cell, as well as others, and had arrested many of their members and leaders and sent them to prison. Azizi and the other 3/11 terrorists interpreted these facts in the context of their Salafist-jihadist worldview, with its fundamentalist, irrational, and bellicose reading of the Quran. This interpretation, with its exhortation to violent action, would have dramatic consequences for Spain, including 191 dead and more than 1800 injured in the Madrid bombings.

The Madrid attacks are not the only case in which the legitimate counterterrorist activities conducted by a given state affected—not necessarily in a deterrent sense—the decisions adopted by individuals implicated in global terrorist actions who were residing in Western Europe. On occasion, those individuals reacted by designating their home countries and hosting societies as targets. One such earlier example, which had less bloody consequences, was the Hofstad Network in the Netherlands. This jihadist network included the Dutch-Moroccan Mohammed Bouyeri, who would murder Dutch film director Theo van Gogh in November 2004. (Earlier in the year, van Gogh had directed and produced *Submission*, a short drama film that criticized the treatment of women in fundamentalist Islam.) In 2003, Dutch security, which was cooperating with its security and intelligence counterparts in Portugal and Pakistan, began to put pressure on individual members of this network, resulting in various arrests and administrative expulsions. In the face of this perceived persecution, the network begin to conspire that same year against Dutch targets in their local immigrant neighborhoods where they resided.[15]

Morocco and Spain as Targets of Jihad

After Azizi and Mourafik met in Karachi in December 2001, another important summit occurred in February 2002. In that month, delegates from the LIFG, MICG, and the Tunisian Combatant Group (TCG) met in Istanbul. This meeting brought together representatives from the Maghrebi jihadist organizations that had lost their bases after the US intervention in Afghanistan. Notably, the Istanbul meeting did not include representatives from the GSPC; unlike the other three organizations, the GSPC had maintained its bases in the interior of Algeria, where it originally had operated.[16] That February in Istanbul, the LIFG, the MICG, and the TCG agreed to modify their operational approach and reorient their respective organizations to work more closely with each other. Deprived of their Afghan facilities, part of their members opted to relocate to the tribal areas in Pakistan, while others dedicated themselves to reinforcing the clandestine structures in their countries of origins or in designated countries in Western Europe.

Moreover, the delegates of all three jihadist organizations took a decision that specifically would alter the parameters of the terrorist threat for Spain.

The organizations, sharing a common Maghrebi origin, resolved that they should not limit the execution of jihadist acts to zones of armed conflict affecting Muslim populations. They agreed instead that these acts also should occur in the places where their members originated or resided, regardless of whether the countries in question were majority-Muslim or were populated mainly by infidels. The sequence of events is telling. The Istanbul summit occurred in February 2002; the Casablanca attacks ensued on May 2003; and the Madrid bombings took place in March 2004. Both the Casablanca and Madrid attacks involved members who belonged to at least two of the jihadist organizations present at this operational meeting in Istanbul.

Sumario 20/2004 of the National Court, the main criminal proceedings opened after the March 11 attacks in Madrid and the April 3 suicide attack in Leganés, includes an interesting note provided by the FCSE on this meeting and the operational reorientation adopted by the Maghrebi jihadist organizations.[17] The literal contents of the note, elaborated in part by information supplied by European and North African security services that regularly cooperate with the respective CNP and Guardia Civil counterterrorist units, is as follows:

> From intelligence reports, it is known that in February 2002, a meeting occurred in Istanbul where the leaders of the Libyan, Moroccan, and Tunisian Islamic Combating Groups agreed that the jihad should happen in those places where they reside, without the "good Muslim" having to leave for places where open conflict with Islam existed, like Chechnya, Kashmir, Afghanistan, Bosnia, Iraq, etc. According to those reports, under the coordination of Abu Musab al-Zarqawi, the terrorist leader associated with al-Qaeda and with the proclamations already made by Osama bin Laden—where he progressively situated Morocco and Spain as objectives for where to attack—the decision appears to have been made, requiring only the moment [to attack], situating the objective, and defining who would execute it.
>
> That is why the attacks in Casablanca were granted legitimacy, and possibly as well those in Madrid.

Notably, Abu Musab al-Zarqwai is suggested here to have played a significant role in the choice to make Morocco and Spain the targets of the jihad. In any case, the proposal that jihadist acts should occur in places where members of terrorist organizations resided would spread throughout jihadist networks in Madrid the month after the Istanbul meeting. By March 2002, meetings were being held to sketch out the framework of what would become the 3/11 network. In these meetings, Mohamed Larbi ben Sellam (an individual already mentioned in the first part of this book) explained to those in attendance—at this point, mainly Moroccans—that it was not necessary to travel to Afghanistan or Chechnya to carry out jihad. It was possible to do so in Morocco and Spain.[18]

Chapter 7's discussion on the formation of the 3/11 network pointed out that Mustafa Maymouni, who until November 2001 had belonged to the Abu Dahdah cell, acted as the local organizer and promoter. Maymouni was not acting on his own initiative, but rather was following orders. These instructions came directly from the meeting that Amer Azizi and Abdelatif Mourafik had held in Karachi in December 2001, instructions which complemented the operative revisions adopted by the three jihadist Maghrebi organizations that met in Istanbul in February 2002. Maymouni acted and carried out the orders given to him by Mourafik.[19] He communicated with Mourafik directly by using a shared email account, the password for which the latter had given him.[20] The instructions that Mourafik gave were the same ones he had acquired from Azizi, the man who originally had brought them together. In this manner, Maymouni received the mission to establish jihadist cells in Morocco and Spain, the former in the port city of Kenitra in northern Morocco and the latter in Madrid.

Maymouni began in Kenitra, as he had moved temporarily to Morocco following Operation Dátil. Jamal Zougam assisted him in this task. Both had met in a café in Tangier in December 2001, with Zougam accompanied by Salaheddin Benyaich, also known as Abu Mughen (see chapter 2).[21] Abu Mughen, who later would be arrested in Morocco for terrorist activities, helped Maymouni find a base for the cell in Kenitra and procured passports to facilitate their activities.[22] This cell intended to attack foreign targets in Morocco, but the Moroccan authorities were able to dismantle it in May 2003, although not before cell members had attacked a mausoleum in the city of Larache. Maymouni was detained and sentenced in Morocco. Given that Maymouni had been indicted previously in Spain, the Spanish National Court attempted to have him transferred temporarily to Spain, but the Moroccan authorities refused, alleging that there had been formal deficiencies in the Spanish request. The Spanish National Court declared Maymouni *en rebeldía*—"in default," a term for a defendant who has absconded and cannot be indicted in person—and suspended the case against him.[23]

"The Tunisian" and His Libyan Acquaintances:
Connections to Serhane ben Abdelmajid Fakhet

After the 2003 Casablanca attacks, the Turkish authorities detained Abdelatif Mourafik in Turkey and extradited him to Morocco, where judges sentenced him for terrorist crimes.[24] Mourafik was one of a number of key members of jihadist Maghrebi organizations that sent delegates to the Istanbul meeting in February 2002. The 3/11 network was linked with the MICG structures in Western Europe, including one of its leaders, Hassan el Haski, as well as Youssef Belhadj, who made frequent trips to Madrid from Brussels to meet with individuals who were preparing to attack the commuter trains. Since at least October 19, 2003, Belhadj had known the designated date for this act of terrorism, and he left the Spanish capital for the last time a few days before the attacks took place.

Mourafik was not the only contact that the LIFG had in the 3/11 network. A few weeks before the train bombings, Serhane ben Abdelmajid Fakhet had contacted Abdelhakim Belhadj on his cell phone. Since 1995, Abdelhakim Belhadj—better known at this time by his alias, Abu Abdullah al-Sadeq—had been acting as the principal leader of the LIFG. The conversations between Abu Abdullah al-Sadeq and Fakhet began not long after Fakhet became the local ringleader of the 3/11 network, following Mustafa Maymouni's arrest in May 2003 during a trip to Morocco and Driss Chebli's detention in Spain due to his ties to the Abu Dahdah cell. Fakhet was calling from Madrid, and al-Sadeq replied from Hong Kong, as he was en route to Southeast Asia.

Shortly after the bombings, in April 2004, Abu Abdullah al-Sadeq was arrested in a Bangkok airport and handed over to Libya, where he was imprisoned. Some years later, the LIFG was on the point of dissolution. Toward the end of 2007, the LIFG members who were located in the tribal zones in Pakistan that had maintained extensive contact with al-Qaeda decided to join with al-Qaeda itself. However, another substantial part of the organization, including the part to which al-Sadeq belonged, opted to dissolve the LIFG in 2009 after prolonged negotiations between its imprisoned leadership and the Libyan government of the time under Muammar Gaddafi. Al-Sadeq left prison on March 23, 2010, alongside the other leaders of the LIFG, notably the second-in-command, Khalid al-Sharif, and the main ideologue, Sami al-Saadi.

The day after Abu Abdullah al-Sadeq's release from prison, I had the opportunity to interview him in Tripoli. I did so in the presence of Rohan Gunaratna, the director of the Centre for Political Violence and Terrorism Research in

Singapore, taking advantage of the fact that we both were attending an international conference on deradicalization and terrorist disengagement focused on the experience of the leadership and a good portion of the membership of the LIFG. When I asked al-Sadeq—who until that point had been the emir, or top leader, of the LIFG—about his relationship with Serhane ben Abdelmajid Fakhet, his initial response (according to his interpreter) was that he did not know Fakhet. At my insistence, apparently fully aware of the specific terms of my question, al-Sadeq admitted directly in English that yes, he personally knew Fakhet, and that they had "social relations." He excused himself due to fatigue and asked to end the conversation.

This line of questioning confirmed existing documentation from the judicial proceedings related to the 3/11 attacks. *Sumario 20/2004* contains a Spanish police report on the alluded telephone conversations between Fakhet and Abu Abdullah al-Sadeq, supplemented with contributions from foreign security services, most notably the British.[25] The fact that al-Sadeq admitted his relationship with Fakhet, in an interview and in front of a witness, underscores the critical importance of this fact. Yet additional evidence shows that on April 3, 2004, minutes before taking his life in the Leganés apartment, Fakhet also contacted another important LIFG member who was based in London.[26] And Fakhet was not the only member of the 3/11 network who had ties to the LIFG. When Mustafa Maymouni first started the 3/11 network, he also completed the necessary arrangements so that one of his sisters would marry Ziyad al-Hashim (alias Imad al-Libi), an important member of the LIFG.

This information indicates that there were significant ties between notorious members of the LIFG and at least two of the individuals who played a fundamental role in the formation of the 3/11 network from at least March 2002 until the suicide blast in Leganés in April 2004. Moreover, these connections confirm the fact that, rather than acting as an independent homegrown jihadist cell, those who carried out the Madrid train bombings maintained important international ties throughout the development of their network. Both the LIFG and the MICG were key components of the 3/11 network, integrated through the organization's Western Europe structures. More crucial was the link to al-Qaeda through Amer Azizi, who since at least the middle of 2003, if not before, acted as the adjunct to al-Qaeda's chief of external operations.

In sum, the initial decision to attack Spain emanated from Azizi's desire for revenge. This desire was complemented with the change in operational orientation adopted by various jihadist organizations of Maghrebi origin, in particular the MICG and the LIFG. Both were obligated to adapt to a less propitious situation following the defeat of the Taliban in Afghanistan in the fall of 2001, which had provided sanctuary to al-Qaeda and its associated entities. As such, revenge and opportunity came together in the decision to attack Spain, taken in Karachi in December 2001 and later ratified, not entirely by coincidence, in Istanbul in February 2002.

Were the Madrid Train Bombings a Response to the US Invasion of Iraq?

The Madrid train bombings often are regarded as being connected to the 2003 US invasion of Iraq, specifically to Spain's participation in the international coalition involved in the invasion. However, Amer Azizi's meeting with Abdelatif Mourafik in Karachi at the end of 2001 predated the initial bombardment of Baghdad on March 20, 2003, by a year and three months. Further, when the delegates of three jihadist Maghrebi organizations met in Istanbul in February 2002 and agreed to transfer their jihad to Morocco and Spain, the United States was still more than a year away from launching its offensive against Iraq, and the prospect of such an invasion was still being debated in US policy circles. Mustafa Maymouni received the instructions from Azizi, handed to him by Mourafik, to instigate the formation of the 3/11 network at least a year before coalitions forces entered Iraq.

Certainly, these jihadist efforts culminated five months after the initial invasion, with the incorporation of Jamal Ahmidan's band of criminals into the 3/11 network. Yet the fact remains that the initial decision to attack Spain was taken in late 2001, well before the events in Iraq. This also holds true for the jihadist reorientation that occurred in February 2002, which designated Spain as a target, and for the terrorist mobilization that began in the following month. The chronological order of events undermines such a neat association between the Iraq war and the Madrid train bombings.

Nonetheless, the terrorists made use of the invasion and occupation of Iraq to justify the attacks. In this sense, they introduced a pretext to explain what happened in a narrative favorable to the interests of al-Qaeda and its web of global terrorism. At the same time, they used the Iraq situation as a way to present 3/11 as a success. First, they claimed that their attack had influenced the results of the general elections held on March 14, three days after the bombings, and held it up as proof of their success. This claim does not hold up to scrutiny, though. As explained in chapter 4, the date of the attack was fixed no later than October 19, 2003, and the date of the Spanish general elections was not announced until January 9, 2004. All the same, this disclaimer is not intended to underplay the impact that the bombings had on the election itself. They influenced the behavior of an important segment of the Spanish electorate, and consequently affected the results of the elections—regardless of the interpretation of the attacks—in a manner detrimental to the governing Partido Popular (Popular Party; PP) but beneficial to the Partido Socialista Obrero Español (Spanish Socialist Workers' Party; PSOE).[27] The terrorists, understandably, sought to exploit the advantageous situation created by their attacks to influence the forthcoming election.

Second, the terrorists also claimed a further victory in the return of the Spanish soldiers who had been present in Iraq since the previous year. Five weeks after the train bombings, the new prime minister, José Luis Rodríguez Zapatero, announced that Spanish troops would be withdrawn from Iraq. It was the first decision that Zapatero took after assuming power following the victory his party achieved during the March 14 elections.[28] Zapatero's decision was not related to the attacks, as he had pledged during the election campaign that he would withdraw the troops if the United States did not hand over power in Iraq to the United Nations by June 30, 2004. All the same, the proximity of the decision to the events in March crystallized across the world the idea that the Spanish government had responded to al-Qaeda's terrorism.

To explain then why Madrid became a target for terrorism, it is important to understand the desires for revenge by the true instigator of the attacks, Amer Azizi, following the judicial and police actions against jihadist terror in Spain that dismantled Abu Dahdah's cell. To his benefit, Azizi's desires for retribution against Spain, its institutions, and its citizens coincided with the desires of the surviving members of Abu Dahdah's cell and others who joined the 3/11 network. Moreover, it is important to note that Maghrebi jihadist organizations like the LIFG and the MICG changed their operational orientation to attack the countries where their members resided after they lost their bases in Afghanistan following September 11. All of these factors complemented Azizi's initial decision.

Even though the true causes of the Madrid train bombings are to be found in the desire for revenge and the opportunity presented to its actors, al-Qaeda's senior leadership adopted Azizi's project for two additional intervening reasons. First, Azizi had ascended to important positions in the organization's hierarchy, becoming the adjutant to Hamza Rabia, the chief of external operations. Second, and no less important, the war in Iraq offered the leaders of the organization an unintentional pretext to accommodate their plans to attack Spain and its citizens as part of al-Qaeda's general strategy. The second point will be discussed in greater detail in chapter 11, but first, it is necessary to address the ties that Azizi maintained with the main initiators of the 3/11 network, including the network's foundation and consolidation, as well as the nature of these connections after he became an important member of al-Qaeda's external operations during the preparation and execution of the Madrid bombings.

10

Amer Azizi and the 3/11 Network

On March 11, 2004, the day that the ten bombs exploded in four commuter trains traveling between the Alcalá de Henares and Atocha stations, Amer Azizi was more than a dedicated jihadist who had once figured prominently in a now-dismantled Spanish al-Qaeda cell. At this point, he was serving as adjunct to Hamza Rabia, the chief of external operations for al-Qaeda. For a fugitive like Azizi, with his well-established jihadist credentials, joining al-Qaeda's central organization in Pakistan had not been difficult. By the time he joined, he had cut his teeth in Spain radicalizing and recruiting youths for the organization, and had gone abroad to the training camps run by al-Qaeda and the Libyan Islamic Fighting Group. These experiences provided him with important contacts across the globe. Some of these contacts derived from his membership in the cell led by Abu Dahdah, and others came from his experiences in South Asia.

Amer Azizi's key achievement in relation to the Madrid bombings, during his transitory phase from the disappearance of Abu Dahdah's cell to his advent as an important member of al-Qaeda's central organization, was his convincing the organization to approve and support his plans, sometime in the middle of 2003. In that time, Azizi went from being an isolated jihadist who had incited and encouraged his former terrorist comrades to retaliate against Spain to becoming an intermediary between the top leaders of al-Qaeda in Pakistan and the 3/11 network. He was the conduit between al-Qaeda's leadership and the local Madrid cell, guiding and facilitating the execution of the attacks in March 2004. Whether acting as an inciter, intermediary, or conduit, Azizi accomplished his task because of the strong interpersonal ties he had cultivated, ties that predated his integration into the hierarchy of al-Qaeda in Pakistan. How had he developed these strong links with Abdelatif Mourafik, with Mustafa Maymouni, or with Driss Chebli? How did he forge connections with Serhane ben Abdelmajid Fakhet, or with Said Berraj, Jamal Zougam, and other members of the 3/11 network?

Azizi and Maymouni: "Intimate friends"

Azizi's ties to Abdelatif Mourafik (often better known at that time as Malek al-Maghrebi), the man who transmitted his orders to Mustafa Maymouni in the local cell in Madrid, arose from their shared time in the same training camps run by al-Qaeda and LIFG in Afghanistan. Mourafik later used Azizi's address in Spain, and a fake name, to receive personal mail from Morocco.[1] Mourafik and Azizi remained in contact over telephone throughout the summer of 2001, right up until September 11.[2] Shortly after Azizi arrived in Pakistan, he asked Mourafik to contact Maymouni in Madrid to arrange travel plans for his wife, Raquel Burgos, so that she could reunite with him in some designated place. Once Maymouni received these instructions from Mourafik, he made the necessary arrangements both inside and outside of Morocco, just as Azizi had ordered.[3] Raquel Burgos finally traveled from Morocco to France in the summer of 2002, and in August of that year, Mourafik confirmed to Maymouni that she had arrived at her destination and was with her husband.[4] The fact that Azizi charged Maymouni with arranging his wife's travel arrangements shows the confidence and trust he had in his local Madrid contact. During an oral hearing at the National Court, a National Police Corps official who was well versed in the activities of both individuals provided the most elegant description of their relationship: "they were intimate friends" (*íntimos amigos*).[5] Both, for example, celebrated jointly the birth of their respective sons in a rural property that Maymouni owned in Cañada Real de Valdemingómez, a shanty town on the outskirts of Madrid. These and other facts included in the judicial order decreeing the indictment of Amer Azizi *en rebeldía* (in default) in *Sumario 35/2001* are evidence of the strong interpersonal ties between these two men.

Azizi and Maymouni had met in 1999 when they attended meetings held by a Tablighi Jamaat congregation in Madrid. Azizi, who at the time already had been established as a member of Abu Dahdah's cell, radicalized

Maymouni, drawing him into the postulates of Salafist-jihadism to recruit him into the cell proper.[6] From this point forward, Maymouni became Azizi's closest collaborator. For example, aside from using standard forms of communication, Azizi visited Maymouni's home no less than five times between September 29 and October 28, 2001.[7] This mutual history made it easy for Maymouni to fulfill the instructions that the fugitive Azizi had sent to him via Mourafik, specifically the order to start a new jihadist cell with decidedly operative purposes. Maymouni duly sought to reunite the other cell members that the Spanish police had failed to arrest in November 2001.

That was the origin of the 3/11 network, in which Maymouni participated fully until he was arrested in Morocco in late May 2003, during a stay in Larache. The Moroccan government, reacting forcefully after the Casablanca bombings earlier that month, acted against him and charged him with terrorist activity. As mentioned earlier, Driss Chebli, another Abu Dahdah acolyte who had evaded arrest during Operation Dátil, replaced Maymouni and assumed responsibility for orders sent by Amer Azizi. Much like Maymouni, Azizi trusted Chebli because they had ties dating back to their membership in Abu Dahdah's cell.[8] Chebli himself noted that he had known Azizi since 2000.[9] Their relationship is much more complex than simple friendship. Azizi guided Chebli in his radicalization process between the end of 2000 and the beginning of 2001, pushing him away from traditional Salafism to a more jihadist orientation.[10] Azizi's and Chebli's connections also went deeper than their common membership in Abu Dahdah's cell, or the fact that Chebli's phone number featured prominently in a planner that Azizi left behind in his abandoned home in Madrid. For instance, Chebli accompanied Maymouni to Casablanca to organize Raquel Burgos' trip to reunite with her husband in Pakistan.[11] Tellingly too, Chebli registered Azizi's abandoned vehicle in Madrid in his own name after Azizi left for Pakistan.[12] Synthesizing the relationship between all three men is the fact that according to Chebli, Maymouni himself delivered Azizi's vehicle to him.[13]

"Amer Azizi knew the people in Lavapiés": Radical Connections in Spain

To understand the relationship between Azizi and Serhane ben Abdelmajid Fakhet, the man who replaced Driss Chebli as ringleader of the local 3/11 network cell after Chebli's arrest in June 2003, it is necessary to realize that

Azizi had radicalized Fakhet into Salafist-jihadism. Toward the end of the 1990s, Azizi had introduced Fakhet into Abu Dahdah's circle and recruited him into the cell, much as he had done with Maymouni and Chebli.[14] Fakhet also attended the celebrations that Azizi and Maymouni held for the birth of their respective children. Exemplary of the nature of their friendship, sometime between the summer and fall of 2001 Azizi and Fakhet jointly reproached publicly the leaders of the M-30 Mosque for not acting as true Muslims, adding pressure by making offensive phone calls to the mosque's imam and his associates.[15]

A similar pattern emerges with Said Berraj, another important member of the 3/11 network who came from Abu Dahdah's cell and who had once shared an apartment with Chebli.[16] Much as with Maymouni, Chebli, and Fakhet, Berraj had deep ties to Azizi that predated the latter's departure to Pakistan. One incident is rather revelatory. Both traveled together to Afghanistan through Istanbul in September 2000, but the Turkish authorities detained them on the night of September 10. They were in the company of Salaheddin Benyaich, known as Abu Mughen, and Lahcen Ikassrien, whom American soldiers would arrest in Afghanistan in 2001 and keep in detention in Guantánamo Bay until July 2005, when the US authorities handed him over to Spain, where the National Court prosecuted him for previously belonging to Abu Dahdah's al-Qaeda cell while he was living in Madrid in the 1990s.[17] Berraj told Turkish police that he wanted "to go to Tehran to study," whereas Azizi claimed during his interrogation that he was traveling to Iran to "inform myself of the conditions to study there and [understand] the common characteristics of the Shias and Malikis."[18] The Turkish authorities had reasons to doubt the two men's claims, as five fake visas to Pakistan were found among their possessions.[19] Surprisingly, the Turkish police let Berraj and Azizi go, and both managed to arrive at their final destination, an al-Qaeda training camp.

According to testimony from the bombing trials, "Amer Azizi knew the people of Lavapiés," and he knew Jamal Zougam "in particular."[20] Much as with their other contacts, Azizi and Zougam had a special relationship dating to before 2000. In June 2001, the Spanish authorities searched Zougam's home and the cell phone shop he managed in Lavapiés, fulfilling a French petition written originally in March 2000. Along with propaganda from Osama bin Laden, al-Qaeda, and various jihadist conflict zones like Dagestan and Chechnya, the Spanish police discovered a piece of paper with Amer Azizi's phone number written on it: 659 869 731.[21] This evidence only touched the surface of their connection. Both men had attended the same jihadist meetings since at least 1998.[22] On August 3, 2001, they jointly called and spoke to Abu Dahdah at 10:46 pm.[23] All evidence indicates that Azizi and Zougam were in contact before the former escaped to Pakistan in November 2001.[24]

Azizi's abiding connections with these five individuals demonstrate his importance to the 3/11 network. It is likely that his relationship with others in the group was similar in nature, but unfortunately the extant evidence is sketchier. It is possible, for example, that Azizi personally knew Youssef Belhadj, the node of the Moroccan Islamic Combatant Group inside the 3/11 network, for reasons other than his ties to the organization in Afghanistan, Spain, and Morocco. On July 11, 2001, Abu Dahdah, accompanied by Azizi, received a phone call from a so-called Abu Dujana, who himself spoke in the company of Driss Chebli.[25] During the call, Abu Dujana spoke of a trip that he was going to take. Abu Dujana is the same nickname linked to the cellphone used by Youssef Belhadj. (Chapter 11 will describe how one of the communiques released after the Madrid bombings was signed by an Abu Dujana al-Afghani, a person also known by that name who spent time in Afghanistan, or at least had ties to the country.)

A further connection ties Azizi to Rabei Osman Es Sayed Ahmed, also known as Mohamed al-Masri. In a recorded conversation between al-Masri and his acolyte Fouad el Morabit Amghar, the former spoke about a person known as "al-Andalusi." This reference, in the context of his previous relationships, likely meant Othman al-Andalusi, a nickname that Azizi used when he was in Madrid.[26] Curiously, in his first official request for Spanish residency in June 2001—months before he made Spain his temporary home—al-Masri claimed that his address was a home in the Francos Rodriguez Street in Madrid, where an individual named Abdallatif Ball resided. Abdallatif Ball appeared in photographs alongside Azizi dating from the same period. On July 9, 2004, Spanish police and intelligence officials gave copies of these photographs to the National Court judge investigating the Madrid train bombings.[27]

"Azizi returned to Spain at the end of 2003": Building the 3/11 Network

Azizi interacted with most of the important members of the 3/11 network during its formation and the planning and preparation of the Madrid bombings. Indeed, this interaction dated to before and after he became adjunct to

Hamza Rabia, the chief of external operations for al-Qaeda. Azizi exploited the interpersonal ties developed during his prolonged stays in training camps run by al-Qaeda and the LIFG, and his years of activity alongside the followers of Abu Dahdah. His personal networks supplied him with a cast of characters who were capable of mobilizing the human and material resources necessary to attack Madrid, and perhaps some other place in Spain.

Initially, Azizi communicated with the main members of the 3/11 network through his intermediary, Abdelatif Mourafik. Later, he used email. A protected witness who temporarily shared a home with Serhane ben Abdelmajid Fakhet, Mustafa Maymouni, and another individual who shared similar jihadist ideas—perhaps Mouhannad Almallah Dabas[28]—between 2002 and 2003, told police about these emails.[29] The protected witness could not read the content of the messages, but according to comments made by her roommates, a so-called "Amer" had been sending emails from Afghanistan. Effectively, at this point, Azizi was already integrated into al-Qaeda's central organization, and was advancing his jihadist activities on the borders of Afghanistan and Pakistan. It is impossible to reconstruct these messages because of the security measures that terrorists adopted when messaging each other. Whether inside Afghanistan, Pakistan, or Spain, the terrorists shared the same email account. To avoid creating electronic traffic that could be intercepted, they would draft and save messages in the account, allowing other individuals to read, delete, and respond to them without the messages ever being transmitted (and therefore vulnerable to police interception). Mourafik and Maymouni used this same technique to share orders from Azizi, as well as with other MICG members who joined the 3/11 network.[30]

Along with private email accounts, Azizi likely used other means to maintain contact with members of the 3/11 network in Madrid. One potential method was the private space of the Global Islamic Media Center website linked to al-Qaeda. Sufficient evidence exists to know that members of the local cell in Madrid, especially the operative nucleus, had access to the center's private forums, where they received restricted information. A series of files found on the cell members' computers came from this forum. Generally, these files dealt with organizational and operational matters, and were available on password-protected pages that the Global Islamic Media Center administrators shared with a private email list.[31]

Azizi's role changed drastically during the more than two-year period between the decision to attack Spain and the March 11 bombings. Taking advantage of the changing circumstances of the world, at this point polarized by the conflicts in Afghanistan and Iraq, he convinced al-Qaeda's leadership to approve and support his plan to attack in Madrid, which ideated primarily out of his desire for revenge. His role in relation to the 3/11 network evolved in accordance with these changes. He became more than the brains behind the Madrid bombings, serving as an intermediary between al-Qaeda's leaders in Afghanistan and Pakistan and the key members of the 3/11 network that formed after March 2002. Once Azizi reached important leadership positions in al-Qaeda's hierarchy, Fakhet, head of the local cell after the middle of 2003, replaced him in this role.[32] Azizi then dedicated himself to the supervision of the planning and the preparations of the attacks with the approval of Hamza Rabia, truly making him the conduit for the attacks.

The previously mentioned National Counterterrorism Center report, "The Case for Al-Qai'da Links to the 2004 Madrid Bombings," which was published on August 2, 2008—nearly one year after the main judicial sentence on the commuter train attacks was handed down by Spain's National Court— after synthesizing the available information about 3/11 from different sources (including testimony from detained al-Qaeda members), cites the following as one of its most important conclusions:

> Azizi was well positioned in 2003—when preparations for the Madrid bombings would have been under way—to act as a conduit between external operations chief Hamza Rabi'a or other al-Qaeda leaders and the Madrid operatives. Through Azizi, al-Qaeda had a vehicle for conveying approval for the Madrid operation or providing detailed instructions.[33]

It was worth asking whether Azizi, both as the creator and instigator of the attacks, might have traveled to Spain before March 11 to supervise the preparations and to contribute final touches to the bombings. Azizi may well have limited his relationship with the network solely to transmitting instructions from Pakistan, which originally came from him before al-Qaeda's external branch brought its influence. However, another form of contact may have occurred between the conceiver of 3/11 and the local cell in Madrid. According to US intelligence services:

> In late 2003 Azizi returned to Spain, possibly for Madrid planning. . . . He could have used this opportunity to convey instructions or approval to Fakhet from al-Qaeda senior leadership.[34]

Why would Azizi, who still had a warrant pending for his arrest, have traveled clandestinely to Spain with a layover in Turkey a few months before 3/11? In this respect—although it is a detail worth considering with caution—one of the persons who negotiated the lease for the Leganés apartment not only correctly identified Mohamed Belhadj as one of the renters, but also identified an individual of Moroccan descent in a photograph shown to him by Spanish intelligence. The authorities had shown the man a long series of photographs before producing a photograph of Azizi.[35]

11

"Free our prisoners and leave our lands": The 3/11 Attacks and Al-Qaeda's General Strategy

On October 18, 2003, Osama bin Laden explicitly threatened Spain for the first time. He did so through a message shared by the Qatari television station Al Jazeera. In a proclamation addressed to the American people and focusing extensively on the Iraq war, he also included a direct warning for Spain.[1] In this light, even though the decision to attack Spain was made at the end of 2001 and the 3/11 network began forming in March 2002, it was not until October 2003 that the then leader of al-Qaeda stepped forward to justify ahead of time, before the world's public opinion, the planned attacks in Madrid that would take place less than five months later.

The following passage is an English translation of the section where bin Laden introduces his clear, although not exclusive, threat against Spain. He does so in reference to a set of nations that were allied with the United States in the ongoing military intervention in Iraq, which had begun in March 2003:

> We reserve the right to [pursue] reprisals, in the appropriate place and time, against all the countries implicated, especially the United Kingdom, Spain, Australia, Poland, Japan, and Italy, without excluding Muslim states that took part, especially the Gulf States, and in particular, Kuwait, that has become a launch pad for the forces of the crusaders.

In this respect, it is plausible that the leaders of al-Qaeda endorsed the plans that Amer Azizi had set in motion once the international context became favorable to incorporating them into the organization's general strategy. Two aspects of al-Qaeda's global strategy, focused on the Western world, stand out. First, the organization sought to provoke divisions among the Western nations that were allied against global terrorism, extending into their societies and taking advantage of the different internal fractures that could be produced by terrorist actions and propaganda. Second, it focused on manipulating its sympathizers, notably individuals and groups within certain European countries, by encouraging their mobilization potential to prepare and execute attacks that would sow panic within populations.[2] The US-led invasion and occupation of Iraq in March 2003 gave Osama bin Laden and Ayman al-Zawahiri a propitious context in which to make their efforts known.

In this sense, al-Qaeda used the pretext of the Iraq war, accommodated to its general jihadist strategy, to support the true causes of 3/11: the desire for revenge resulting from Spanish counterterrorism, and the decision by Maghreb jihadist organizations to carry out terrorist acts where their militants resided. Even though Amer Azizi had only recently become a part of al-Qaeda's central organization in Pakistan, he was able to use the opportunity to bring in the Moroccan Islamic Combatant Group, which introduced its own component into the 3/11 network, and the Libyan Islamic Fighting Group, which adopted his decision to attack driven by revenge. By the time he had become the adjunct to Hamza Rabia, the chief of al-Qaeda's external operations, "the son of Casablanca" had won approval for his plans from al-Qaeda's top leaders for reasons dealing with strategic motives in relation to the war in Iraq.

This is not to say that the invasion by and continued presence of a multinational force in Afghanistan after September 11 was less important for the leaders of al-Qaeda, but Western nations were more unified in support of this mission, and in 2003 the internal Afghan situation had not yet devolved into chaos and armed confrontation—the opposite of what was happening in Iraq.[3] Along this line, the desires for revenge postulated by Azizi and others associated with Abu Dahdah's former cell were not necessarily contrary to al-Qaeda's ideology. With the initiation of the Iraqi conflagration, these individuals could merge their desires for revenge with the more pragmatic interests of al-Qaeda's central command. Al-Qaeda did not order the operational reorientation adopted in February 2002 by three Maghrebi jihadist organizations, but the May 2003 Casablanca attacks met with a negative reaction among the population of the Arab world, as the majority of the victims in Casablanca were Moroccans. It was necessary to respond to this backlash with a terrorist attack against non-Muslims—those who were considered to be infidels—to generate popular goodwill once again in the Arab world. In addition, Osama bin Laden's declaration, released through Al Jazeera on October 18, 2003, was a missive directed toward al-Qaeda members who were active in Western Europe, in particular those who were close to the 3/11 network.

It should be remembered, in this respect, that the earliest known record of the proposed March 11 date for the Madrid bombings goes back to October 19, 2003—one day after Al Jazeera transmitted bin Laden's statement. This information was put on paper not in Madrid, but in a municipality close to Brussels known as Molenbeek, on a document related to Youssef Belhadj, the node for the MICG's involvement in the attacks, who likely was a member of both MICG and al-Qaeda.[4] Additional indicators suggest that other levels of al-Qaeda knew that a plot, approved by the top leadership, to execute a major attack in a country like Spain was at hand. On October 26, 2003, Abu Mohamed al-Ablaj, acting as an al-Qaeda spokesperson, sent a message to the Arabic weekly *Al-Majallah* (which was edited in London) where he announced, "We are preparing ourselves for a great day," in "a place in one of the Western countries"—excluding the United States, which bin Laden had mentioned explicitly eight days earlier.[5]

"It is part of settling old scores with the Crusader Spain, allied with America in its war against Islam": Justifications for the Madrid Train Bombings

After executing the 2004 attacks, four messages claimed responsibility for the bombings. The Abu Hafs al-Masri Brigades (al-Qaeda) signed two of them, one on the evening of March 11 and the other on March 15. The local cell within the 3/11 network released the other two statements, the first on March 13 and the second on April 3, and also filmed a video (dated to March 27) that they never released to the press. The content and sequence of these messages help to unravel the real causes of the attacks and the accidental pretexts, and demonstrate the subordination of the local cell to a higher instance present outside of Spain.

On March 11, 2004, around 7:30 p.m. in London and 8:30 p.m. in Madrid, the well-known London-based Arabic-language newspaper *Al-Quds al-Arabi* received an email that claimed responsibility for the events in Madrid. The editor of the newspaper would later explain that earlier in the day he had received a phone call from a country in the Gulf that he did not name, notifying him that a message about the Madrid attacks would be forthcoming.[6] The newspaper considered this message, like previous messages it had received from al-Qaeda, as authentic and published the claim on its front page. The Spanish authorities, thanks to help from British intelligence, later learned that the message came from Iran.[7]

The message sent to *Al-Quds al-Arabi* was written in Arabic and signed by the Abu Hafs al-Masri Brigades (al-Qaeda). The name references the Egyptian Mohamed Atef, nicknamed Abu Hafs al-Masri, who served as the first chief of al-Qaeda's military committee and died during the US bombardment of Afghanistan at the end of 2001.[8] Al-Qaeda had used this title in various occasions to claim responsibility for attacks before 3/11. It did so following the attacks against the United Nations headquarters in Baghdad in August 2003 that left twenty-four people dead, and the bombing of a Marriott Hotel in Jakarta where twelve people died. It did so as well after the attacks against members of the Italian Carabinieri (military police) in Nasiriya, Iraq, that killed nineteen, and after the attacks in Istanbul where it bombed a synagogue, the British consulate, and an HSBC bank, resulting in fifty-eight deaths.[9] The following text is an English translation of the original communique sent to the *Al-Quds al-Arabi* newspaper on the afternoon of March 11, 2004:

In the name of Allah, Clement and Merciful, when they punish you, you need to punish those that punished you in the same way. Kill them where you find them, expel them like they expelled you; sedition is more grave than assassination. To those that commit aggressions against you, you should do the same to them.

The Abu Hafs al-Masri Brigades promised in their last message in reference to the explosions in Karbala and Baghdad on the 2nd of March, that they were preparing themselves for the next operations, and we have fulfilled our promise. The squadron of death has achieved this in the profoundness of Crusader Europe, hitting one of the pillars of the Crusaders and their allies, Spain, with a painful blow. *It is part of settling old scores with the Crusader Spain, allied with America in its war against Islam.*

Where is America, Aznar? Who will protect you, Great Britain, Italy, Japan, and other agents? When we hit the Italian troops in Nasiriya, we sent the agents of America a warning: withdraw from the alliance against Islam. But you did not understand the message. Now we dot the "I's." We hope that you understand the message. We, the Abu Hafs al-Masri Brigades, do not mourn the death of civilians. Is it legitimate that they kill our children, women, elders, and youths in Afghanistan, Iraq, Palestine, and Kashmir, while it is a sin that we kill them? Almighty Allah says, "To those that do you harm, you should harm."

Take your hands off us; *free our prisoners and leave our lands*. We will leave you in peace. The nations allied with the United States should force their governments to end their alliance in the war against terrorism, which means war against Islam. If you cease [your] war, we will cease ours.

We say to you: the Squadron of the Smoke of Death will reach you soon in a place where you will see thousands dead, if Allah wills it, and this is a warning. We tell Muslims all around the world that the strike by the Winds of Black Death is in its final phase, at 90 percent, if Allah wills it, at the appropriate moment.

In another operation, the Squadrons of the Soldiers of Jerusalem hit the Jews and Masons in Istanbul, and three important Masons died in that operation, and if it had not been for a technical failure, more Masons would have died.

Allah is Great. God is Great. Islam comes now.

Abu Hafs al-Masri Brigades (al-Qaeda)

Thursday 20 Muharram 1425 – 11 March 2004[10]

This is not the first time that the leaders of al-Qaeda used different titles to claim responsibility for terrorist plots against Western targets. When referring to the attack against German tourists that was perpetrated on the Tunisian island of Djerba in 2002, they claimed that it had been carried out by the Liberation Army of Holy Places. In reality, important members of al-Qaeda, including the mastermind of 9/11, Khalid Sheikh Mohammed, had conceived, planned, and prepared the attack. Further, the above message matters not only because of its claim of responsibility but because it provides two different justifications for the bombings. On the one hand, the message presented the Madrid bombings as a reprisal against Spain as "one of the pillars of the Crusaders and their allies," and in particular, as a country allied with the United States in "its war against Islam." On the other hand, it referred to 3/11 as "part of settling old scores with the Crusader Spain." Furthermore, the references to Baghdad, Karbala, and Nasirya underscore the ongoing conflict in Iraq. In doing so, al-Qaeda situated this conflict, and other ongoing conflicts in South Asia and the Middle East, as part of an imagined war against Islam, in which Spain participated, as the jihadist narrative goes, when José María Aznar was premier. The mentioned attacks in Nasiriya on November 12, 2003, were attributed to al-Qaeda nine days after their execution by the aforementioned Abu Mohamed al-Ablaj, who did so through an email sent to the weekly *Al-Majallah*. This data point contains an interesting link between the attacks in Nasiriya and the 3/11 network, a point that will be discussed further in chapter 13.

The matter of "settling old scores," as mentioned in order to explain the Madrid bombings, is not an allusion to Iraq specifically. There are two possible interpretations that are not, in principle, mutually exclusive. The "old scores" might refer to the Reconquista, or the recovery of the Iberian Peninsula from Islamic dominion, which took place between the eighth and fifteenth century and concluded with the Catholic monarchs' conquest of Granada in 1492. This interpretation would situate the message within the inherent Salafist-jihadist contents of al-Qaeda's ideology. Likewise, it might refer to counterterrorist activities against individuals implicated in al-Qaeda's Spanish cell in the fall of 2001, or more broadly, members of other, al-Qaeda–related jihadist entities who had been detained in Spain since 1995.[11]

Nevertheless, both justifications for the Madrid attacks mentioned in the March 11 message released by the Abu Hafs al-Masri Brigades (al-Qaeda) combined strategic interest with eagerness to revenge. First, al-Qaeda's strategic interest in confronting Western troops on territory defined as Islamic was meant to exploit dissenting opinions in open societies. Second, Azizi and the most notorious leaders of the 3/11 network were pursuing revenge for the imprisonment of leaders like Abu Dahdah; numerous coreligionists; and sometimes, as in the case of Allekema Lamari, themselves.[12] The phrase "take your hands off us; free our prisoners and leave our lands" most neatly synthesizes both motivations.

"We have prepared ourselves to instill terror in your hearts": The Local Cell's Insistence That the 3/11 Attacks Corresponded with 9/11

The local cell within the 3/11 network had no reason to release its own message regarding the bombings, but it did so anyway on the afternoon of March

13.[13] In all likelihood, the cell members acted because in the fervor surrounding the attacks and the forthcoming general elections, the media outlets they visited on their computers could not settle on one organization to which they would attribute the bombings. In spite of the message released by the Abu Hafs al-Masri Brigades (al-Qaeda), other speculations about the identity of the attackers were rife. Was it ETA, which had been waging violent terrorist campaigns against Spain since the 1960s?[14] Alternatively, could it have been jihadists, whose penetration into Spanish society had hitherto escaped the public notice?[15] These rhetorical questions aside, none of these potential culprits had done anything to indicate that the terrorists who had attacked Spain on March 11 had done so to influence the elections. (As noted before, the terrorists had chosen the date of the attack long before the Spanish government had fixed March 14 as the date of the next elections.)

Undoubtedly, al-Qaeda's strategic interest, once it coopted the plan to attack Spain, was to influence public opinion to affect the Spanish government's foreign policy, independent of elections. This consideration explains why the message released on March 11 by the Abu Hafs al-Masri Brigades (al-Qaeda) does not allude to the upcoming elections, either implicitly or explicitly. The message did request that the citizens of Western countries like Spain "force" their respective governments to "end" an imaginary "war against Islam." Regardless of al-Qaeda's interests, the timing of the general elections was an unexpected but fortuitous circumstance for the orchestrators of the 3/11 attacks, as it gave them an exceptional opportunity to achieve more from their efforts than they had expected, well beyond any conscious decision to affect Spanish public opinion.

In this sense, it is worth mentioning that the US decision to invade Iraq and depose Saddam Hussein, as well as Spanish participation in the conflict, had become very unpopular among the Spanish public. The question of withdrawing Spanish troops from Iraq was an important electoral issue.[16] It is not surprising then that the local cell in Madrid, specifically Serhane ben Abdelmajid Fakhet (acting as ringleader) and Jamal Ahmidan (the operational chief), made all haste to insist on the jihadist nature of the Madrid train bombings, doing so on the afternoon of March 13, hours before the polling booths opened. The speed and the technical manner in which they prepared their message show that they initially had not intended to release their own messages. Rather, this task belonged to the Abu Hafs al-Masri Brigades (al-Qaeda). It is logical to suppose that they acted once they realized that the question of attributing responsibility for the events of March

11 had created a very heated discussion among Spanish politicians, as well as the public.[17]

This chain of circumstances helps to explain why members of the local 3/11 network cell recorded their unanticipated first message a little over two hours after Interior Minister Ángel Acebes held a press conference in which he explained that in relation to the attacks, the police investigation was prioritizing ETA as a prime suspect. Around 7:30 p.m., an individual with a strong Arabic accent called the Madrid public broadcasting station Telemadrid, and said that there was a videotape inside a trash can next to the M-30 Mosque, the largest Islamic worship site in the city and a familiar site for most of those who had been integrated into the 3/11 network. In the video, three individuals from the local cell appear. The three, all hooded and dressed in white, are standing in front of a green banner on which is printed the *shahada*, the profession of the faith in Islam. The person in the middle holds a rifle and reads in Arabic the following proclamation:

In the name of Allah, the Merciful, the Compassionate.

Combat them! Allah will punish them through your hands and will humiliate them; he will give you victory over them and will cure the chests of the believing people . . .

We make ourselves responsible for the attack that occurred in Madrid, it two and a half years after the holy conquests of New York and Washington, in response to your alignment with global terrorist organizations and those organizations by Bush and his followers that killed our children and women and left them without homes in Iraq and Afghanistan.

Today we kill you in your own homes and we have more of the same, Allah willing. You should know that we choose death as our path towards life, but you choose life as your path to death.

We swear by Almighty Allah that if you do not cease in your injustice and the death of Muslims with the excuse of combating terrorism, we will blow away your homes from the air and we will spill your blood like rivers. We have prepared ourselves for what will fill your hearts with terror.

[Realize] that these attacks are only a small sample and a warning that we make to you as part of our plan for jihad against your terrorism until you abandon our land with your tail between your legs as a sign of defeat, exactly as it happened to your Pharaoh in Somalia and in Lebanon. If you return, we will also return.

This is a notice by the spokesperson of the military wing of Ansar al-Qaeda in Europe, Abu Dujana al-Afgani.[18]

In consonance with their unexpected purpose, only a few short hours before the polling booths opened, the principal members of the local cell insisted that the 3/11 attacks corresponded with those of 9/11. Carefully choosing their words in the message, they avoided explicit allusions to other polemical issues that they perceived as divisive to the Spanish public, such as the question of the Spanish government's policy toward ETA. It is significant that they did include a few key words like "Bush," "Iraq," and "Afghanistan," perhaps supposing that their conjectural significance would make more sense to the Spanish electorate. The message reflected the terrorists' preferred outcome—namely, the loss of the incumbent PP in the elections.

It is not possible to know with any degree of certainty the true identity of "Abu Dujana al-Afghani," the man who acted as an al-Qaeda spokesperson. Among the various possibilities, the most convincing hypothesis is that it was Youssef Belhadj, a notable member of al-Qaeda and the MICG, the latter organization reflecting al-Qaeda's so-called military wing. If not him, then other MICG leaders such as Hassan el Haski or Abdelkader Hakimi are equally likely possibilities.[19] But the name "Aboudojanah" appeared on the various cell phones seized from the MICG in Belgium, and was associated with Youssef Belhadj's phone number (which he used until his detention), possibly making it a secure number used by leaders of the MICG. Regardless, the member or members of the local cell and the operating nucleus of the 3/11 network who wrote the message included a clear warning indicating what they would do in Spain if their expectations were not met: We have prepared ourselves to fill your hearts with terror. With those words, the terrorists paraphrased a passage from the Quran, surah 3, verse 151:

We will cast terror into the hearts of those who disbelieve for what they have associated with Allah of which He had not sent down [any] authorization. And their refuge will be the Fire, and wretched is the residence of the wrongdoers.[20]

"Suspension of the operations in the lands of Al-Andalus": The Local Cell Recognizes the Preeminence of the Abu Hafs al-Masri Brigades (al-Qaeda)

Immediately after the March 14 general elections, it became clear that those who had planned the Madrid bombings wanted not only to create the largest number of casualties but also to exploit the ensuing situation. One other aspect also became evident: the local jihadist cell, in addition to its connections that extended to Brussels and Milan, was following directives from a location far outside the external borders of the European Union.

On March 18, a second communique from the Abu Hafs al-Masri Brigades (al-Qaeda), dated March 15, the day after the elections, appeared on the website of the Global Islamic Media Center, an al-Qaeda internet portal. The day before, another slightly, but not significantly, different message arrived in London's *Al-Quds al-Arabi* newspaper and by fax at another London-based Arabic newspaper, *Al-Hayat*:

NOTIFICATION FOR THE NATION IN RESPECT TO THE SUSPENSION OF THE OPERATIONS IN THE LAND OF AL-ANDALUS

The suspension of all operations in the land of Al-Andalus for the moment.

Praise be to Allah who has facilitated us the conquest with the battle of Madrid, who has destroyed one of the pillars of the axis of the Crusaders of evil. Thanks be to Allah. Glorified and sanctified be His name for the mujahedin that found themselves in the field of battle, and for the participants in that struggle, including those who contributed simply with invocations of Allah.

We have given the Spanish nation the choice between war and peace, and they have chosen peace, voting for the party that was against the North American alliance in its war against Islam. For that, *the directorate has decided to suspend all operations on Spanish territory* against those known as civilian targets until [we are certain] of the path of the new Government, which has promised the withdrawal of its troops, [assuring] ourselves that there will be no interference by the new Executive in matters [concerning] Muslims. With this motive, we reiterate the decision to all battalions on European land, to suspend all operations.

A few words for the American satellites:

This is Aznar, agent of the North Americans. He has ruined your [future] with his alliance with the tyrant of the century, America. The same Aznar who suffers from hysteria since the strike in Madrid, because his intelligence services [report] that it was al-Qaeda who was responsible for the attack, and at the same time he insists on ETA's responsibility. Aznar, who will be written in the worst pages of history; what can America do for this man? . . .

You, agents! [Be ready], for the squadrons of death await you at the doors of your homes, and we will hit you with an iron fist without mercy at an opportune time and place. . . . Who will be the next target this time? Will it be Japan, America, Italy, Great Britain, Australia or . . .?

Who will protect you from our ire? Who will stop the cars, the trains, and the planes of death? Who?

Out of our lands, free our prisoners, and stop interfering in our affairs . . . we will stop the squadrons of death.

The entire world [should] know that we form part of the world order. We change states and destroy others with the [help] of Allah. Moreover, we decide over the fortunes of the world's economy and we do not accept in any way being passive subjects of this world, rather active and very active, with His grace . . .

The UN, the organization at the service of the Americans. . . . The last assembly of the Security Council, in an unheard of resolution, [blamed] ETA for the attack in Madrid, with the surprise of the politicians and the media, in an attempt to save the government of the [lapdog] Aznar following American instructions. . . . The duty of every Muslim is to combat this Zionist crusader organization allied with the Jews in Palestine.

And before finishing this communique, we want to tell those that were surprised by the speed of publication of the message following the battle of Madrid, [this time] other circumstances exist, [because] beforehand we had the reprisals against the Taliban government [to worry about], but given their withdrawal to the mountains, we have nothing to fear. But it is a worse strategic error that the Americans have committed. For this reason, some operations were not communicated due to political or security reasons. In the case of the battle of Madrid, the time factor was too important to end with the government of the ignoble Aznar, [the] tail of the American tyrants.

The mujahedin follow the ongoing events, taking into account the changes of place, time, and circumstances.

Allah is great. Islam rises.

The Abu Hafs al-Masri Brigades (al-Qaeda)[21]

This second communique explains why al-Qaeda assumed responsibility for the Madrid train bombings on the same day as the attacks—an uncommon practice for the organization, which usually does not admit its involvement immediately following an act of terrorism. The message admits that al-Qaeda wanted to take advantage of the situation to influence the results of the general elections on March 14. Their celebration was a "circumstance," in the literal language of the terrorists, which varied in respect to the initial planning of the attacks. As mentioned in their original message, they insist on the same terms of releasing prisoners and the withdrawal from Islamic territories. To this standard demand, the new message adds the rhetorical question of which country would serve as a target after Spain. One of the European countries listed in the communique, the United Kingdom, would experience an attack on its own capital city's public transit system shortly over a year later, in July 2005. The Abu Hafs al-Masri Brigades—meaning al-Qaeda—would claim responsibility for this attack as well. However, this second message contains a revelatory statement that is important for understanding the functioning of the 3/11 network and its international connections. As the message details, the terrorists evaluated the bombing's success by its ability to sway the results of the forthcoming elections; implicitly, they discarded alternative explanation for Spanish electoral behavior. Moreover, the message authors announced that as a result of their success, they would call for a truce "in the land of Al-Andalus."

Someone from the local cell downloaded the message the day after it appeared on the internet, at exactly at 10:16 a.m. on March 19. (This information came from a laptop found in the home of Jamal Ahmidan, the operational chief for the local cell.) This sequence of events reflects the significance of the second message released by the local cell. This time, Serhane ben Abdelmajid Fakhet wrote the message by hand and sent it to the Madrid newspaper *ABC* on the morning of April 3. This text, which alludes to preparations to attack the Spanish high-speed AVE train (see chapter 12), announces "the annulment of the previous ceasefire":

Thanks to Allah who never breaks his promises.

After the Spanish state continued with its injustices and aggression against Muslims with its deployment of new troops to Iraq and its intentions to send more [troops] to Afghanistan;

And after we have demonstrated our power to hit you again and be merciless with you after the holy attacks of March 11;

Given that we have placed bombs on the rails of the high-speed train near Toledo and we had the possibility to make the trains that passed by there on Thursday afternoon and Friday morning explode, and we have not done so, because our objective was solely to warn you and announce to you that we have the strength and capacity, with permission of Highest Allah, to attack you when we want to and however we want to;

We, the Battalion of Death, announce the annulment of the previous ceasefire and we give a deadline to the Spanish government of midday of next Sunday, the 14th of Safar of 1425 (April 4, 2004) to satisfy our follow significant [demands]:

The immediate and complete withdrawal of your troops from Afghanistan and Iraq, and the promise never to return to those countries.

To cease supporting the enemies of the Islamic Ummah (the United States and its allies) opposed to Islam and Muslims.

If you do not comply, let there be sadness between you and us, for we declare war, and we swear by Highest and Sublime Allah that we will convert your country into a hell and we will make your blood flow like rivers.

We consider this our last warning to the Spanish nation and its government. Allah help he who helps himself. Allah is strong and powerful. Let peace fall on those who follow the right path.

Abu Dujana al-Afgani.[22]

This message, a written letter, was sent to a national newspaper by the head of the local cell of the 3/11 network, and endorsed once more by Abu Dujana al-Afghani. It announced the suspension of a truce, threatening to convert Spain into "a hell." It should be noted at this point that the *local* cell had never announced the truce that it annulled with the April 3 message. The Abu

Hafs al-Masri Brigades (al-Qaeda) had declared the truce in their March 18 message, and the local cell members had downloaded the message onto their laptops the following day. In other words, the local cell recognized the preeminence of the Abu Hafs al-Masri Brigades (al-Qaeda) in issuing orders. Even though it is not clear why the local cell members decided to annul the truce, evidence suggests that they made the decision to do so as early as March 27. The date announced in the cell's second message concluded on April 4, and it coincided with a date that the cell members had announced in a separate recording made on March 27 but had never released.[23]

Besides the message by the Abu Hafs al-Masri Brigades (al-Qaeda), the cell extracted other messages from the Global Islamic Media Center page. As early as February 2003, cell members had downloaded a series of videos in Arabic, titled "Preparations for the Struggle," that included lectures on the fabrication and use of explosives. The group accessed these videos from a private forum on the website available only to those with passwords.[24] However, there is no evidence that the local cell ever accessed or downloaded a number of other critical documents, also published by the Global Islamic Media Center, that threatened Spain because of its military presence in Iraq.[25] Moreover, there can be no connection between these documents and the Madrid attacks, since the first of these documents became available between October and December 2003, and at that point the 3/11 network was already complete and the preparations for the Madrid train bombings were nearing their final stages.

What Did Osama bin Laden and Ayman al-Zawahiri Say about 3/11?

On April 15, 2004, Osama bin Laden finally issued a statement about the supposed truce in Al-Andalus. His response came after the Madrid police had arrested various individuals following the suicide explosion in Leganés that attenuated the possibility of another attack by the 3/11 terrorists. In a message shared by the Arabic channels Al Jazeera and Al Arabiya, bin Laden outlined the matter and proposed a truce to the whole of Europe. His message has two revelatory bits of information. First, he situated the Madrid bombings as part of a continuum with the September 11 attacks in New York and Washington, definitively stating al-Qaeda's responsibility for the attack on the commuter trains:

What happened on 11 September and 11 March is that your own merchandise was returned to you.[26]

Second, bin Laden offered the countries of Western Europe a sort of peace, "whose essence is our compromise to stop actions against whatever country that promises to abstain from attacking Muslims or intervening in their affairs." Alluding once more to 3/11, this time implicitly, he added, "The killing of Europeans only happened after the invasions of Iraq and Afghanistan." In the next line, he gave a three-month deadline to the European governments—excluding the United States and the United Nations—to either accept or reject his offer. By trying to take advantage of the Madrid train bombings to distance the United States from Western Europe, bin Laden continued al-Qaeda's strategic efforts to divide open societies.[27]

On November 16, 2005, long after bin Laden's deadline, Ayman al-Zawahiri, still in his role of second-in-command, referred to 3/11 in similar terms. In a video eulogizing the al-Qaeda terrorists who had committed four coordinated suicide attacks on the London public transit system on July 7 of that year, Zawahiri referenced this latter event—known as 7/7—as the next in the sequence following 9/11 and 3/11, and contextualized the earlier attacks as a precedent for the events in the British capital:

The holy attack, like its illustrious predecessors in New York, Washington, and Madrid, took the battle to the enemy's own territory.[28]

In a new recording broadcast through Al Jazeera on January 19, 2006, bin Laden once more mentioned the March 2004 attacks. As part of his propaganda, he described the Madrid and London bombings as a reaction to the invasion of Iraq, which at this point had been ongoing for three years. Osama bin Laden did not mention either Madrid or London directly, but the reference to both was clear enough when he said that "the war against America and its allies has not been limited to Iraq. Proof of this are the explosions that you have witnessed in the capitals of the most important European countries that are part of this hostile coalition."[29] These are obvious references to the Spanish and British capital cities.

Yet another message from bin Laden, dated September 25, 2009, refers openly to the Madrid train bombings. Since he had announced the truce in April 2004, various European counterterrorism units had foiled important plots by al-Qaeda, including a plan to bomb the Barcelona Underground in

January 2008.[30] But this new message once more addressed Europeans. With a less than favorable situation in Iraq for al-Qaeda, Osama bin Laden urged Europeans to leave Afghanistan, where the situation had changed with the burgeoning Taliban insurgency. This is how he referred to 3/11:

> If you had seen how your American allies and those that helped them rounded up thousands of Taliban in containers, packing them like sardines, then keeping them prisoners until they died or were thrown into rivers, then you would understand the bloody events of Madrid and London.[31]

Close to a year later, on July 27, 2010, Ayman al-Zawahiri recorded another audio message that further explicitly exalted the Madrid and London attacks.[32] On November 1, 2015, four years after he had replaced Osama bin Laden as the leader of al-Qaeda, another al-Zawahiri audio communiqué threatened the West with more attacks like those of 9/11, 3/11, and 7/7.[33] Among the tranche of documents recovered by the US Navy SEALs from the compound used to hide Osama bin Laden in Abbottabad, Pakistan, released as declassified materials in 2015 and 2016, several refer to the Madrid attacks—but there is in particular an undated letter, from all accounts by Osama bin Laden himself, that is particularly relevant to the Madrid train bombings. The letter, addressed to what is termed as "occupying countries," clearly was written in a relatively short period of time following the bombings, where these attacks are undoubtedly linked to 9/11 and literally referred to as "3/11."[34]

12

"I invoke Allah and ask him to facilitate my martyrdom": Other Facets of the 3/11 Attacks

Why were the Madrid bombings not a suicide attack? This is a reasonable question to ask, given that most people assume that attacks planned and prepared with the involvement of al-Qaeda usually result in the voluntary death of their perpetrators. This scenario happened most vividly in the 9/11 hijackings, but it was not the only case. Between September 11, 2001, and March 11, 2004, al-Qaeda was directly or indirectly involved in many suicide attacks across the globe. In 2002, suicide attacks were carried out on the Tunisian island of Djerba on April 11; in Bali, Indonesia, on October 28; and in Mombasa, Kenya, on November 28. In 2003, al-Qaeda–linked suicide attacks struck three capital cities: Riyadh on May 12, Jakarta on August 5, and Istanbul on November 20. The case of the Madrid bombings differs, because in spite of the connections between the perpetrators and al-Qaeda's external operations command, the terrorists intended to attack other targets in Spain beyond the Madrid rail network, and needed to maintain their manpower and keep their identities secret from the authorities. To this end, they rented a flat in Leganés on March 1 and a house in Albolote, close to the city of Granada, on March 4.[1] Evidence suggests that the terrorists did not plan to stay in Leganés for more than a month and half.[2] Is it possible that they wanted to carry out a spectacular jihadist attack near the Alhambra, the Granada palace complex built by the Muslim rulers of Al-Andalus—an emblematic locale for the Islamic world? This volume's author cannot answer this question satisfactorily beyond pointing out that members of the 3/11 network's operative nucleus hoped to use a property near Granada.

Chapter 11 mentioned the 3/11 network's clear intention to attack the high-velocity AVE train line between Madrid and Seville, specifically in the province of Toledo. In this sense, it is worth reiterating the message from Spanish intelligence's assessment of Allekema Lamari, reproduced in chapter 3, which described his previous desires to commit terrorist acts involving "derailing trains." On April 2, 2004, rail maintenance workers discovered an explosive device on the high-speed rail line connecting Madrid and Seville, near the town of Mocejón in Toledo. Notably, the explosives and detonators found on the undetonated bomb were identical to the ones used on 3/11. However, evidence from the subsequent investigation suggested that, rather than having been set to explode on April 4 or in the following days, the bomb actually had failed to go off two days earlier, preventing the network from triggering another massacre.[3]

In addition to the network's plans for further attacks on Spain's rail lines, it had compiled information on potential targets in and around Madrid. The list of targets recovered by the Spanish authorities included a recreational facility owned by the Jewish community in Hoyo de Manzanares, a town around thirty-five kilometers north of Madrid; a British school in the affluent Madrid neighborhood of La Moraleja; and the grounds of the Spanish Agency for International Cooperation (Agencia Española de Cooperación Internacional), in the Madrid district of Moncloa.[4] The network also pinpointed targets in Segovia and Ávila, particularly those with Jewish symbolism.[5] To carry out these new attacks, the group had ample operational space in the two properties they had rented, as well as the arms and explosives already in their possession. Their financial reserves approximated €1.5 million euros—four times the cost of the materials that had been used to commit the Madrid bombings, which were estimated at around €105,000.[6]

The police action by the National Police Corps, which had begun on March 13, did not necessarily prevent the execution of other attacks, as the group threatened in their message dated April 3, 2004. Instead, the collective suicide explosion in Leganés on 9 p.m. on April 3, in which seven of the terrorists died, ended their plans. The attack showed how far the terrorists were willing to go to fulfill their common martyrdom jihadist ideology. Instead of surrendering themselves to the police, they carried out the first incident of suicide terrorism related to the current wave of global terrorism in Western Europe.[7]

Testament of a Suicide Terrorist: Abdenabi Kounjaa

It is possible to adduce why the seven terrorists trapped in the flat in Leganés reacted the way they did, immolating themselves in an act of suicide terrorism, after seeing themselves surrounded by the police, which had dispatched members of their Special Operations Group (Grupo Especial de Operaciones; GEO). As an aside, the GEO actually lost a member during the event: Assistant Inspector Francisco Javier Torronteras, who died in the explosion while the terrorists shouted out Islamic slogans. The act itself is not the only revealing bit of information of the final intentions of the terrorists. Serhane ben Adbelmajid Fakhet expressed his will in an Arabic manuscript discovered by the UCIE in his home in Madrid. It contained stanzas such as these, translated into English:

We are partisans, the partisans of Allah.

We are going to the jihad.

We have not come to stay.

To achieve martyrdom we have come.[8]

Some among those who, as shown in the text written by the ringleader of the 3/11 local cell, sought to achieve martyrdom by carrying out attacks, left behind written evidence of their will to leave behind testimonies. Investigators know of two testaments, one definitely written before March 11 and the other written at some unknown date, but likely preceding the bombings. The one dated with certainty was written by local cell member Abdenabi Kounjaa, and includes an explicit appeal to his two daughters that demonstrates his desire for the jihadist mentality to continue in the next generation.[9] This is the translation of the testament:

In the name of Allah, the Clement and Merciful. I am Abu Yusra Abdullah Bin Ahmed Kounjaa. This is my testament and hope it is read with prudence. It is written to my mother, my father, my brothers and sisters, as well as my wife and my daughters.

I will not extend myself much to not bore you. You need to cry for yourselves and repent for the opportunity that you have lost, given that

140

none of you had the merit to encourage me to join the path of jihad. Moreover, you have put yourself against my thoughts and wishes. I have sacrificed myself, departing from my total conviction.

As such, because jihad is an obligation. If you ask yourself why, then you will have return to the sayings of the Prophet (Allah pray for his soul) to read them, and then you will know why jihad is an obligation for the believers.

For that reason, it has been my will that opted for the path of jihad. It is not necessary to bring in texts, nor arguments from the Quran or the Sunnah, nor the sayings of the ulema [clerics], nor the wise on the topic of jihad, because I have already spoken about it to you repeatedly.

They were like shouts in the desert, or like blowing ashes; everything was in vain. *If I had called on living ones, you would have heard me, but I [called on] dead ones.* Have patience because of that goodbye and do not become sad. I swear by Allah that I invoke Allah and ask that he facilitate my martyrdom and that he join me with you in Paradise, and like that, you all [should] invoke Allah in all your prayers.

I swear by Allah, I cannot stand living in this world, humiliated and [feeling] weak before the eyes of the infidels and the tyrants. And I am afraid that Allah will judge me on the Day when money and children will not serve me. Neither will I have a legitimate excuse for him to forgive me.

Therefore, I give thanks to Allah, who brought me to this path. Be devoted to Allah. I have already left my children in the hands of Allah. He will have them in his blessings. If He did that when I did not fight for him, how can he forget them while I fight in the path of Allah? In this sense, I tell you:

Do not be sad, brothers,
I am the martyr of the (divine) word,
Our hopes are limited,
And our meeting will happen in Paradise.

If Allah predestines me for prison, I will tell you the same thing that Shayk Ibn Taimiyaa said: *What can my enemies do to me? If they imprison me, it will be for my retirement; if they banish me, it will be a journey; and if they kill me, I will be a martyr.* I ask that you care for the good education of my children. Teach them to read the Quran and the

141

Prophet's Sunna (Allah pray for his soul). My wish is that they be wise and [become] mujahedin.

For my wife: Your husband has lived yearning for this commitment, and I give thanks to Allah for having oriented me on this path. I want to tell you that you do not need to come to Spain. Be grateful to Allah that you are fine with your family. It would be illicit if you came. Take care of your children, teach them the Book of Allah and the Sunna of the Prophet of Allah (Allah pray for his soul) until you find Allah. Know with certainty that I have left my children, not from my own desire, but to comply with an order from Allah, the Almighty and Highest. Return to the surah of At-Tawbah (verses 9–24): *Say yes to your fathers.*

To my in-laws: I confirm to you that I have left this world because it is not worth as much as you think, and because I want to meet with my god and that He be happy with me. I ask that you take care of your daughter. Do not let her go to the land of infidels. You do not know where the Good is. Guard yourself and your families from Hell, if you really do feel responsible for your daughter and her children. Do not become saddened by my goodbye; thanks to Allah, I feel happy on this path. Let peace and mercy be with you.

To my daughters: Your father has been a man of moral values, and has always thought about jihad. The rest wanted to intimidate me with suffering and jail. Notwithstanding, thanks to Allah, He guided me to carry out that [which happened]. I ask you that you be devoted to Allah, and that you follow our brothers, the mujahedin, there where they are, and maybe, you can become part of them. This is the hope I leave with you, given that religion triumphs through the blood and sacrifice. Do not become attached too much to this life. Let peace be with you. Your father, Abdullah.

I ask that all those that love me, that they invoke Allah so that he can facilitate the martyrdom in the path of Allah for them and all the Muslims.

To my brothers in the Path of Allah, [wherever they maybe]: Many people take life as a path to death. I have chosen death as a path to life. You need to attach yourself to Islam, in word and deed, like activity and jihad. Islam does not reduce itself to a couple of prayers in the mosque, like some think, but it is a religion that encompasses everything. Abstain from following Satan's [lies], from humiliating yourself, and from believing the lies of despots, in a fashion that the whole world, from east to west, laughs at you. Curse the tyrants and fight them with all your strength alongside its flunkies, the human beings.

Let Allah's curses fall upon the unjust.

This testament, though left behind by a jihadist terrorist of the 3/11 network, made no mention of the war in Iraq. Instead, Kounjaa's words underscored his belief that jihad, understood as violence against infidels, is "an obligation" for believers in Islam. This conception of jihad, in its most bellicose and imperative sense from a religious perspective for Muslims, acts as a basic ingredient for the ideology of Salafist-jihadism. As Kounjaa's case demonstrates, marriage and children do not inhibit the decision to lose one's life on the path of jihad, because "martyrdom" is a way of "fulfilling an order from Allah."[10]

Not mentioned, but also very important, is that those who opt for suicide to become "martyrs" also have other nonworldly incentives for their actions. Abudllah Azzam, one of the founders of al-Qaeda and noted Salafist-jihadism ideologue, enumerated before his death the special favors that Allah granted to "martyrs": the forgiveness of all his or her sins, the vision of his place in heaven while his blood is split and before his soul leaves his body, enjoying the sweetness of faith, marriage with seventy-two virgins, protection against the penalties of purgatory, salvation from the great terror of the Day of Judgment, the right to wear a crown of honor worth more than anything on earth, and finally, permission to intercede for seventy members of his or her family to take them to paradise and to save them from the fires of hell.[11]

Kounjaa also expressed in his testamentary letter an emotional, personal sense of individual motivation that drove him to the extremes of jihadism. Specifically, he spoke of his sensation of feeling "humiliated and weakened before the eyes of the infidels," something very difficult to accept for those indoctrinated to believe in the superiority of the Islamic creed over all others. This sentiment also emerges in the second recovered testament belonging to the 3/11 terrorists. Although its author has not been identified, it likely belongs to a member who was part of the operational nucleus of the network, as the document was found among the ruins of the destroyed Leganés flat. This is a translation of a fragment of the text:

I have chosen this path from my own personal will, the path of the prophets and those sent by Allah, because the time of humiliation and dishonor has reached its end. For Allah! For me, it is more dignified dying honorably than living humiliated, seeing my brothers decapitated and assassinated and detained in all corners of the world, while we feed ourselves, quench our thirst, and live like beasts.

From this second testament written by a member of the 3/11 network, it is impossible to deduce the origin of the author's jihadist radicalization as belonging to economic privation or social exclusion. Complementing the hostile sentiments at the core of the 3/11 network toward the counterterrorism measures adopted by the Spanish authorities since 2001, the author instead mentioned his "brothers" who were "detained." Like most jihadists, the author nonetheless fails to mention that most of the victims of al-Qaeda and its territorial branches are in fact Muslims from North and East Africa, the Middle East, and South Asia, who are condemned as apostates by the extremists and therefore are regarded as deserving of death.[12]

Before discussing the next epigraph, it is worth mentioning that on April 19, 2004, fifteen days after the burial of Assistant Inspector Torronteras in the Cementerio Sur in Madrid, unknown individuals desecrated his grave. Several persons took his coffin to an obscure spot in the cemetery, and brutally ravaged the body and burned it. Private guards who were stationed in the cemetery became aware of what was happening and notified the police, who then informed the judicial authorities. The authorities dropped the case because of a lack of evidence identifying the culprits, although there are reasons, besides simple intuition, to suggest that those involved may have been individuals related to the 3/11 network, and, by implication, those who carried out the suicide attack in Leganés.

Sophisticated Planning and Mass Victimization: Distinctive Features of an Al-Qaeda Attack

Even though the Madrid bombings had not been conceived as suicide attacks, other facets of the 3/11 operation fit with the modus operandi of al-Qaeda—and not merely because the attack materialized on the eleventh day of March. Al-Qaeda chose the eleventh of September to attack New York and Washington, as well as other targets on the eleventh of April (Djerba in 2002 and Algiers in 2007) and July (Mumbai in 2006). The calendar date is revelatory, but not especially determinant, as al-Qaeda has planned attacks for days that did not correspond to the eleventh of a given month. It does merit mentioning, however, that exactly 911 days passed between 9/11 and 3/11.

The modality of the bombings is itself consistent, particularly in the use of coordinated explosions to cause the largest number of casualties possible. Much as in the September 11 attacks, where al-Qaeda used four planes, on March 11, the local cell attacked four trains. These were commuter trains with a departure time between 7:37 and 7:41 in the morning, their busiest period, allowing for greater lethality. In fact, the number of dead would have been higher if several other bombs that failed to detonate had exploded, and if one of the trains had not been slightly delayed—the four bombs on that train exploded before it entered Atocha station, which at the time was brimming with people.

One further symbolic detail illuminates with clarity the cognitive framework that informed the thought process of the 3/11 terrorists in desiring that their activities create the largest number of casualties. Among the various papers recovered from the debris of the apartment in Leganés, the authorities found a piece of paper with annotations in both Arabic and Spanish, largely illegible, that contained a drawing of 9/11 and a poem that praised the large number of victims.[13]

In relation to all of this, the final analysis of 3/11 by the US National Counterterrorism Center is relevant. This volume has already alluded to this NCTC report, "The Case for Al-Qai'da Links to the 2004 Madrid Bombings," which was written in 2008. After assessing the Madrid bombings, and compiling new intelligence pieces from American and foreign intelligence services after 2006 from Western and non-Western countries, the report concludes that the known data about the preparation and execution of the Madrid attacks indicate "evidence of sophisticated planning and a focus on mass casualties, both hallmarks of an al-Qaeda attack."[14]

Concerning the thirteen bombs used on 3/11, one of their essential components, the use of cell phones as detonators synchronized through alarms, clearly evokes al-Qaeda's terrorist practices. Jemmah Islamiyah, one of al-Qaeda's associated entities in Southeast Asia, collaborated directly with al-Qaeda's central organizations in the October 12, 2002, Bali bombings. In those attacks, the terrorists used the same Mitsubishi Trium cell phones that the Madrid bombers used.[15] The assistant director of Indonesia's national counterterrorist agency confirmed in an interview that he personally had interrogated Umar Patek, the individual who designed the phone-triggered bombs used in the Bali attacks, when Patek was detained in Abbottabad in

2011. He said that Patek had learned to use these phones to make components for explosions in an al-Qaeda training camp in Afghanistan.[16] The Spanish authorities had already recovered similar items in November 2001 and January 2003 during the police operations that had dismantled Abu Dahdah's cell, as well as during another operation against a jihadist cell based in Catalonia, in northeast Spain, which was indirectly related to al-Qaeda.[17] Al-Qaeda taught the use of cell phones in explosives in one of the training camp that Said Berraj, an operative member of the 3/11 network, attended.

Nonetheless, with respect to the explosives used in the Madrid bombings, it is not possible to argue that the similarities to other al-Qaeda actions persisted. The samples recovered from the train bombings and the remains of the Leganés apartment indicate that the terrorists used dynamite, specifically Goma 2 Eco.[18] Chapter 6 discussed how the terrorists acquired this substance from a group of Spanish delinquents, who extracted it and later traded it for drugs and other unknown economic incentives offered by Jamal Ahmidan's criminal group. Therefore, the terrorists fabricated the bombs using the dynamite and other items acquired in the areas they intended to perpetrate the attacks—in this case, in Spanish territory. However, before Ahmidan joined the network and assumed operational responsibilities in the group, taking on the responsibility for acquiring the explosives, other members of the group received instructions through a restricted internet forum on how to make bombs using triacetone triperoxide (TATP), an organic explosive. It is very likely that if the terrorists had not acquired the dynamite from the quarry, they would have used TATP to prepare the explosives used in the Madrid bombings. The terrorists in the 2003 Casablanca attacks and the 2005 London bombings used TATP, which in essence consists of mixing hydrogen peroxide, sulfuric acid, and acetone.[19]

Later in 2004, another jihadist cell in Spain tried to emulate the same model of terrorist action that the operational cell of 3/11 had accomplished. An agent for the Salafist Group for Preaching and Combat, Abderrahmane Tahiri (alias Mohamed Achraf), prepared a suicide attack against the grounds of the National Court in the center of Madrid. The plot, intended for the end of 2004, involved a vehicle loaded with hundreds of kilos' worth of explosives. In the summer of that year, Achraf had asked a Mauritanian member of his group, Kamara Birahima Diade, to acquire the explosives, specifically Goma 2. He wanted emulate 3/11, and perhaps believed that Goma 2 would be an easier item to acquire on the black market than another explosive like TATP would be. The authorities detained Achraf and Diade, along with others in their cell, in October 2004, unraveling the group and their goals.[20]

It is worth noting that jihadist terrorists groups outside of Western Europe have analyzed the use of dynamite by the 3/11 terrorists. In January 2006, the seventh issue of the *Al Fursan* magazine published by the Islamic Army of Iraq included a bulletin written by the so-called Brigades of the Supreme Paradise, a subset of the World Islamic Front for the Jihad against Jews and Crusaders. The World Islamic Front, the umbrella structure for all groups established by al-Qaeda, analyzed the "blessed attacks in Madrid." The group included the following analysis, not entirely accurate, on the use of dynamite:

It was an [accomplishment] that the brothers managed to acquire this component of military [origin] and used it instead of any other product, like homemade explosives, whose preparation requires more time and money—apart from having a safe location available for its preparation that, in its way, could have exposed the brothers before the Spanish intelligence services.

For that reason, we are going to examine here the most important characteristics and the positive aspects, which [enabled] the use of this explosive material and the differences between this and other types of explosives.

1. Talking from a military perspective, it is considered that this substance has a greater explosive capacity than TNT, capable of generating the foreseen destruction. Further, the use of this material has provided the brothers with an experience perhaps beneficial, or not, for operations of this type, because this is a substance that can be used without the need of assays or tests, given its proven detonative capacity.

2. This substance offers the mujahedin a strong camouflage because of its similarity to items used by the ETA organization. The Spanish security services tend to find this substance in the places where explosions perpetrated by this separatist organization happened, leading them to believe that it was executed by this separatist organization. This permits the mujahedin to move with freedom and without fear to prepare other attacks.

3. The ease of preparing the explosive package without the interferences presented by the construction of homemade explosives, because it is sufficient to place the material in a pan for the explosion, introducing a detonator and connecting it to a cell phone.

4. The explosive material is stable, meaning that one can place a fuse on it without it exploding immediately. Friction does not affect it, either, which guarantees that while the mujahedin transport it to the chosen place, passing among the people or over the bumps of the trains, it will not explode [until] the established time.

It is telling how the authors of this analysis understand the confusion generated by the explosives used in 3/11, but more importantly how they relate it to the Spanish public's misunderstanding of the nature of the attack in the days after the bombings. They remember in particular the transfer of culpability (to which terrorists aspire when they commit crimes) by pointing out that such an explosive substance was "similar to the one used by the ETA organization." Perhaps, in other circumstances, this type of confusion could have provided the terrorists with effective "camouflage." For example, if Spain had not been scheduled to hold elections three days after the bombings, the terrorists would not have needed to claim responsibility for them immediately. Alternatively, this misidentification would have helped to hide the terrorists from immediate scrutiny; in this case, because several of the explosive devices failed, the police had been able to identify the first suspects of the bombings.

Passenger Trains as Targets: Madrid, London . . . and Elsewhere

Among the various after-the-fact analyses by groups and organizations embedded in the global terrorist web, one interesting testimony produced by the al-Qaeda central organization itself is highly revealing. It demonstrates that Hamza Rabia, the al-Qaeda operations chief who was Amer Azizi's superior, had a true fixation with making passenger trains targets for terrorism. In 2005, while being interrogated by the American authorities in Guantánamo Bay, Abu Faraj al-Libi, who until recently had been third in command for al-Qaeda, declared that Rabia "wanted strongly to attack passenger trains in the US or UK following the March 2004 bombing of commuter trains in Madrid."[21]

On July 7, 2005, one year and four months after the Madrid bombings, suicide terrorists attacked multiple subway lines on the London Underground and a double-decker London bus just outside Russell Square station, the latter occurring after one of the bombers failed to immolate himself underground. Initially, the British authorities were reluctant to consider al-Qaeda's leaders as the plotters of the attack, but subsequent evidence shows that al-Qaeda was indeed behind it.[22] In December 2005, a CIA-piloted drone killed both Rabia and Azizi in North Waziristan. At the time, both were training individuals recruited by al-Qaeda to carry out attacks similar to the Madrid train bombings of 2004 or the London Underground bombings of 2005 in an important place in the United States, very likely New York City.[23]

13

Fleeing to Join Al-Qaeda's Mesopotamian Branch: The Fugitives of the 3/11 Network

After the events in Leganés on April 3, 2004, which conclusively disrupted the future plans of the 3/11 network, at least six of those who had been involved in the Madrid train bombings fled Spain. Mohamed Afalah, Mohamed Belhadj, and Abdelmajid Bouchar went on the run on the same night that their comrades blew themselves up in their apartment; the first two left together, and the third went on his own. These three had joined the 3/11 network with the component added by the Moroccan Islamic Combatant Group. The Algerian Daoud Ouhnane and the Moroccans Abdelilah Hriz and Othman el Mouib, all three of whom also were linked to the terrorist network, fled Spain in the following months. A seventh suspect was already out of the country: Hicham Ahmidan, one of the delinquents-turned-jihadists who had belonged to Jamal Ahmidan's gang, the third and final component of the 3/11 network, had left Spain and reached Morocco four or five days before the bombings took place.[1] At least five, though probably six, of the 3/11 network fugitives headed to Iraq.

Their choice of destination, and the behavior exhibited by most of these known fugitives—there may well be other unidentified fugitives whose names have not made the news—are both evidence of the widespread willingness to become suicide bombers shown by the members of the 3/11 network. The flight of these men, apart from confirming the intensity with which they adopted the martyrdom ideal inherent in Salafist-jihadism, aligns with the arguments laid out in previous chapters on the 3/11 network's international connections. As demonstrated earlier, these international connections derived from the constituent components' alignment with then-rising jihadist movements in and outside of Western Europe.

In March 2004, the Iraq war was the principal armed conflict involving jihadist organizations, and it attracted individuals who had been radicalized and recruited in certain sectors of the Muslim communities in European societies.[2] The terrorist campaign in Iraq had begun in 2003, shortly after the country's invasion and occupation by the US-led multinational coalition forces. The George W. Bush administration justified the intervention by arguing that Iraqi leaders had colluded with al-Qaeda in its terrorist activities, including the September 11 attacks, and alleged that Saddam Hussein had an arsenal of weapons of mass destruction. (Both of these assertions later proved to be false.) Following the US invasion, a terrorist campaign began in Iraq, frequently targeting the coalition forces. Many of these attacks on the coalition forces were suicide attacks, and involved militants of Tawhid wal-Jihad.

Tawhid wal-Jihad, as its name implies, combined the concepts of monotheism, or unity of Allah (*tawhid* means "oneness"), with jihad, in a warlike sense. Founded by a Jordanian known as Abu Musab al-Zarqawi, its membership originally consisted mainly of Jordanians and Palestinians. The group moved to northern Iraq in late 2001 or early 2002, from Herat, Afghanistan, where al-Qaeda and the Taliban provided sanctuary for them. Zarqawi, by his own admission, had met Abdelatif Mourafik (also known as Malek al-Andalusi) in Afghanistan.[3] Mourafik, introduced in earlier chapters as a member of the Libyan Islamic Fighting Group, was the intermediary for Amer Azizi when Azizi directed Mustafa Maymouni to form a new jihadist cell in Madrid from the remnants of the dismantled Abu Dahdah cell, which ultimately became the 3/11 network. Once established on Iraqi soil, Tawhid wal-Jihad incorporated foreign jihadists from Muslim countries and Western societies.

Zarqawi is thought to have played a role in the aforementioned meeting held by the delegates of the LIFG, the MICG, and the Tunisian Combating Group in February 2002, in which they all decided to practice jihad in their countries of origin because they had better opportunities for doing so, as their members resided there. In Iraq, Tawhid wal-Jihad's terrorist activity against foreign troops, international organizations, and, above all, Iraqi Shiites (whom the organization considered to be apostates), acquired such frequency and intensity that the leaders of al-Qaeda and Tawhid wal-Jihad agreed to merge. Thus in September 2004, al-Qaeda in Mesopotamia (AQM) was formed under the leadership of Zarqawi himself. Zarqawi swore allegiance to Osama bin Laden through the Global Islamic Media Center, an instrumental website for the 3/11 network's local cell. From then on, the individuals who had been recruited and radicalized in the Western European countries and had joined Tawhid wal-Jihad aligned themselves to the newly created Iraqi branch of al-Qaeda.[4]

"It's Mohamed, I'm in Iraq; forgive me": 3/11 Fugitives as Suicide Bombers in Iraq

One of the 3/11 fugitives, Daoud Ouhnane, had had an international capture-and-arrest warrant out on him since May 2004. He arrived in Iraq in the beginning of 2005 and incorporated himself into the recently formed Iraqi branch of al-Qaeda. He quickly gained notoriety in the ranks, becoming one of the organization's important leaders next to Zarqawi.[5] In 2005, in one of the various telephone conversations intercepted by the UCIE, he reached out to a fellow Algerian with Spanish residency, Djilali Boussiri. In their conversation, Ouhnane referred to a weapon that was frequently used in Iraq, and spoke of the feeling he had when he carried it. He said, "When you have it, you can finish anyone."[6]

However, it was Ouhnane who lost his life in a confrontation with coalition soldiers at the end of 2006, or beginning of 2007. He died at a time when he had ascended far enough in the AQM ranks to combine its connections with his own networks to organize and plan various attacks on European soil, most likely another major terrorist attack on Spain, again most likely motivated by revenge.[7] Because of his experience in terrorist activities and his knowledge of the counterterrorism measures employed by the Spanish authorities, Ouhnane aligned himself with a faction of AQM led by Abdallah Najim Abdallah Muhammed al-Juwari, who was campaigning to extend AQM operations into Western Europe—contrary to Zarqawi's plans to focus more on terrorist activities in Iraq.[8]

On June 6, 2005, the British Embassy in Madrid confirmed in writing to the Spanish authorities that British intelligence had found another fugitive member of the 3/11 network, the Moroccan Mohamed Afalah, in the Iraqi city of Tikrit between the end of March and the beginning of April that same year. The British stated that Afalah had died carrying out one of the ten suicide attacks that had taken place around the outskirts of Baghdad between May 13 and May 19. An international warrant had been issued for Afalah in April 2004. On May 12, before he committed his final act of terrorism, he attempted unsuccessfully to contact his father in Morocco through a cell phone number that was unknown to the Spanish police, but finally called his father at a phone number that his father regularly used, saying, "It's Mohamed, I'm in Iraq; forgive me."[9] AQM claimed responsibility for the suicide attack that Afalah committed. Through this same al-Qaeda branch, Said Berraj, another of the 3/11 escapees, also channeled his desire for martyrdom. Trained in terrorist tactics alongside Amer Azizi in a camp run by al-Qaeda in Afghanistan before 9/11, Berraj is believed to have died in a suicide attack inside Iraq in 2006. Othman el Mouhib followed a similar path, and blew himself up in Iraq on April 17, 2005.[10] His international warrant dated to April 2004. The latter had escaped from Spain with his fellow countryman Abdelilah Hriz, whom the Spanish authorities were seeking for his involvement in the Madrid train bombings.

Abdelilah Hriz fled Spain at the end of 2004, hoping to travel to Iraq to practice jihad, but the Syrian authorities arrested him in 2005. The National Court in Spain had indicted him and ordered his imprisonment earlier that same year, but the Syrian authorities extradited him to Morocco, his home country, instead. It is interesting to note that when Spanish police traveled to Syria to interrogate Hriz during his detention there, he insisted to the officials that the 3/11 attacks had not been decided on in Spain, but rather had been initiated far away.[11] In 2008, a Moroccan court sentenced Hriz for his actions in the Madrid attacks.[12]

The Moroccan Mohamed Belhadj met a fate similar to that of Abdelilah Hriz: imprisonment in his home country. He sought refuge in Belgium even though the Belgian authorities had positively identified him twice before, first in 2004 and again in 2005. He managed to receive the necessary help to travel to Syria, but when he arrived there, the Syrian authorities detained and extradited him to Morocco. In 2010, the Moroccan courts convicted him for his participation in the Madrid attacks.[13] Morocco does not extradite its citizens, which is why Moroccan courts were involved in the sentences imposed on Hriz and Mohamed Belhadj for their actions in Madrid. Hicham Ahmidan, who had also fled to Morocco, also was caught and sentenced in Morocco; unlike the others implicated in the Madrid attacks, however, he seemed not to have aspired to become a martyr.[14]

As such, it is significant that some of the individuals who fled Spain following their participation in the Madrid train bombings integrated themselves directly into al-Qaeda's Iraq branch, where they became suicide terrorists. Their actions highlight the ongoing connections between the 3/11 network and al-Qaeda, through Amer Azizi's dual role as an instigator of the attacks in

Spain and as the conduit for al-Qaeda's external operations. No less relevant is the complex connections through which the remnants of the 3/11 network were able to travel to Iraq. Escaping from Madrid, to avoid detection, all the fugitives traveled through the town of Santa Coloma de Gramanet in the province of Barcelona—a fact that deserves closer examination.

Al Kalaa: The Fortress

In Santa Coloma de Gramanet, on a street named San Francesc (in the local Catalan vernacular), there was a building that its occupants and the Maghrebis who passed through it called *Al Kalaa* (roughly, "the fortress" in Arabic). The people living in Al Kalaa had dedicated themselves to Salafist-jihadism, assisting those who shared their ideology and who needed a temporary hiding place, or were seeking to go to Iraq or another country to practice jihad.[15]

Through various trials, the National Court sentenced five individuals for aiding, hiding, and providing money and false documents to the fugitive members of the 3/11 network in Al Kalaa prior to their escape from Spain.[16] Two of the five individuals sentenced were Moroccan: Souahir Kadiri and Samir Tahtah. Two others were Algerian: Kamal Ahbar and the previously mentioned Djilali Boussiri, who knew the 3/11 fugitive Daoud Ouhnane. The fifth, Tarek Hamed Hamud, was Spanish, and had come from the autonomous Spanish city of Ceuta on the border with Morocco. Mohamed Afalah was carrying Hamud's passport when the Turkish authorities briefly stopped him before he arrived in Iraq in 2004. During a search of Hamud's house before his arrest on April 2, 2005, the authorities found a pistol, two hundred rounds of ammunition, a fake driver's license, documents about arms and munitions, an axe, and an Arabic-language book titled *Introduction to Jihad*. The book was subdivided into chapters with titles such as "Jihad: Fight to the Death," "Any Form of Death Becomes Martyrdom if Allah Desires," "Jihad Will Last Until the Day of Final Judgment," "The Acts Will Erase All Sins," and "The Merits of Dying in the Name of Allah."[17]

From Al Kalaa, aid flowed toward Iraq. The journey from Spain normally required stops in Belgium, Turkey, and Syria. Mohamed Afalah, as mentioned above, was detained in the Istanbul airport in the summer of 2004 when he tried to use fake documents to board a plane to Damascus. He was held for several months in a detention center for illegal immigrants, until a collaborator in Al Kalaa sent him €600 that he used to bribe a guard. Abdelilah Hriz and Othman el Mouhib also received money during their journey through Turkey, as did Mohamed Belhadj during his stay in Belgium, with Al Kalaa members providing the funds generally through a Western Union operator in Santa Coloma de Gramanet. During his CGI hearing on October 19, 2008, Kamal Ahbar, one of the individuals sentenced for aiding members of the 3/11 network, acknowledged that he had provided help from Al Kalaa to the fugitive suspects so they could escape from Spain and travel to Iraq. He also affirmed that he was convinced that "jihad realized by the mujahedin is totally justified" and that he was "proud" to be called a "terrorist," and added that "when he leaves prison" he wanted to go "directly to Iraq or Somalia to fight the coalition troops." He maintained that the "authors of the attacks of 3/11 in Madrid had their reasons for committing them," and made it clear "he [did not] regret" having helped them escape.[18]

Two Moroccans developed special management and support roles in the jihadist activities related to Al Kalaa: Mohamed Larbi ben Sellam, himself a member of the 3/11 network, and a second, unidentified person who was considered to be an important MICG member residing in Spain.[19] In 2004, that second individual regularly contacted one of the then supposed chiefs of al-Qaeda in Europe, an Algerian known by his nickname of Abu Bassir.[20] The latter was associated with the leaders of the Salafist Group for Preaching and Combat, with Abu Musab al-Zarqawi, and with Osama bin Laden himself.[21] Mohamed Larbi ben Sellam, acting on his own, collaborated in the beginning of a new jihadist cell in Madrid in March 2002, and attended meetings in which he adamantly justified jihadist acts in countries such as Morocco or Spain.[22] He also had a very good relationship with Rabei Osman es Sayed Ahmed, better known as Mohamed al-Masri. Larbi ben Sellam was convicted for his role in the 3/11 network.

Additional Links with Ansar al-Sunna

From Santa Coloma de Gramanet—more concretely, from Al Kalaa—links were also cultivated with al-Qaeda's affiliate Ansar al-Islam, a connection that proved to be an important point of contact for the majority of the fugitive members of the 3/11 network. Ansar al-Islam had first taken root in Iraqi Kurdistan in December 2001, but after May 2003 it was forced to reorganize after the US-led invasion of Iraq greatly reduced the power of its infrastructure and its membership. In September 2003, it changed its name to Ansar al-Sunna. It attracted Iraqi Arabs and foreign volunteers, and proceeded to wage a violent terrorist campaign in Iraq from its bases in the north of the country, where the population is predominantly ethnic Kurdish and Sunni.[23]

Al Kalaa had been in place in Santa Coloma de Gramanet since 2003. The initial head of the group was Abdelahim Akoudad (also known as Nadufel), a prominent member from the MICG structures in Western Europe who had traveled to Spain from Belgium to assume the role and who was already in contact with Kamel Ahbar. In October 2013, Akoudad was detained in the city of Badalona and extradited shortly after to Morocco, where he was convicted for terrorist activities.[24] Akoudad and his associates were in permanent contact with Ansar al-Islam and Ansar al-Sunna members who were based in Damascus, where they helped aspiring terrorists and suicide bombers who had arrived from Spain and other European countries to make the final part of the journey into Iraq. Therefore, Al Kalaa, through their arrangements with Ansar al-Islam/Ansar al-Sunna, helped supply the organizations with Western European assets, mobilizing and transferring human and material resources to these and other jihadists operating in Iraq.

Ansar al-Islam and its successor, Ansar al-Sunna, were well-known entities to the members of the 3/11 network. In the ruins of the Leganés apartment, the authorities recovered videos from both al-Qaeda and Ansar al-Sunna. One of these recordings focused on the terrorist attacks committed on November 29, 2003, against Spanish intelligence members in Iraq. Of the eight CNI members who were attacked as they were traveling through an area south of Baghdad in two all-terrain vehicles, only one survived. Ansar al-Sunna claimed responsibility for the attack through a communique released through the Global Islamic Media Center website. The hard drive in one of the computers used by the operational nucleus of the 3/11 network, also recovered from the Leganés rubble, contained documents with speeches in favor of jihad and images of suicide attacks, which in large part came from an Ansar al-Sunna web page. The hard drive also held an Ansar al-Sunna video that showed images of one of the Spanish intelligence members who had been killed in Iraq. In Leganés, the authorities also found a document that appeared to be a second incomplete message written by the local cell. The writing style corresponded to that of Jamal Ahmidan, although it was clear that Serhane ben Abdelmajid Fakhet had drafted it originally. In the document, the cell members styled themselves as "Ansar Al Sunna in Europe."[25]

It is also important to consider that before the so-called Abu Hafs al-Masri Brigades (al-Qaeda) claimed to be responsible for the Madrid train bombings, the same organization also claimed responsibility for other attacks, such as one that occurred in November 2003 in the Iraqi city of Nasiriya. The communiqué, signed with the name Abu Hafs al-Masri Brigades (al-Qaeda), was sent by email to the Arabic-language London-based *Al-Quds al-Arabi* newspaper on the afternoon of March 11, 2004. It contained the following message: "When we hit the Italian troops in Nasiriyah, we sent the American agents a warning: retire from the alliance against Islam. But you didn't understand the message. Now we dot the 'I's.'"[26] A message communicated to the Saudi-owned London-based *Al-Majalla* newspaper by Abu Mohamed al-Ablaj, nine days after the Nasiriya attack, also linked the attack to al-Qaeda. The Al Kalaa group was responsible for sending one of the suicide bombers who committed the November 2003 attack in Nasiriya.[27]

In sum, the paths through which at least five but probably six of the 3/11 network fugitives used to leave Spain, with the help of Al Kalaa, involved three types of individual and collective actors related to those who prepared and executed the Madrid train bombings. First, there was the MICG, which had incorporated its own component into the 3/11 network. Second was Abu Musab Zarqawi, who had exercised his influence over the change in strategy that had been agreed upon in Istanbul in February 2002 by Maghreb jihadist organizations. The third was al-Qaeda's central organization, connected to the 3/11 network through its adjunct to the external operations commander and former prominent member of Abu Dahdah cell, Amer Azizi.

14

After the 2004 Madrid Train
Bombings: The Fallout in Spain

The 3/11 attacks in Madrid, which killed 191 and injured over 1800 people, had other domestic consequences beyond their already-mentioned impact on the Spanish general elections that took place three days later, on March 14. Again, there is little doubt that the mobilization of a significant segment of the electorate, spurred by the terrorist massacre and its aftermath, secured the victory of the Partido Socialista Obrero Español at the polls. The incumbent Partido Popular government's insistence that the Basque terrorist group ETA was behind the attacks, when emerging evidence clearly pointed toward jihadist terrorism, also proved counterproductive to the ruling party. After the Madrid train bombings and the elections, Spanish society became deeply divided over who to blame for the train blasts. Yet counterterrorism in Spain underwent an important reform, so as to adapt the state's internal security structures to better face the threat posed to its citizens and interests by the persisting and evolving phenomenon of jihadism.

Why Did 3/11 Divide Spaniards, Instead of Uniting Them?

Contrary to what happened in the United States after September 11 or in the United Kingdom after the London attacks on July 7, 2005, the March 11, 2004, Madrid train bombings profoundly divided Spanish society. The aftereffects of that disunity persisted for well over a decade, although they have become less manifest with time. The disunity stemmed from differing attributions of blame for the commuter train massacre. Yet it proved to be a spurious division resulting from a politicization of the attacks. This situation, in turn, was made possible by specific features of the Spanish political system—such as, for instance, its greater penchant for polarization, or the recurring absence of cross-party consensus on matters of defense, foreign affairs, or counterterrorism—but above all because citizens were unaware of a terrorist threat that had been present in Spanish society for a full decade before the bombings.

Some Spaniards, particularly those whose political beliefs lie on the right of the spectrum, believed, and partly still do, that ETA was somehow implicated in the Madrid attacks. The most common version of this argument goes that the so-called *moritos de Lavapiés* ("little Moors from Lavapiés")—a derogatory and oddly dismissive way to talk about a group of people who set up such a complex and sophisticated terrorist network—lacked the knowledge and ability to carry out the attacks. According to this argument, even though these *moritos de Lavapiés* took part in the events, they must have been induced to act and supported from within Spain by other, more experienced terrorists.[1] This argument is typically supplemented with speculation about the way in which José Luis Rodríguez Zapatero—the new PSOE prime minister who came to power in the general elections held three days after the attacks—later offered ETA a transformative way out of its decades-long terrorist trajectory by means of a negotiation process, instead of trying to defeat the terrorist organization.

Other Spaniards, mostly on the left of the political spectrum, believed, and more than a few surely still do, that the March 11 attacks were a direct consequence of the "Azores photograph"—a reference to a photograph taken on March 16, 2003, on one of the Portuguese islands, that illustrated the affinity between the then Prime Minister José María Aznar of the PP and US president George W. Bush, and Spain's support for Bush's war on terror. In addition to Bush and Aznar, the picture includes the then British prime minister Tony Blair, a strong supporter of the US action in Iraq. This affinity led to the subsequent deployment of Spanish troops in Iraq shortly after the United States invaded the country and toppled its dictator, Saddam Hussein.[2] It has not been unusual for this sector of Spanish society to criticize the PP for its insistence on associating ETA with 3/11, even after the evidence pointed elsewhere, in order to protect its voting expectations at an election that was to be held just three days after the bombings.

As explained and documented in this book, both interpretations of the Madrid train bombings were erroneous, and the lacerating rift that divided Spaniards, including the surviving victims themselves, continues to be deceiving. There is no direct or indirect evidence that ETA was somehow involved in the bomb attacks. Nor is it true that the idea of perpetrating a massacre in Madrid originated in response to the presence of Spanish soldiers on Iraqi soil. The decision to carry out that act of terrorism was made in December 2001 in Karachi, Pakistan, and ratified at a meeting that delegates from three jihadist organizations from the Maghreb region held in Istanbul in February 2002. The initial recruitment efforts for the nascent 3/11 network began the following month, March 2002, well over a year before the Iraq invasion would take place.

But it was not really necessary to investigate the March 11 attacks, or to unveil new information about them, to avoid this division between Spaniards—even though doing so has helped narrow the gap. It would have been enough if, like the British, the Spanish had been sufficiently aware of the threat of jihadist terrorism since well before the invasion and occupation of Iraq. It should be remembered that, as mentioned earlier, since at least 1997, reports sent in by the UCIE of the National Police to magistrates at the National Court—in charge of authorizing wiretaps of jihadists active in Spain—were warning about the need for investigations "to prevent the highly probable perpetration of attacks in our country."[3] Even among citizens with an interest in the issue who were adults when the Madrid bombings took place, there was a huge lack of awareness about the expansion of jihadism in Spain since the mid-1990s. Hardly anybody had in mind that back in 1994, al-Qaeda had founded in Spain one of its most important cells in all Western Europe, or that this cell was broken up in November 2001 after it was shown to have ties with the people who committed the September 11 attacks. Likewise, almost no one was aware that throughout 2003, the year before the Madrid train bombings, more than forty individuals had been arrested in Spain for their involvement in jihadist terrorism activities. That figure had not been so high since the first jihadist arrest in Barcelona in 1995 and the first breakup of a jihadist cell in Valencia in 1997.

This lack of awareness about these and many other incidents relating to the evolution of jihadist terrorism in Spain in the decade prior to the Madrid attacks, and the fact that Spanish public opinion did not perceive the existing threat until much later—and then only after the Iraq crisis of 2003—can be explained in part by the fact that ETA's frequent terrorist attacks had received the most public attention and media coverage. But as far as jihadist terrorism was concerned, the political class did not provide the public with adequate information and education regarding the problem, and even trivialized it on occasion. As a result, when the attacks occurred in March 2004, Spaniards sought to explain the terrorist bombings using familiar concepts, since they could not do so using unfamiliar ones. What was familiar? On the one hand, ETA, and on the other, Iraq. If 3/11 divided Spaniards, it was because Spanish society lacked the necessary resilience against large-scale terrorist attacks beyond the immediate crisis and emergency responses.

Spain's Counterterrorism Reformed

At the time of the 2004 Madrid train bombings, Spain was equipped with well-developed internal security structures that were highly efficient in the fight against ETA terrorism but not as well adapted to dealing with a type of terrorism related directly or indirectly to al-Qaeda. The reason for this deficiency was not so much because this phenomenon was unknown to the few expert officials dealing with this issue in the CNP's central intelligence unit, but rather was because only a very few individuals had been dedicated to this task, and they had limited resources to carry out their work.[4]

Things likely would have been different if the problem of jihadist terrorism had been given the importance and resources it deserved since at least the mid-1990s, especially after the September 11 attacks in the United States and the May 2003 attacks in Casablanca. But the Spanish government, then formed by the conservative PP, did not do so. Its leader, José María Aznar, acknowledged shortly after leaving office in March 2004 that "the very successes achieved in the struggle against ETA in recent years may have led us to lower our guard against the fundamentalist threat."[5] Indeed, the Madrid train bombings made it clear that the fight against jihadist terrorism had not received due priority from the government, and that as a result, the police information and intelligence services were not able to cope with the existing needs. In spite of the previous knowledge that both the CNP and the Guardia Civil had of a substantial portion of those who belonged to the 3/11 network, even to the point where the authorities were keeping tabs on some of these individuals, the terrorists showed a remarkable ability—surely derived from the skills that some of them had acquired in al-Qaeda's Afghanistan training camps prior to 9/11—to conceal their true intentions.

It also became clear that there were serious problems of coordination, not only among police forces but also within each of them. In fact, adequate coordination efforts between the corresponding sections of the CNP and of the Guardia Civil that were dedicated to combating terrorism, illicit drug trafficking, and the illegal trade in explosive substances likely would have enabled them to share data, to sound the alarm, and possibly even to thwart the preparations to perpetrate the 3/11 attacks in Madrid.

In April 2004, the new authorities that took charge of the Ministry of Interior—Spain's central institution for counterterrorism policy—within the new PSOE government understood from the very beginning that jihadist terrorism posed a lasting threat to Spain.[6] The ministry's first decisions were aimed at correcting observed counterterrorism weaknesses. But to do so, they were not able to refer back to the electoral program on which the PSOE had campaigned in the general elections, because it contained no specific proposals in this regard to countering terrorism. Initially, decisions involving the changes that subsequently would be made to Spain's internal security structures were shaped by the security forces themselves, as stated by the newly appointed minister of the interior before the corresponding parliamentary committee:

> . . . when we got to the Interior Ministry, we told the professionals at the Police and Guardia Civil information services: We have a serious problem in terms of Islamic terrorism, al-Qaeda terrorism, or new international terrorism. Do we have sufficient resources? Do we have a strong enough structure? . . . Basically, the Police and Guardia Civil information services told us two things: one, that we clearly have to increase the resources and personnel available to the external information units, that is, the Police and Guardia Civil units that focus on international terrorism; and two, they also told us that we should create a professional structure that can receive information, analyze it, assess the risks of the new terrorism, and consequently make operational recommendations to the Police and Guardia Civil.[7]

By May 2004, the Interior Ministry authorities had approved a wide-ranging counterterrorism plan with a special focus on al-Qaeda and related jihadist terrorism. Over the entire four-year term of the legislature that began a few weeks after 3/11, about a thousand police and Guardia Civil agents were added to central units and local brigades dealing with jihadist terrorism. Based on the initial number of police agents who were dealing with international terrorism at the time of the Madrid bombings, the increase in personnel may be in the order of six- to tenfold, depending on the criteria used to calculate.[8] Likewise, two months after the train bombings and more than a quarter of a century since the Spanish democracy was faced with the terrorism of ETA, both agencies with nationwide counterterrorism competences finally were able to secure joint and shared access to each other's databases. At the same time, a National Center for Counterterrorism Coordination (Centro Nacional de Coordinación Antiterrorista) was established. Both innovations intended to strengthen coordination among national security forces, in light of the weaknesses in this area that became clear on examination of the events leading up to the Madrid train bombings.[9]

Prior to the attacks, existing Spanish antiterrorism legislation, crafted in response to several decades of ETA terrorism, was inadequate in the face of the challenges of jihadist terrorism. Different individuals linked to jihadist cells and groups in Spain had been able to evade detention or conviction, which ultimately enabled them to involve themselves in the preparation and execution of the Madrid attacks. Yet no significant modifications were introduced in the legislation, except for an increase in the penalties for trafficking and illegal use of explosive substances, until December 2010. It was only then, more than nine years after 9/11 and almost seven years since 3/11, that provisions on terrorism offenses included in the Spanish Criminal Code were revised. Even so, the reform was done to comply in a timely manner with the amended EU Council Framework Decision on combating terrorism, approved on November 2008, which provided for the criminalization of certain activities that lay the groundwork for violent radicalization, recruitment, and terrorist training.

In spite of the advances made since the 9/11 attacks and the fact that international terrorism was a field to which Spain's police (especially within the CGI) were paying careful attention, intergovernmental cooperation could not help prevent the Madrid train bombings. A number of red flags should have been raised earlier: those directly or indirectly involved in the plot were resident or nonresident foreigners, mainly Moroccans; a good number of them were known to the security services in their countries of origin; and several well-known members of the 3/11 network had even been arrested in France, Morocco, or Turkey. Increasing and diversifying international cooperation against global terrorism became a top goal of Spanish internal security after 3/11. The first cooperation partners were Spain's immediate European neighbors, working within the EU context. The international cooperation against terrorism developed by the

Spanish authorities also led to an increased cooperation with the United States. Further priorities for counterterrorism cooperation were the predominantly Muslim countries where al-Qaeda, its territorial extensions, or associated groups or organizations were established, and which could penetrate Spanish territory, mainly though not only in the Maghreb. As an obvious result of the 3/11 attacks, Morocco would receive Spain's top attention.[10]

Efforts to enhance intelligence capabilities, foster counterterrorism coordination, and advance international cooperation combined, after the Madrid train bombings, with a number of other initiatives, adopted since 2005. Such initiatives included the elaboration and implementation of a Terrorism Prevention and Protection Plan; a National Plan for the Protection of Critical Infrastructures; and a Prevention and Reaction Plan to deal with possible terrorist incidents involving nuclear, radioactive, bacteriological, or chemical components. Other developments in Spain have included new interdepartmental measures in the area of terrorism financing, and the application of a special disciplinary and monitoring regime in prisons to inmates charged with or convicted of jihadist terrorism offenses.[11]

The success of the Spanish government measures taken against international terrorism perpetrated by those who claim to be followers of Islam depends to a large extent on how the Muslim communities in Spain perceive both these terrorists and the state's counterterrorist activities. It should not be ignored that a good part of the individuals involved in the 3/11 network were known within Madrid's Muslim communities precisely because of the extremism of their attitudes and beliefs. Enough people inside these communities, who regularly frequented places of worship with or had other contact with these well-known figures, may have been aware that people they knew or were friends with were among those preparing to commit terrorist attacks in or outside Spain. Yet two years after the Madrid train bombings, 16 percent of Muslims living in Spain still expressed positive attitudes toward terrorist attacks against civilians in alleged defense of Islam or toward al-Qaeda and Osama bin Laden specifically.[12]

The Spanish Interior Ministry, particularly the Office of the Secretary of State for Security, has made efforts to develop a free exchange of views with the leaders of the Islamic Commission of Spain. The commission has been in dialogue with the Spanish state since the two entities signed a cooperation agreement in 1992, and these talks have been renewed by efforts on the part of the General Directorate of Religious Affairs to regulate Islam in Spain since 2004. However, this dialogue is limited by problems of representation that affect the leaders of the main Muslim associations, who strive—not without interference from beyond Spain's borders—to articulate the interests of Muslims living in Spain. It is also limited by the divisions found both within each association and between associations.

All in all, the action that the Spanish government has taken against jihadist terrorism since 3/11 is both multifaceted and multidepartmental, and goes beyond the measures adopted in the internal security sector. However, even though other European and Western countries have been formalizing integrated, national strategies to deal with this issue, in Spain's case the need to deal with two simultaneous terrorist threats—the ETA on one hand and al-Qaeda–related terrorism on the other—was an obstacle to developing a national strategy and an integrated plan to prevent radicalization. It was not until 2010 that the Spanish government, still under the control of the PSOE, approved an Integrated Strategy against International Terrorism and Radicalization (Estrategia Integral contra el Terrorismo Internacional y la Radicalización), which then was ratified in 2012 under a new PP executive leadership. The adoption of a more specific National Strategic Plan to Fight Violent Radicalization (Plan Estratégico Nacional de Lucha contra la Radicalización Violenta) had to wait until January 2015, more than ten years after 3/11.

A survey carried out by the Elcano Royal Institute in June 2006 showed that, on the whole, Spanish public opinion strongly supported the adoption of these measures.[13] (By this point, most of the above-mentioned initiatives already had been adopted and were at an advanced stage of implementation.) The survey also showed that there were solid grounds for an explicit and stable political consensus on this important issue, at least between Spain's then two main political parties. Such a political consensus concerning the fight against jihadist terrorism, however, did not exist until a decade following the Madrid train bombings. Known as the Pact against Jihadism (Pacto contra el Yihadismo), officially called the Agreement to Strengthen the Defense of Freedoms and Fight against Terrorism (Acuerdo para Afianzar la Defensa de las Libertades y en la Lucha contra el Terrorismo), the agreement was signed on February 2015—again, a decade after 3/11.

Jihadism in Spain after 3/11

Between the first arrest in 1995 and 2003—that is to say, in the nine years preceding the Madrid train bombings—slightly over one hundred individuals were detained in Spain for offenses related to jihadist terrorism, an average of twelve arrests per year. By contrast, over a similar nine-year period after the attacks (2004 to 2012), the number of arrests resulting from police operations against jihadist terrorism in the country exceeded 470. The annual average of detentions thus climbed to fifty-two, more than four times higher than during the previous period.

In the nine years before 3/11 and throughout the nine years following the attacks, Spain essentially had the same antiterrorist legislation, since new criminal provisions were not introduced in the Criminal Code until the end of 2010 and only took effect from the beginning of 2011. Thus, even when counterterrorism efforts intensified following 3/11, data on detentions should to be considered a reliable, relevant indicator of the extent to which the phenomenon of jihadist terrorism and its inherent threat persisted in Spain following the Madrid train bombings.

All fifty jihadists who were arrested and ultimately convicted for terrorism offenses from 2004 thorough 2012 were men. [14] No less than half of them were twenty-five to thirty-four years old at the time of their detention. Eight out of every ten were under forty, and more often than not were married and had children. Up until 2012, jihadist terrorism in Spain was not a home-grown phenomenon; 90 percent of the individuals involved were foreigners, and just 10 percent were Spanish nationals (although only 6 percent actually had been born in Spain). Six out of every ten were natives of geographically close Maghreb countries—43 percent were Moroccan and 19 percent were Algerian—but 28 percent were from Pakistan. Notwithstanding their diverse educational and occupational backgrounds, those with primary or no formal education, as well as those employed as services personnel, unskilled laborers, or in unknown occupations, were particularly represented among these individuals arrested and convicted for activities related to jihadist terrorism in Spain between 2004 and 2012. In addition, about one-third of those in this group had criminal records as ordinary delinquents before they were detained and charged with terrorist offenses.

Around seven out of every ten of the convicted who were sent to prison in the nine years following 3/11 resided in or around the metropolitan areas of Madrid and Barcelona. They typically had been radicalized at least in part in these areas, though others had been radicalized outside the country as well. [15] Radicalization took place in top-down or to a lesser extent in horizontal processes, starting usually between their mid-teens and late twenties. The circumstances of their radicalization were mainly, though not exclusively, inside private homes or in places of business or worship; prisons also played a role, as did the immediate influence of charismatic or religious figures and previously existing kinship, friendship, or neighborhood ties.

An overwhelming majority of these individuals were involved alongside others as parts of cells either integrated in or linked to jihadist organizations such as al-Qaeda and its then Iraqi branch, or associated North African and South Asian entities such as the Moroccan Islamic Combatant Group, the Algerian-based Salafist Group for Preaching and Combat, or Therik e Taliban Pakistan.[16] Indeed, Therik e Taliban Pakistan claimed responsibility for a plot, thwarted in January 2008, to carry out a highly lethal explosive-based attack against Barcelona's public transit system.[17] Eleven individuals—ten from Pakistan (one of whom was a naturalized Spaniard) and one from India, of whom slightly more than half resided in Barcelona—were convicted in connection with a terrorist plot that was meant to be Spain's second 3/11.[18]

From 2013, in the context of the worldwide mobilization prompted by jihadist insurgencies in Syria and Iraq, jihadist terrorism experienced a major transformation in Spain. Spain is not affected as strongly as other Western European nations by such mobilization, but jihadist activity is no longer a phenomenon overwhelmingly associated with foreigners living in the country. Data on some 140 suspected jihadists arrested between 2013 and May 2016 show that nearly half the detained were Spanish nationals and had been born in Spain. Though most of the rest were Moroccan, these findings clearly indicate the rise of homegrown jihadism in Spain.[19] This homegrown component has its main focus among second-generation descendants of Moroccan immigrants who reside in the North African Spanish enclaves of Ceuta and Melilla, though Barcelona's metropolitan area remains the leading national geographical focus overall. In contrast with past findings, though jihadism in Spain (as elsewhere) is still a phenomenon dominated by young men, the percentage of women involved in jihadist activity has grown significantly, along with the proportion of converts. Only 5 percent of all individuals arrested for jihadist terrorism activities in Spain between 2013 and May 2016 were acting alone. The vast majority (95.5 percent) were embedded in new or reconstituted cells and networks connected mainly with major jihadist organizations such as Al Nusra Front but, above all, with the former Iraqi branch of al-Qaeda, which throughout 2013 and 2014 morphed into the so-called Islamic State, rivaling al-Qaeda for hegemony within global jihadism.

Meanwhile, the propaganda disseminated by the main jihadist organizations persistently continues to make specific references to Spain. Among the most frequently mentioned points in the decade since 2004 are those alluding to Al-Andalus and to the Madrid train bombings.[20]

Notes

Prologue

1. Spain's Audiencia Nacional (National Court), Juzgado Central de Instrucción (Central Investigative Court) no. 6, *Sumario 20/2004*, vol. 161, 60,764 and 60,771.

2. National Court, Sala de lo Penal (Criminal Division), Sección Segunda (Second Section), *Sentencia 65/2007*, 229–422.

3. On the immediate material damages, see *Sumario 20/2004*, vol. 216, 84,062. On the direct economic costs, see Mikel Buesa, Aurelia Vilariño, Joost Heijs, Thomas Baumert, and Javier González, "The Economic Cost of March 11: Measuring the Direct Economic Cost of the Terrorist Attack on March 11, 2004 in Madrid," *Terrorism and Political Violence* 19, no. 4 (2007): 489–509.

4. See Bruce Hoffman and Fernando Reinares; "Introduction" and "Conclusions," in *The Evolution of the Global Terrorism Threat: From 9/11 to Osama bin Laden's Death*, ed. Bruce Hoffman and Fernando Reinares (New York: Columbia University Press, 2014).

5. See Marc Sageman, *Leaderless Jihad: Terror Networks in the Twenty-First Century* (Philadelphia: University of Pennsylvania Press, 2008), in particular, chaps. 4 and 7; a similar interpretation is given by Mitchell D. Silber, *The Al Qaeda Factor: Plots Against the West* (Philadelphia: University of Pennsylvania Press, 2012), 184–205. More scholarly, cautious, and ultimately meritorious approaches to understanding the 3/11 attacks have been offered, among others, by Lorenzo Vidino, *Al Qaeda in Europe: The New Battleground of International Jihad* (New York: Prometheus Books, 2005), chap. 11; Alison Pargeter, *The New Frontiers of Jihad: Radical Islam in Europe* (London: I. B. Tauris, 2008), chap. 8; and Seth G. Jones, *Hunting in the Shadows: The Pursuit of Al Qa'ida Since 9/11* (New York: W. W. Norton, 2012), chap. 7.

6. A second sentence on the Madrid train bombings, though limited in scope to a series of appeals and based on no different evidence than existed previously, came from the Second Section of the Criminal Division of the Tribunal Supremo (Supreme Court) in 2008. Other criminal proceedings and sentences concerning the 3/11 attacks are listed and discussed throughout this book.

7. Fernando Reinares, "Jihadist Radicalization and the 2004 Madrid Bombing Network," *CTC Sentinel* 2, issue 11 (2009): 16–19; Fernando Reinares, "The Madrid Bombings and Global Jihadism," *Survival* 52, no. 2 (2010): 83–104; Fernando Reinares, "The Evidence of al-Qa'ida's Role in the 2004 Madrid Attack," *CTC Sentinel* 5, issue 3 (2012): 1–6; Fernando Reinares, "The 2004 Madrid Train Bombings," in *Evolution of the Global Terrorism Threat*, ed. Hoffman and Reinares, 29–60; Fernando Reinares, *¡Matadlos! Quién estuvo detrás del 11-M y por qué se atentó en España* (Barcelona: Galaxia Gutenberg, 2014).

Chapter 1

1. National Court of Spain, Central Investigative Court No. 5, *Sumario 35/2001*, which concluded in June 2004.

2. Marc Sageman, *Understanding Terror Networks* (Philadelphia: University of Pennsylvania Press, 2004), chaps. 1 and 2; Abdel Bari Atwan, *The Secret History of Al-Qa'ida* (London: Abacus, 2006), 31–82; Bruce Riedel, *The Search for Al Qaeda: Its Leadership, Ideology, and Future* (Washington, DC: Brookings Institution Press, 2008), chaps. 1-4; and Jean-Pierre Filiu, *Les neufs vies d'Al-Qaida* [The nine lives of al-Qaeda] (Paris: Fayard, 2009), 23–54.

3. On the concept of defensive jihad, see Atwan, *The Secret History of Al-Qa'ida*, 62–63; and Devin R. Springer, James L. Regens, and David N. Edger, *Islamic Radicalism and Global Jihad* (Washington, DC: Georgetown University Press, 2009), 42, 54, and 93.

4. Rohan Gunaratna, *Inside Al Qaeda: Global Network of Terror* (New York: Columbia University Press, 2002), 98; and Filiu, *Les neufs vies d'Al-Qaida*, 55–71.

5. National Court of Spain, Criminal Division, Third Section, *Sentencia 36/2005*, 442–45.

6. Supreme Court of Spain, Criminal Division, *Sentencia 556/2006*, 298–99 and 302–3.

7. A reference that I believe has been given more importance than it deserves, but see Brynjar Lia, *Architect of Global Jihad: The Life of Al-Qaida Strategist Abu Mus'ab al-Suri* (New York: Columbia University Press, 2008).

8. Abu Musab al Suri, "The Call to Global Islamic Resistance," reproduced in Jim Lacey, ed., *The Canons of Jihad: Terrorists' Strategy for Defeating America* (Annapolis, MD: Naval Institute Press, 2008), 174.

9. Quintan Wiktorowicz, "Anatomy of the Salafi Movement," *Studies in Conflict and Terrorism* 29, no. 3 (2006): 207–39; Rohan Gunaratna, "Al Qaeda's Ideology," *Current Trends in Islamist Ideology*, vol. 1 (2005), 59–67; David Aaron, *In Their Own Words: Voices of Jihad* (Santa Monica, CA: RAND Corporation, 2008), especially chap. 4; and Antonio Elorza, *Los dos mensajes del Islam: razón y violencia en la tradición islámica* [The two messages of Islam: Reason and violence in the Islamic tradition] (Barcelona: Ediciones B, 2008), 289–312.

10. On the origins and evolution of the GIA, see Camille Tawil, *Brothers in Arms: The Story of Al-Qa'ida and the Arab Jihadists* (London: Saqi Books, 2010), 67–87 and 127–35.

11. Tawil, *Brothers in Arms*, 115–16

12. Peter L. Bergen, *Holy War, Inc.: Inside the Secret World of Osama bin Laden* (New York: The Free Press, 2001), 88–89 and 205; Tawil, *Brothers in Arms*, 112; and United States District Court, Southern District of New York, *Indictment S(9) 98 Cr. 1023 (LBS)*, 17–18, 20–24, 27–28, 30–32, and 116–17.

13. Jarret M. Brachman, *Global Jihadism: Theory and Practice* (London: Routledge, 2009), 72–74 and 169–71.

14. Tawil, *Brothers in Arms*, 120.

15. Quoted in Brachman, *Global Jihadism*, 73.

16. Atwan, *The Secret History of Al-Qa'ida*, 19. Interestingly, in February 2015, during the terrorism conspiracy trial of Khaled al-Fawwaz in a US federal court in New York City, a set of photographs introduced as evidence showed Osama bin Laden in Tora Bora, a mountainous area of Afghanistan, in November 1996. In at least three of these images, Abu Musab al-Suri is pictured next to the then emir of al-Qaeda. "Rare Photos Offer Look Inside Osama bin Laden's Afghan Hideout," CNN, March 12, 2015, http://www.cnn.com/2015/03/11/world/gallery/osama-bin-laden-rare-photos.

17. Al-Suri's videos were available on the *Saowt* (Voice) online forum, www.saowt.com/forum/showthread.php?t=16158, audiovisual recording number 22, from 00:06:45 to 00:06:50 and from 00:07:13 to 00:07:17, and audiovisual recording number 23, 00:19:40-00:19:46 (site discontinued, accessed January 2006).

18. Ibid., audiovisual recording number 23.

19. Ibid., audiovisual recording number 25, especially from 00:21:20 to 00:21:40.

20. Lia, *Architect of Global Jihad*, 347–484.

21. A Directorate General of Police (Dirección General de la Policía; DGP), General Commissariat for Intelligence (CGI) report, dated October 28, 2004 and transmitted to the judge in charge of the judicial procedure for the Madrid bombings, indicated that "there is no evidence suggesting the implication of Setmarian Nasar in the preparing and planning of the terrorist acts in Europe," adding that "given the role he played in Afghanistan and his links to Spain, and to some of those al-Qaeda [members] detained in Spain, it is supposed that he could have had some kind of implication in operational activities in our country." See National Court of Spain, Central Investigative Court No. 6, *Sumario 20/2004*, vol. 85, 26,781.

22. "Syria Releases Al-Qaeda Strategist," *Jane's Terrorism and Security Monitor*, January 20, 2012; and Ignacio Cembrero, "La liberación de Setmarian" [The release of Setmarian], *El País*, January 29, 2012, http://politica.elpais.com/politica/2012/01/29/actualidad/1327841128_442958.html. In April 2014, however, Ayman al Zawahiri released an audio message, in which he used the phrase "May Allah release him" to refer to Abu Musab al-Suri, suggesting that Setmarian remained imprisoned. See www.longwarjournal.org/archives/2014/04/zawahiri_eulogizes_a.php.

23. The wiretap was authorized by the National Court of Spain, Central Investigative Court No. 5. DGP, CGI, Unidad Central de Información Exterior (UCIE), "Informe sobre la iniciación y continuación de investigaciones en España sobre los miembros de la organización o infraestructura de Osama bin Laden asentados en nuestro país" [Report on the initiation and continuation of research in Spain on the members of the Osama bin Laden organization or infrastructure settled in our country], October 17, 2003, 2.

24. Gunaratna, *Inside Al Qaeda*, 18.

25. "Informe sobre la iniciancíón y continuación de investigaciones"; *Sentencia 36/2005*, 29.

26. Gunaratna, *Inside Al Qaeda*, 39; and US Department of Defense, Joint Task Force Guantánamo, "JTF-GTMO Detainee Assessment on Abu Zubaydah," November 11, 2008, 2, 4, 9, and 12.

27. Gunaratna, *Inside Al Qaeda*, 118.

28. In this respect, see the message sent to the National Court police on August 2003 by the Special Central Unit 2 of the Guardia Civil Information Service Headquarters, with reference to ILL/ams, in the context of the *Diligencias Previas 154/2003*.

29. DCP, CGI, UCIE, "Informe ampliatorio a escrito de fecha 06-11-01 en relación con una red de infraestructura en España de la organización terrorista Al Qaida vinculada a Osama bin Laden" [Supplemental Report, dated 11/1/06, regarding an infrastructure network in Spain of the terrorist organization al-Qaeda linked to Osama bin Laden], November 12, 2001, 9.

30. Yoginder Sikand, "Islamist Militancy in Kashmir: The Case of the Lashkar-e-Taiba," in *The Practice of War: Production, Reproduction and Communication*, ed. Aparna Rao, Michael Bollig, and Monika Böck (New York, Berghahn Books, 2007), 215–38; and Mariam Abou Zahab, "'I Shall be Waiting for You at the Door of Paradise': The Pakistani Martyrs of the Lashkar-e-Taiba (Army of the Pure)," ibid., 133–58.

31. DCP, CGI, UCIE, "Informe ampliatorio a escrito de fecha 06-11-01"; *Sentencia 36/2005*, 28.

32. DGP, CGI, UCIE, "Informe sobre la iniciación y continuación de investigaciones en España sobre los miembros de la organización o infraestructura de Osama bin Laden asentados en nuestro país," 5–19.

33. The wiretap was successively authorized by the National Court of Spain, Central Investigative Courts Nos. 5, 1, and 3. See DGP, CGI, UCIE, "Informe sobre la iniciación y continuación de investigaciones en España sobre los miembros de la organización o infraestructura de Osama bin Laden asentados en nuestro país," 2–13.

34. Brachman, *Global Jihadism*, 112–13.

35. The citation was extracted from page 12 of a digital edition of the text in Arabic obtained on February 1, 2012, from the Tawhed.ws jihadist website: http://tawhed.ws /dl?i=fx7ze2mm (site discontinued). The original document was not dated but had to have been written between January 1987 and November 1989.

36. The text of the referenced letter is included in Bruce Lawrence, ed., *Messages to the World: The Statements of Osama bin Laden* (London: Verso, 2005), 4–14. The reference to Al-Andalus as an Islamic territory that must be recovered is on page 14.

37. The cited paragraph is found from extracts of the referenced work reproduced in Gilles Kepel, ed., *Al-Qaida dans le texte: Écrits d'Oussama ben Laden, Abdallah Azzam, Ayman al-Zawahiri et Abou Moussab al-Zarqawi* [Al-Qaeda in its texts: Writings of Osama bin Laden, Abdallah Azzam, Ayman al-Zawahiri, and Abu Moussab al-Zarqawi] (Paris: Presses Universitaires de France, 2005), 287. For an English translation, see Gilles Kepel and Jean-Pierre Milelli, eds., *Al Qaeda in Its Own Words* (Cambridge, MA: Harvard University Press, 2008), 194.

38. Fernando Reinares, *¿Cuál es la amenaza que el terrorismo yihadista supone actualmente para España?* [What is the threat that jihadist terrorism currently poses to Spain?], ARI 33/2007 (Madrid: Real Instituto Elcano, March 8, 2007), 2.

39. Ibid.

40. The video appeared, among various well-known sites, at www.as-ansar.com (last accessed April 22, 2009). Abu Yahya al-Libi was killed on June 2012 in a drone strike against a home in North Waziristan. At the time, about a year after Osama bin Laden's death, he acted as the second-in-command of al-Qaeda, after Ayman al-Zawahiri.

41. Gilles Kepel, *The War for Muslim Minds: Islam and the West* (Cambridge, MA: Harvard University Press, 2004), 146. A current well-known ideologue of Salafist-jihadism, Omar Bakri Muhammad, in his 2004 work *The World Is Divided into Two Camps* (published initially by www.salafimedia.com), includes Spain in the category *Daar ul-Kufr Taari'*—meaning Islamic territories that were usurped by the infidels and will return to Islamic dominion and "will be conquered at the first [possible] opportunity" (page 62).

42. DGP, CGI, Unidad Central de Inteligencia, and UCIE, "Informe general de conclusiones, atentados del 11 de marzo, Sumario 20/04" [General report of findings, March 11 attacks, Sumario 20/04], July 3, 2006, 19 and 21.

43. DGP, CGI, UCIE, "Informe sobre registro del domicilio de Luis José Galán González, Yusuf Galán" [Report on the domicile registration of Luis José Galán González, Yusuf Galán], 2002, 71.

44. See Abdennur Prado, "Yusuf Galán: 'Mi crimen es creer en laa ilaha il-lá Al-láh'" [Yusuf Galán: "My crime is believing in *laa ilaha il-la Al-lah*"], WebIslam, December 8, 2012, http://www.webislam.com/articulos/65526-yusuf_galan_mi_crimen_es_creer_en _laa_ilaha_illa_allah.html.

45. Ibid.

46. *Sentencia 36/2005*, 44, 78–88, and 90.

47. *Sentencia 36/2005*, 29–30; and DGP, CGI, UCIE, "Informe ampliatorio escrito de fecha 06-11-01," 19–20.

48. DGP, CGI, UCIE, "Informe general de conclusiones, atentados del 11 de marzo, Sumario 20/04."

49. *Sentencia 36/2005*, 65.

50. *Sentencia 36/2005*, 31–40 and 45–60.

51. DGP, CGI, UCIE, "Informe ampliatorio escrito de fecha 06-11-01," 50.

52. DGP, CGI, UCIE, "Informe solicitado en virtud de Auto de fecha 31 de marzo de 1997, Diligencias Previas 209/96, solicitado por el Juzgado Central de Instrucción número 5 de la Audiencia Nacional" [Report requested under the order of March 31, 1997, preliminary investigation 209/26, requested by the National Court of Spain, Central Investigative Court No. 5], April 14, 1997, 5, 10, and 11.

53. DGP, CGI, UCIE, "Informe sobre la iniciación y continuación de investigaciones en España sobre los miembros de la organización o infraestructura de Osama bin Laden asentados en nuestro país," 5.

54. *Sumario 35/2001*, vol. 36, 11.717; and *Sentencia 36/2005*, 66.

55. By annulling the German law transposing the European Arrest Warrant, the European Union norm on judicial cooperation facilitates extradition requests for claimed individuals between EU countries for criminal judgments or the execution of a sentence. The German court ruled that the law infringed on the right of German citizens to receive a court hearing in Germany before extradition could take place. See Richard Bernstein, "German High Court Overrules Spanish Judge's Order for the Extradition of a Qaeda [*sic*] Suspect," *New York Times*, July 19, 2005.

56. The Attorney General of the Federal Republic of Germany, "Ermittlungsverfahren gegen Mamoun Darkazanli, Sadel Borrmann, weitere, bisher unbekannte Personen wegen des Verdachts der Mitgliedschaft in einer terroristischen Vereinigung und der Geldwäsche; hier: Anzeige des spanischen Justizministeriums vom 17 Februar 2006," [Investigation into Mamoun Darkazanli, Sadel Borrmann et al., previously unknown persons on suspicion of membership in a terrorist organization and money laundering; Spanish Ministry of Justice, February 17, 2006], July 14, 2006.

57. *Diario Oficial de las Comunidades Europeas* [Official journal of the European Community], May 29, 2002, L 139/13.

58. *Sentencia 36/2005*, 96–97.

59. United States Department of Defense, "Verbatim Transcript of Combatant Status Review Tribunal Hearing for ISN 10013," US Naval Base Guantánamo Bay, Cuba, March 9, 2007, 4–5.

60. National Commission on Terrorist Attacks upon the United States, *The 9/11 Commission Report* (New York: W.W. Norton and Company, 2004), 244.

61. *Sentencia 36/2005*, 203–11; DGP, CGI, UCIE, "Informe de las investigaciones realizadas en torno a las visitas a España de Mohamed Atta y Ramzi Binalshibh" [Report of the investigations conducted around the visits to Spain of Mohamed Atta and Ramzi Binalshibh], October 15, 2002, and "Informe ampliatorio de las investigaciones realizadas en torno a las visitas a España de Mohamed Atta y Ramzi Binalshibh" [Expanded report of the investigations conducted around the visits to Spain of Mohamed Atta and Ramzi Binalshibh], October 16, 2002; Guardia Civil General Directorate, Information Service Headquarters, "Informe sobre el estado de las Diligencias Previas 367/01 y solicitud de comisión rogatoria internacional" [Report on the status of Preliminary Investigation 367/01 and request for international letters rogatory], September 16, 2002; and *Sumario 35/2001*, vol. 6, 1823–69, and vol. 53, 16,614–16 and 16,625.

62. DGP, CGI, "Informe sobre Mohamed Belfatmi, sus relaciones con Amer Azizi y la célula de Abu Dahdah" [Report on Mohamed Belfatmi, his relationships with Amer Azizi and the Abu Dahdah cell], April 16, 2004, 11–13.

63. Ibid. See also *Sentencia 36/2005*, 94–95.

64. "Verbatim Transcript of Combatant Status Review Tribunal Hearing for ISN 10013," 5.

65. See the request sent to the National Court of Spain, Central Investigative Court No. 1, by the Special Central Unit 2 of the Guardia Civil Information Service Headquarters, reference MPMR/jlpp., dated February 23, 2004, in the framework of *Diligencias Previas 79/2003*.

66. *9/11 Commission Report*, 244.

67. DGP, CGI, UCIE, "Informe de las investigaciones realizadas en torno a las visitas a España de Mohamed Atta y Ramzi Binalshibh," 7; and "Informe ampliatorio de las investigaciones realizadas en torno a las visitas a España de Mohamed Atta y Ramzi Binalshibh."

Chapter 2

1. The *Auto* (court procedure) that decrees the referenced search and capture order, national and international, is found in *Sumario 20/2004*, vol. 18, 4681–89.

2. National Court of Spain, Criminal Division, Second Section, *Sentencia 12/2006*, 3–7 and 54–55.

3. Information contained in *Atestado número 01/2002*, 66–68, concluded April 17, 2002, by Special Central Unit 2 of the Guardia Civil Information Service Headquarters.

4. In this respect, see the April 15, 2002, report by the US Federal Bureau of Investigation (FBI) that figures in the abovementioned *Atestado número 01/2002*, 149–55.

5. *Sentencia 12/2006*, 31 and 34.

6. Ibid., 35–37.

7. The interview was conducted by Eduardo S. Molano and published in *ABC* on October 11, 2009, 28–29.

8. Ibid.

9. Regarding Wahhabism, see Natana J. Delong-Bas, *Wahhabi Islam: From Revival and Reform to Global Jihad* (Oxford: Oxford University Press, 2004); and David Commins, *The Wahhabi Mission and Saudi Arabia* (London: I. B. Tauris, 2006). On Salman al-Ouda, see Brachman, *Global Jihadism*, 56–57.

10. On August 23, 1996, various Arabic media sites received a faxed document that read, "Message from Osama bin Laden and his Muslim brothers in the whole world, and in particular in the Arabic Peninsula, dated April 9, 1417/ August 23, 1996. From the mountains of the Hindu Kush, Khorasan, Afghanistan." It also included this other title: "Expel the Jews and the Christians from the Arabian Peninsula." See Kepel, *Al-Qaida dans le texte*, 50 and 53; and Kepel and Milelli, *Al Qaeda in Its Own Words*, 48. With the passage of time, and probably influenced by the Saudi authorities, Salman al-Ouda modified his opinion. In September 2007, during a television interview, he expressed disagreement with Osama bin Laden and al-Qaeda.

11. National Court of Spain, Criminal Division, Second Section, *Rollo 09/03, Sumario 7/2003* "Acta de Juicio Oral" [Oral judgment act], Third Session, January 18, 2006, 5.

12. *Sentencia 12/2006*, 37–38.

13. *Sumario 20/2004*, vol. 91, 29, 202–10; and DGP, CGI, UCIE, "Informe general de conclusiones, atentados del 11 de marzo, Sumario 20/04," 9.

14. *Sumario 20/2004, Auto*, April 10, 2006, 1349.

15. DGP, CGI, UCIE, "Informe general de conclusiones, atentados del 11 de marzo, Sumario 20/04," 73.

16. Jan Ali, "Islamic Revivalism: The Case of the Tablighi Jamaat," *Journal of Muslim Minority Affairs* 32, no. 1 (2003): 173–81; and Yoginder Sikand, "The Tablighi Jamaat and Politics: A Critical Re-Appraisal," *The Muslim World* 96, no. 1 (2006): 175–95.

17. Bruce Hoffman, "Radicalization and Subversion: Al Qaeda and the 7 July 2005 Bombings and the 2006 Airline Bombing Plot," *Studies in Conflict and Terrorism* 32, no. 12 (2009), 1107 and 1110.

18. *Sumario 20/2004; Auto*, April 10, 2006, 1348–49; "Declaraciones ante el juez de Abdenabi Lebchina" [Statements to the judge by Abdenabi Lebchina], April 6, 2005, folio

2; and DCP, CGI, UCIE, *Diligencias 8494*, "Acta de declaración del detenido Abdelkrim Lebchina" [Affidavit of detainee Abdelkrim Lebchina], April 31, 2005, folio 5. See also DCP, CGI, UCIE, *Diligencias 8470*, folio 4, "Acta de declaración de Abdulkarim Rahman Awleya" [Affidavit of Abdulkarim Rahman Awleya], April 17, 2004; and declaration by the same before the investigative judge, April 20, 2004, 3.

19. *Sumario 20/2004*; *Auto*, April 10, 2006, 1350; and testimony before the judge by Basel Ghalyoun, March 24, 2004; separate piece 4, 4534.

20. Testimony before the police by Khalid Zeimi Pardo, April 20, 2004. See *Sumario 20/2004*, separate piece 5, 9,196.

21. "Acta de declaración del detenido Abdelkrim Lebchina," folio 5; and *Sumario 20/2004*, separate piece 12, 92.

22. DCP, CGI, UCIE, "Remitiendo informe sobre la iniciación y continuación de investigaciones en España sobre los miembros de la organización o infraestructura de Osama bin Laden asentados en nuestro país," 15.

23. "Declaraciones ante el juez de Abdenabi Lebchina," folio 3; and "Acta de declaración del detenido Abdelkrim Lebchina," folio 5.

24. Serhane ben Abdelmajid Fakeht was one of the individuals investigated in the context of the National Court, Central Investigative Court No. 5, *Diligencias Previas 53/2002*, in relation to the activities and the circle of Rabei Osman es Sayed Ahmed. See DGP, CGI, UCIE, "Informe general de conclusiones, atentados del 11 de marzo, Sumario 20/04," 69.

25. *Sumario 20/2004*, vol. 86, 26,985–86.

26. DGP, CGI, UCI, "Informe atentados 11 de marzo", October 11, 2004, 74.

27. Testimony before the judge by Basel Ghalyoun, March 24, 2004. See also *Sumario 20/2004*, separate piece 4, 4,534; and DGP, Superior Headquarters of the Madrid Police, Provincial Information Brigade, Police Statement by Fouad el Morabit Amghar, *Diligencias 8470*, March 28, 2004, folio 3.

28. *Sumario 20/2004*, vol. 85, 26,747, and vol. 92, 29,646–48.

29. "Informe atentados 11 de marzo," 74.

30. "Informe atentados 11 de marzo," 35. See also *Sumario 20/2004*, vol. 92, 29,646.

31. *Sentencia 36/2005*, 443.

32. "Informe atentados 11 de marzo," 75.

33. Ibid.

34. US Department of Defense, Joint Task Force Guantánamo, "Administrative Review Board Input for Guantánamo Detainee ISN: US9MO-000072DP (U)," November 8, 2004, 1 and 2, in the Guantánamo Docket, "Laacin Ikassrin," *New York Times*, http://projects.nytimes.com/guantanamo/detainees/72-laacin-ikassrin/documents/11.

35. *Sumario 20/2004*, vol. 99, 32,897–98.

36. Ibid.; and "Declaración de Assad Mohamedeid Abd el Maksoud" [Declaration of Assad Mohamedeid Abd el Maksoud], April 20, 2004, folio 5.

37. *Sumario 20/2004*, vol. 92, 29,683.

38. I thank Commissioner Rafael Gómez Menor for these and other details that he kindly reiterated to me during an interview in Madrid on December 20, 2012.

39. For the indictment that decrees the search and capture order, both national and international, see *Sumario 20/2004*, vol. 18.

40. National Court of Spain, Criminal Division, Second Section, *Sentencia 65/2007*, 716.

41. Testimony by Mohamed Chaoui, Jamal Zougam's brother by his mother, and by Mohamed Bakali, respectively, March 19, 2004, in *Sumario 20/2004*, separate piece 3, 2047 and 2050.

42. Testimony of a Spanish resident detained in Afghanistan at the end of 2001 during an operation against al-Qaeda and held as an enemy combatant in Guantánamo Bay. According to his testimony, Zougam had given him financial help to travel to Afghanistan. See "Administrative Review Board Input for Guantánamo Detainee ISN: US9MO-000072DP (U)," 1 and 2.

43. *Sumario 20/2004*, vol. 163, 61,703.

44. DCP, CGI, UCIE, "Informe sobre el Grupo Islámico Combatiente Marroquí (GICM)" [Information on the Moroccan Islamic Combatant Group (MICG)], undated document elaborated by the National Court instructing judge, *Sumario 9/2003*, 8.

45. Ibid., 5–6.

46. The UCIE report releasing documents relative to the International Letter Rogatory solicited by France on Jamal Zougam are found in *Sumario 35/2001*, 28,477–585.

47. Testimony by Jamal Zougam on March 19, 2004, in *Sumario 20/2004*, separate piece 3, 2055.

48. *Sumario 20/2004*, vol. 122, 43,501–2.

49. Ibid., vol. 123, 43.696–702.

50. Ibid., vol. 99, 32.895.

51. Ibid., vol. 99, 32.895, and vol. 163, 61,796.

52. Until shortly before 9/11, Mohamed Fizazi had been the imam of the Al-Quds Mosque in Hamburg. The al-Qaeda members who orchestrated the September 11 attacks lived in Hamburg and frequently attended this mosque. See Lorenzo Vidino, *Al Qaeda in Europe: The New Battleground of International Jihad* (New York: Prometheus Books, 2005), 255–56.

53. Conclusions presented by the public prosecutor, June 4, 2007, to National Court of Spain, Criminal Division, Second Section, modifying a statement from November 2006, 18.

54. *Sumario 20/2004*, vol. 163, 61,790.

55. Ibid., vol. 109, 37.080, and vol. 163, 61,732.

56. Declarations by Abdelouahid Berrak Soussane, to the DGP, CGI, March 21, 2004, in *Sumario 20/2004*, separate piece 3, 2493–94.

57. Declarations by Mohamed Bakali, March 19, 2004, in *Sumario 20/2004*, separate piece 3, 2046.

58. "Informe atentados 11 de marzo," 94.

59. "Comparecencia de Mariano Rayón Ramos, jefe de la Unidad Central de Información Exterior, sobre la investigación de las tramas del terrorismo islamista en el periodo anterior a los atentados y en concreto sobre los antecedentes y circunstancias de la masacre del 11 de marzo (número de expediente 212/000080)" [Appearance of Mariano Rayón Ramos, head of the Central Unit for External Intelligence, on the investigation of Islamist terrorist plots in the period before the attacks and specifically on the background and circumstances of the March 11 massacre (file number 212/000080)], *Diario de Sesiones del Congreso de los Diputados, Comisiones de Investigación, VIII Legislatura, Sobre el 11 de marzo de 2004* [Journal of the sessions of the Congress of Deputies, Commissions of Inquiry, VIII Legislature, March 11, 2004], no. 3 (2004), 34.

60. *Sumario 20/2004*, vol. 1, 174–75.

61. Document-based interview with functionary charged with penitentiary oversight and monitoring, conducted in Madrid between November 2008 and March 2009.

62. "Comparecencia de Mariano Rayón Ramos," 50.

63. Interviews with a CNP commissioner who participated in the investigation into Abu Dahdah's cell, Madrid, November 2008 and December 2012. Further, see *Sumario 20/2004*, vol. 99, 32,907–11.

Chapter 3

1. Tawil, *Brothers in Arms*, 67–87 and 127–35.

2. National Court of Spain, Criminal Division, Third Section, *Sentencia 14/2001*, 33–34.

3. National Court of Spain, Criminal Division, Third Section, *Sentencia 26/2003*, 17–18.

4. *Sentencia 14/2001*, 16–18.

5. DGP, CGI, UCIE, "Remitiendo Informe sobre Allekema Lamari" [Remitting report on Allekema Lamari], April 29, 1997, 1.

6. *Sumario 20/2004*, vol. 99, 32,893 and 32,995.

7. Ibid., *Auto*, April 10, 2006, 1351–52.

8. Superior Police Headquarters of Valencia, Provincial Information Brigade, "Acta de declaración de Safwan Sabagh" [Affidavit of Safwan Sabagh], July 1, 2004, folio 3.

9. Ibid., folio 2.

10. Tawil, *Brothers in Arms*, 35.

11. CGI, UCIE, *Diligencias 25,401*, "Acta de declaración de Safwan Sabagh", July 1, 2004, folio 4.

12. Ibid.

13. *Sumario 20/2004*, separate piece of declassified documents, 790–92.

14. This fact appears in a report on Allekema Lamari prepared by the CGI, Unidad Central de Inteligencia, dated November 26, 2004. See *Sumario 20/2004*, vol. 91, 29,222.

15. *Sumario 20/2004*, separate piece of declassified documents, 793–96.

16. Ibid., 797–99.

17. On the September 2001 CNP operation that dissolved the GSPC cell, see the Spanish government's press release at "Desarticulada en España una célula terrorista islámica relacionada con Osama Ben Laden" [An Islamic terrorist cell linked to Osama bin Laden dismantled in Spain], Spanish Ministry of the Interior, September 26, 2001, available at http://www.interior.gob.es/.

18. *Sumario 20/2004*, "Declaración del testigo protegido número 2323" [Statement of protected witness no. 2323], December 29, 2004, 2.

19. Ibid., December 30, 2004, 2.

20. Ibid., 2.

21. Ibid., 6.

22. Ibid.

23. Ibid.

24. Ibid.

25. National Court of Spain, Criminal Division, Section Three, *Sentencia 6/2008*, especially 11–65, 127–222, and 240–47; and Supreme Court of Spain, Criminal Division, *Segunda Sentencia 618/2008*, 45-46.

26. *Sentencia 6/2008*, especially 138–39.

Chapter 4

1. *Sentencia 65/2007*, 718. In the months before he was notified of his conviction, Youssef Belhadj was implicated with incidents such as "resisting passive orders," or "hunger strikes," and the authorities also recovered "prohibited material," according to documented information provided by a functionary charged with penitentiary oversight and monitoring in the course of interviews conducted in Madrid between November 2008 and March 2009.

2. *Sentencia 65/2007*, 717–18; and Supreme Court of Spain, Criminal Division, *Segunda Sentencia 503/2008*, 955.

3. Mohamed Belhadj was sentenced to twenty years in prison in Sentence number 8 dictated on January 28, 2010, by the Court of Appeal, Criminal Division, in Rabat, Morocco (case number 24-200927).

4. *Sentencia 65/2007*, 718.

5. Anneli Botha, *Terrorism in the Maghreb: The Transnationalisation of Domestic Terrorism*, ISS Monograph Series 144 (Pretoria: Institute for Security Studies, June 2008), 91–93. For a summary of the MICG's formation and the evolution of its leadership, see *Sumario 20/2004*, vol. 97, 31,850–55, and vol. 163, 61,577–78.

6. *Sumario 20/2004*, vol. 208, 81,201–2.

7. Tawil, *Brothers in Arms*, 51–66, 93–97, and 135–40.

8. Evan F. Kohlmann, "Dossier: Libyan Islamic Fighting Group," (New York: NEFA Foundation, 2007), 13–15, www.nefafoundation.org/miscellaneous/nefalifg1007.pdf (site discontinued; accessed July 2008).

9. Atwan, *Secret History of Al-Qa'ida*, 47–48.

10. *Sumario 20/2004*, vol. 208, 81,205.

11. Jeffry R. Halverson, "The Tariq ibn Ziyad Master Narrative," Report #1101, Consortium for Strategic Communication (Tempe: Arizona State University, 2011), http://csc.asu.edu/wp-content/uploads/pdf/126.pdf.

12. DGP, CGI, Unidad Central de Inteligencia, "Investigaciones del piso de Leganés 03.03.04" [Investigations of the Leganés apartment, March 3, 2004], May 3, 2004, 43, in *Sumario 20/2004*, vol. 42, 11,961.

13. *Sumario 20/2004*, vol. 157, 58,978 and 59,267–69, and vol. 191, 74,612.

14. Ibid., vol. 123, 43,700.

15. Ibid., vol. 208, 81,207.

16. Jean-Claude Santucci, "Le pouvoir à l'épreuve du choc terroriste: entre dérives autoritaires et tentation de l'arbitraire," [The power of testing the terrorist shock: Between authoritarian tendencies and the temptation of arbitrariness], in *Annuaire de l'Afrique du Nord 2003* (París: CNRS Éditions, 2005), 245.

17. For a conceptual essay on global terrorism, see Fernando Reinares, *Terrorismo global* [Global terrorism] (Madrid: Taurus, 2003).

18. Ibid., 117–19.

19. National Court of Spain, Criminal Division, Second Section, *Sentencia 20/2006*, 26.

20. To this end, see chap. 7, dedicated to the Spanish case, in Luis de la Corte Ibañez and Javier Jordán, *La yihad terrorista* [The terrorist jihad] (Madrid: Editorial Síntesis, 2007), especially 236–46; Pedro Canales and Enrique Montánchez, *En el nombre de Alá. La red secreta del terrorismo islamista en España* [In the name of Allah: The secret network of Islamist terrorism in Spain] (Barcelona: Planeta, 2002); José M. Irujo, *El agujero. España invadida por la yihad* [The hole: Spain invaded by jihad] (Madrid: Aguilar, 2005), above all chaps. 1 through 9; and Javier Jordán and Nicola Horsburgh, "Mapping Jihadist Terrorism in Spain," *Studies in Conflict and Terrorism* 28, no. 3 (2005): 169–91.

21. See the annex on "Atentados suicidas de Casablanca" [Suicide attacks in Casablanca], included in *Sumario 20/2004*, vol. 123, 43,695–96.

22. Jeffrey B. Cozzens, "Al-Takfir wa'l Hijra: Unpacking an Enigma," *Studies in Conflict and Terrorism* 32, no. 6 (2009): 489–510.

23. National Court of Spain, Central Investigative Court No. 5, *Sumario 9/2003*.

24. *Sumario 20/2004*, vol. 123, 43,690–708.

25. DGP, CGI, UCIE, *Diligencias 38,366, Diligencia Informe*, December 17, 2004, folio 1. This document is found in *Sumario 20/2004*, vol. 94.

26. Europol, "Valoración de amenaza sobre terrorismo extremista islámico, Sexta edición" [Threat assessment of Islamist extremist terrorism, 6th edition], January 29, 2004, 8; in *Sumario 20/2004*, separate declassified document, 12.

27. DGP, CGI, UCIE, *Diligencias 38.366, Diligencia Informe*, folio 18.

28. National Court of Spain, Central Investigative Court No. 6, *Auto*, April 10, 2006, 1258.

29. Ibid., 1306.

30. See the files from the French courts, Tribunal de Grande Instance de París, 16ème chambre/1, No. d'affaire 0313739016, *Jugement du 11 juillet 2007* [Judgment of July 11, 2007], 55, 71, and 73; as well as *Sumario 20/2004*, vol. 97, 31,898–99, and vol. 163, 61,580–608.

31. Ibid.

32. Ibid.

33. *Sumario 20/2004, Auto*, April 10, 2006, 1265.

34. *Sumario 20/2004*, vol. 106, 35,601–14; vol.115, 39,970–73; vol. 133, 48,728–33; and vol. 163, 61,608–24.

35. Ibid., vol. 180, 69,863.

36. Ibid., vol. 106, 35,613; and vol. 163, 61,622–23; see also *Sentencia 65/2007*, 216–17.

37. Saheeh International translation, available at www.webislam.com/quran (accessed April 30, 2016).

38. Richard A. Serrano, *One of Ours: Timothy McVeigh and the Oklahoma City Bombing* (New York: W. W. Norton, 1998), 192.

39. Thomas Hegghammer, "Al-Qaida Statements 2003–2004: A Compilation of Translated Texts by Usama bin Laden and Ayman al-Zawahiri," FFI/Rapport 01428 (Kjeller: Norwegian Defence Research Establishment, 2005), 42–44.

40. Youssef Belhadj's nephew, Ibrahim Moussaten, affirmed and reiterated in his testimony (including a session in front of his uncle), that Youssef had confirmed that he was part of al-Qaeda. See *Sumario 20/2004*, vol. 130, 47,033.

41. *Sumario 20/2004*, vol. 106, 35,612; and vol.163, 61,621–22.

42. "Informe atentados 11 de marzo," October 11, 2004, 45.

43. *Sumario 20/2004*, vol. 115, 39,971.

44. Ibid., vol. 86, 26,985–86.

45. "Acta de declaración de Safwan Sabagh," July 1, 2004, folio 3.

46. DGP, CGI, UCIE, "Acta de declaración del ciudadano extranjero Ibrahín Afalah" [Affidavit of foreign citizen Ibrahín Afalah], March 17, 2004, folio 5, included in *Sumario 20/2004*, separate piece 5.

47. Ibid., folio 4. This document is also included in *Sumario 20/2004*, separate piece 5.

48. Moroccan police obtained a more detailed summary of Mohamed Afalah's activity in November 2005, after the arrest in Morocco of Khaled Azig, an al-Qaeda member who was with Mohamed Afalah in Istanbul and in Syria before Afalah entered Iraq. Azig stated that he had kept Afalah's passport and gave it to an Algerian known as Abu Bassir, a prominent member of al-Qaeda in Europe. See National Court of Spain, Central Investigative Court No. 6, *Sumario 49/2009*, vol. 6, 1283–1352. Interestingly, further evidence on the active participation of Mohamed Afalah in the Madrid train bombings emerged in March 2016, as part of thousands of leaked Islamic State organization archives, which included the registration file of Ismail Afalah, Mohamed's other, younger brother. He left Madrid, where he resided, and entered Syria on May 30, 2014, the day when the Islamic State border agent who filled Ismail Afalah's record file wrote in Arabic the following observation at the bottom of the document: "His brother is a perpetrator of the operations in the metro [sic] in Madrid". See Fernando Reinares, "Más evidencia sobre el 11-M en document de Estado Islámico," Madrid: Blog Elcano, June 1, 2016, http://www .blog.rielcano.org/mas-evidencia-11-m-documento-estado-islamico.

49. *Sumario 20/2004*, vol. 180, 69,863.

50. *Sumario 20/2004*, "Declaración del imputado Jaouad el Bouzrouti" [Statement of the accused Jaouad el Bouzrouti], March 11, 2005, folio 3.

51. "Acta de declaración del ciudadano extranjero Ibrahín Afalah," folio 3.

52. Interview with functionaries charged with penitentiary oversight and monitoring, conducted between November 2008 and March 2009.

Chapter 5

1. Milan Questura, General Investigations and Special Operations Division, Antiterrorism Section, *Procedimento penale n. 17596/04 r.g.n.r. mod. 21* [Criminal proceeding no. 17596/04 r.g.n.r. mod. 21], March 8, 2005, 17–24.

2. *Sumario 20/2004*, vol. 48, 13,905.

3. Khalil Gebara, "The End of the Egyptian Islamic Jihad?" *Terrorism Monitor* 3, no. 3 (Washington, DC: The Jamestown Foundation, February 9, 2005), http://www.jamestown .org/single/?no_cache=1&tx_ttnews%5Btt_news%5D=27523.

4. *Sumario 20/2004*, vol. 48, 13,905.

5. Ibid., 13,921.

6. Ibid., 13,906.

7. *Procedimento penale n. 17596/04 r.g.n.r. mod. 21*, 61 and 112.

8. *Sumario 20/2004*, vol. 48, 13,906–7 and 13,920.

9. Ibid., 13,910 and 13,920.

10. See UCIE, *Diligencias 840/04*, official correspondence, folio 2, June 18, 2004, in *Sumario 20/2004*, vol. 61, 18,281.

11. *Sumario 20/2004*, vol. 48, 13,919.

12. *Sentencia 65/2007*, 718.

13. *Sumario 20/2004*, vol. 48, 13,925; and "Declaración del detenido Fouad el Morabit Amghar" [Declaration of the detained Fouad el Morabit Amghar], March 30, 2004, folio 1, in *Sumario 20/2004*, separate piece 4.

14. *Sumario 20/2004*, separate piece 9, 17–18, 35, and 43.

15. Ibid., 17–18.

16. Ibid., 25 and 48.

17. Ibid., 50.

18. *Sentencia 65/2007*, 718.

19. On the Islamic Cultural Institute in Milan and the jihadist activities related to it, see Vidino, *Al Qaeda in Europe*, 215–31.

20. Vidino, *Al Qaeda in Europe*, 217–18; and Anneli Botha, "Politics and Terrorism: An Assessment of the Origin and Threat of Terrorism in Egypt," ISS Paper 131 (Pretoria: Institute for Security Studies, December 2006), 5, https://www.issafrica.org/uploads/Paper131pdf.pdf.

21. Vidino, *Al Qaeda in Europe*, 221–26.

22. *Sumario 20/2004*, vol. 48, 13,909.

23. Ibid., 13,908.

24. *Procedimento penale n. 17596/04 r.g.n.r. mod. 21*, 23.

25. Ibid., 68 and 130.

26. Ibid., 23.

27. Ibid., 42 and 134.

28. Ibid., 133–34.

29. *Sentencia 39/2007*, 4–5 and 48.

30. *Procedimento penale n. 17596/04 r.g.n.r. mod. 21*, 33.

31. *Procedimento penale n. 17596/04 r.g.n.r. mod. 21*, 55–56; and *Sumario 20/2004*, *Auto*, April 10, 2006, 1278.

32. *Procedimento penale n. 17596/04 r.g.n.r. mod. 21*, 54–55.

33. Ibid., 43.

34. DGP, CGI, UCIE, "Remitiendo traducción de la conversación ambiental mantenida por Rabei Osman El Sayed a.k.a. Mohamed el Egipcio, facilitada por las autoridades italianas" [Remitted translation of ambient conversation by Rabei Osman El Sayed, a.k.a. Mohamed the Egyptian, provided by the Italian authorities], folio 3, in *Sumario 20/2004*, vol. 51, 15,048.

35. *Procedimento penale n. 17596/04 r.g.n.r. mod. 21*, 114.

36. Ibid., 114–15.

37. "Informe atentados 11 de marzo," October 11, 2004, 107; and *Sumario 20/2004*, vol. 48, 13,910.

38. In reality, Rabei Osman es Sayed Ahmed was born on July 22, 1971. *Procedimento penale n. 17596/04 r.g.n.r. mod. 21*, 26, 48, and 128.

39. *Sumario 20/2004*, "Declaración del imputado Rabei Osman El Sayed," December 13, 2004, folio 5.

40. *Procedimento penale n. 17596/04 r.g.n.r. mod. 21*, 142.

41. National Court of Spain, Central Investigative Court No. 5, *Sumario 21/2006*, *Auto*, October 23, 2007, 32.

42. First Court of Assizes, Milan, *Sentenza 10/2006*, 66.

43. Third Court of Assizes of Appeal, Milan, *Sentenza 38/2007*, 75–76 and 85.

Chapter 6

1. The *Auto* decreeing the corresponding search and capture orders, both national and international, are found in *Sumario 20/2004*, vol. 18.

2. *Sentencia 65/2007*, 717–18.

3. Hicham Ahmidan was sentenced to ten years in prison in Sentence no. 6 dictated on February 18, 2009, by the Rabat Court of Appeal, Criminal Division (case number 5-2009-28).

4. DGP, CGI, Unidad Central de Inteligencia, "Acta de declaración de Rosa María Aguayo de Inés" [Affidavit of Rosa María Aguayo de Inés], March 26, 2004, folio 3, in *Sumario 20/2004*, vol. 17, 4302; CGI, Unidad Central de Inteligencia, "Análisis de datos derivados de la investigación relativa a hermanos Ahmidan y Abdelilah el Fadual" [Analysis of data from the investigation of the brothers Ahmidan and Abdelilah el Fadual], June 2005, 6, in *Sumario 20/2004*, vol. 149, 56,712.

5. "Análisis de datos derivados de la investigación relativa a hermanos Ahmidan y Abdelilah el Fadual," 5, in *Sumario 20/2004*, vol. 149, 56,711.

6. *Sumario 20/2004*, vol. 91, 24,174.

7. Ibid.

8. Ibid., 24,175.

9. Ibid.

10. Ibid.

11. As claimed by the affidavit of a protected witness on May 13, 2004. See *Sumario 20/2004*, vol. 43, 12.229.

12. Ibid. See also "Análisis de datos derivados de la investigación relativa a los hermanos Ahmidan y Abdelilah el Fadual," 102, in *Sumario 20/2004*, vol. 149, 56,868.

13. *Sumario 20/2004*, vol. 43, 12,228.

14. *Sumario 20/2004*, vol. 43, 11,227–12,229; and vol. 149, 56,710–11.

15. Peter R. Neumann, *Joining Al-Qaeda: Jihadist Recruitment in Europe* (London: International Institute for Strategic Studies, 2008), 25–28.

16. Ibid., 26–27.

17. *Sumario 20/2004*, vol. 98, 32,652–53.

18. Karim Serraj, "Dans le fief islamiste de Fizazi" [In the Islamist stronghold of Fizazi], *La Gazette du Maroc*, June 16, 2003, http://www.lagazettedumaroc.com/articles.php?id _artl=2900 (accessed July 24, 2009).

19. DGP, CGI, Unidad Central de Inteligencia, "Análisis de datos derivados de la investigación relativa a los hermanos Oulad Akcha" [Analysis of data from the investigation on the Oulad Akcha brothers], May 2005, 52, in *Sumario 20/2004*, vol. 139.

20. Ibid., 57.

21. Ibid., 5.

22. Ibid.

23. Ibid., 6.

24. *Sumario 20/2004*, vol. 42, 11,928.

25. "Análisis de datos derivados de la investigación relativa a los hermanos Oulad Akcha," 9 and 51.

26. *Sumario 20/2004*, vol. 92, 29,681–83.

27. DGP, CGI, UCIE, *Diligencias Previas 16388*, June 14, 2005, folios 52 to 58.

28. "Análisis de datos derivados de la investigación relativa a los hermanos Ahmidan y Abdelilah el Fadual," 43, in *Sumario 20/2004*, vol. 149, 56,809.

29. Ibid., 102, in *Sumario 20/2004*, vol. 149, 56,868.

30. *Sumario 20/2004*, vol. 91, 29,276.

31. Ibid.

32. Interviews conducted with a functionary charged with penitentiary oversight and monitoring, held in Madrid between November 2008 and March 2009.

33. "Informe atentados 11 de marzo," 36.

34. Ibid., 42-43.

35. DGP, CGI, UCIE, "Informe general de conclusiones, atentados del 11 de marzo, Sumario 20/04," 116–19.

36. "Informe atentados 11 de marzo," 27–29 and 32–33.

37. DGP, CGI, UCIE, "Informe general de conclusiones, atentados del 11 de marzo, Sumario 20/04," 107.

38. "Informe atentados 11 de marzo," 11.

39. Ibid., 6.

40. Ibid., 11.

41. *Sumario 20/2004*, separate piece 29, annex II, documents 15 and 16.

42. "Informe de 19 de agosto de 2004 de la Unidad Central de Droga y Crimen Organizado, de la Comisaría General de Policía Judicial" [August 19, 2004, report of the Drug and Organized Crime Central Unit of the Judicial Police Commissioner General], in *Sumario 20/2004*, separate piece 10, vol. 8, 2572–75.

43. *Sumario 20/2004*, separate piece 10, vol. 5, 1630–31, 1846, and 1869; vol. 6, 1939; and vol. 7, 2360.

44. DGP, General Commissary of Scientific Police, "Informe técnico-policial núm. 116-IT-04" [Technical police report no. 116-IT-04], July 27, 2004, in *Sumario 20/2004*, separate piece 10, vol. 8, 2577–92.

45. *Sumario 20/2004*, separate piece 10, vol. 8, 2364.

46. "Informe atentados 11 de marzo," 26–27.

47. Ibid., 27–29 and 32–33.

48. DGP, CGI, UCIE, "Informe general de conclusiones, atentados del 11 de marzo, Sumario 20/04," 103.

49. Ibid.

50. CGI, UCIE, "Acta de declaración de Hamid Ahmidan" [Affidavit of Hamid Ahmidan], March 21, 2004, folio 6, in *Sumario 20/2004*, separate piece 4.

51. "Declaraciones del detenido José Emilio Suárez Trashorras" [Statement of the detainee José Emilio Suárez Trashorras], May 22, 2004, folio 4, in *Sumario 20/2004*, separate piece 10, vol. 8, 2366.

52. Ibid.

53. *Sumario 20/2004*, vol. 15, 3662 and separate piece 3, 2698.

Chapter 7

1. *Sumario 20/2004*, vol. 98, 32,656–57.

2. *Sumario 6/2005*, vol. 2, 258; and CGI, UCIE, *Diligencias 37,552*, "Acta de declaración de Mohamed el Ouazzani" [Affidavit of Mohamed el Ouazzani], December 15, 2004, 2.

3. National Court of Spain, Criminal Division, First Section, *Sentencia 22/2007*, 22.

4. "Acta de declaración de Mohamed el Ouazzani."

5. *Sumario 20/2004*, vol. 111, 37,972–75.

6. Ibid., vol. 98, 32,657.

7. Testimony by CNP functionary No. 18403, instructor in preliminary investigation 396/2002 of the Central Investigative Court No. 5., National Court of Spain, Criminal Division, Section One, *Acta de juicio oral*, February 23, 2007, session, 84–85.

8. Ibid., 86.

9. *Sentencia 65/2007*, 718.

10. *Sumario 20/2004*, vol. 85, 26,747; and vol. 92, 29,646–48.

11. Ibid.

12. DGP, CGI, UCIE, "Informe general de conclusiones, atentados del 11 de marzo," 74.

13. Ibid., 75.

14. Fernando Reinares and Carola García-Calvo, *Los yihadistas en España: perfil sociodemográfico de condenados por actividades terroristas o muertos en acto de terrorismo suicida entre 1996 y 2012* [Jihadists in Spain: Sociodemographic profile of those convicted of terrorist activities or killed in an act of suicide terrorism between 1996 and 2012], DT 11/2013 (Madrid: Real Instituto Elcano, June 26, 2003). These kinship, neighborhood, and friendship ties are determinants in the radicalization and recruitment of terrorists, both in general and with regard to jihadist terrorism. In this respect, see Sageman, *Understanding Terror Networks*, chaps. 4 and 5; as well as Carola García-Calvo and Fernando Reinares, *Procesos de radicalización violenta y terrorismo yihadista en España: ¿Cuándo? ¿Dónde? ¿Cómo?* [Processes of violent radicalization and jihadist terrorism in Spain: When? Where? How?], DT 16/2013 (Madrid: Real Instituto Elcano, November 18, 2013).

15. Reinares and García-Calvo, *Los yihadistas en España*, in particular the passages on the distribution based on sex, age, and civil status.

16. Ibid., especially the passages on administrative situation, nationality, and origin.

17. Ibid., specifically the passages on level of education, occupation, and previous criminal record.

18. Ibid.

19. Fernando Reinares, "Jihadist Radicalization and the 2004 Madrid Bombing Network," *CTC Sentinel* 2, no. 11 (2009): 16–19. See also the biographical reconstructions of Serhane ben Abdelmajid Fakhet and Jamal Ahmidan in Justin Webster and Ignacio Orovio, *Conexión Madrid. Cómo y por qué Serhane y Jamal se convirtieron en terroristas yihadistas* [The Madrid connection: How and why Serhane and Jamal became jihadist terrorists] (Barcelona: Debate, 2009).

20. See the Cuatro television program *11-M: retrato de los asesinos* [11-M: Portrait of the killers], Cuatro, March 10, 2007, 00:00:17 to 00:01:42.

21. DGP, CGI, Unidad Central de Inteligencia, "Análisis del disco duro recuperado en la Carmen Martín Gaite, 40. Leganés (Madrid)" [Analysis of the hard drive recovered from 40 Carmen Martín Gaite Street, Leganés (Madrid)], *Sumario 20/2004*, vol. 88, 27,993–28,091.

22. On these links, see Sageman, *Understanding Terror Networks*, chaps. 4 and 5; and García-Calvo and Reinares, *Procesos de radicalización violenta y terrorismo yihadista en España*.

Chapter 8

1. On the counterterrorism program using drones developed by the United States in Pakistan since 2004, see the information offered by the New America Foundation in "Drone Wars Pakistan: Analysis," New America Foundation, last accessed July 15, 2016, http://securitydata.newamerica.net/drones/pakistan-analysis.html.

2. Rohan Gunaratna and Anders Nielsen, "Al Qaeda in the Tribal Areas of Pakistan and Beyond," *Studies in Conflict and Terrorism* 31, no. 9 (2008), 786–88.

3. Ibid.

4. Ibid., 780 and 783. See also Rohan Gunaratna and Aviv Oreg, "Al Qaeda's Organizational Structure and Its Evolution," *Studies in Conflict and Terrorism* 33, no. 12 (2010), 1057.

5. Verbal confirmation given to the author in November 2009 by CIA sources present in Pakistan when the attack in Haisori occurred, and written in December 2008 by sources in Spanish police intelligence.

6. Crown Court at Manchester, T20087479, "The Honourable Mr. Justice Saunders, Regina v. Rangzieb Ahmed, Habib Ahmed, Mehreen Haji," *Hearing Including Short Judgement, Veredicts and Mitigation*, December 18, 2008. In this judicial proceeding, see specifically pages 3 and 4 of *statement number S555*, April 23, 2008. Michael Clarke, director of the Royal United Services Institute, erroneously considers "Ilyas the Spanish" to be Mamoun Darkazanli, the Syrian-born businessman and major al-Qaeda financier mentioned in chap. 1. Nonetheless, Darkazanli continued living in Hamburg, as Guido Steinberg of the Stiftung Wissenschaft und Politik in Berlin confirmed to me by email in July 2009.

7. *The Moroccan Connection* (documentary on Dateline, SBS, Sydney), first broadcast July 14, 2004, 10:45:00 to 11:57:01.

8. Ibid., 03:05:00 to 03:12:00.

9. Ibid., 03:45:02 to 03:51:00.

10. *Sumario 35/2001*, "Declaración judicial de Abdula Jayata Kattan" [Affidavit of Abdula Jayata Kattan], February 4–5, 2004, 19.

11. *Sumario 35/2001*, vol. 57, 18 and 322–418.

12. DGP, Madrid Police Superior Headquarters, Provincial Information Brigade, *Diligencias 8470*, "Acta de declaración de Mouad Benkhalafa" [Affidavit of Mouad Benkhalafa], March 29, 2004, folio 2. Included in *Sumario 20/2004*, vol. 19.

13. DGP, CGI, UCIE, *Diligencias 8470*, "Acta de declaración de Khalid Zeimi Pardo" [Affidavit of Khalid Zeimi Pardo], April 20, 2004, folio 4. Document included in *Sumario 20/2004*, separate piece 5.

14. "Declaración del detenido Abdulkarim A. Rahim Awleya" [Affidavit of detainee Abdulkarim A. Rahim Awleya], April 20, 2004, folio 3. Document included in *Sumario 20/2004*, separate piece 5.

15. DGP, CGI, UCIE, "Formularios rellenados en campos de Al Qaida por mujahidín [*sic*] enviados desde España a través de Othman el Andalusi (Amer Azizi), hombre de confianza de Imad Eddin Barakat Yarkas a.k.a. Abu Dahdah" [Forms filled out in al-Qaeda camps by mujahedin sent from Spain through Othman al-Andalusi (Amer Azizi), confidant of Imad Eddin Barakat Yarkas a.k.a. Abu Dahdah], March 29, 2004, *Sumario 35/2001*, vol. 126, 35,668–79.

16. Bruce Riedel, "The Mysterious Relationship Between al-Qa'ida and Iran," *CTC Sentinel* 3, no. 7 (2010): 1–3; and Paul Hastert, "Al Qaeda and Iran: Friends or Foes, or Somewhere in Between?," *Studies in Conflict and Terrorism* 30, no. 4 (2007): 327–36.

17. DGP, CGI, UCIE, *Diligencias 18*, May 25, 2003.

18. CGI, "Informe del registro de Amer Azizi (Sumario 35/01)," [Log report of Amer Azizi (Sumario 35/01)], n.d. (very likely written in November or December 2001), 9.

19. Ibid.

20. Ibid., 15–17 and 31–37.

21. Ibid., 9, 15–17, 19, and 20–30.

22. Ibid., 17.

23. Personal interview with relevant CGI member in November 2009. Personal interview with intelligence officials of two Western countries (one European) in December 2011 and February 2012.

24. "Declaración del imputado Rachid Bendouda" [Statement of the accused Rachid Bendouda], February 7, 2005, folio 3. Document included in *Sumario 20/2004*, separate piece 11; see also testimony by Mouad Benkhalafa in *Sumario 20/2004*, vol. 129, 46,635.

25. CGI, UCIE, *Diligencias 8470*, "Acta de declaración de Abdelouahid Berrak Soussane" [Affidavit of Abdelouahid Berrak Soussane], March 21, 2004, folio 11. Document included in *Sumario 20/2004*, vol. 10, 2497.

26. *Sumario 35/2001*; *Auto*, April 28, 2004, 30–31.

27. Daniel Klaidman, *Kill or Capture: The War on Terror and the Soul of the Obama Presidency* (Boston: Houghton Mifflin Harcourt, 2012), esp. 37–63.

28. Personal interview conducted with relevant CGI member in November 2009. Personal interviews with intelligence officials in two Western countries (one European) in December 2011 and February 2012.

29. Syed Saleem Shahzad, *Inside Al Qaeda and the Taliban: Beyond Bin Laden and 9/11* (New York: Palgrave Macmillan, 2011), 51 and 180.

30. Personal interview in October 2007 with intelligence officials dealing with external relations, based in Brussels, then working for the EU Common Foreign and Security Policy community.

31. The jihadist sites where this passage was shared included http://shamikh1.net/vb /showthread.php?p=295528 and www.majahden.com/vb/showthread.php?t=29399.

32. Some of the contents of this passage were anticipated in a 2010 *El País* op-ed; see Fernando Reinares and Ignacio Cembrero, "¿España fue blanco de Al Qaeda antes del 11-S?" [Was Spain an al-Qaeda target before 9/11?], *El País*, September 11, 2010, http://elpais.com/diario/2010/09/11/opinion/1284156011_850215.html.

33. Said Bahaji was prosecuted by the National Court of Spain for the crimes of belonging to a terrorist organization and terrorist plots in the context of *Sumario 35/2001, Auto*, September 17, 2001. As mentioned in chapter 1, Bahaji also had Abu Dahdah's phone number, which was found in a planner that he had left behind in Hamburg.

34. *9/11 Commission Report*, 164 and 167.

35. Ibid., 249.

36. In this respect, see the information provided on March 27, 2012, in the Indian newspaper *Hindustan Times* at http://www.hindustantimes.com/world/al-qaeda-suspect-met -sept-11-figure-in-pak/story-QRoPXeGl9xj9dXeZFOmfaI.html (accessed March 27, 2012), and the Pakistani newspaper *The News*, at http://goo.gl/jWq8n0 (accessed April 6, 2012).

37. See Katherine Tiedemann, "Passports Linked to 9/11 Found in Northwest Pakistan Military Operations," *Foreign Policy*, October 30, 2009, http://foreignpolicy .com/2009/10/30/daily-brief-passports-linked-to-911-found-in-northwest-pakistan -military-operations/.

Chapter 9

1. In this respect, see Imtiaz Ali, "Karachi Becoming a Taliban Safe Haven?," *CTC Sentinel* 3, no. 1 (2010): 13–15; and Zia Ur Rehman, "Taliban Recruiting and Fundraising in Karachi," *CTC Sentinel* 5, no. 7 (2012): 9–12.

2. *Sumario 20/2004*, vol. 208, 81,215.

3. National Counterterrorism Center (NCTC), "The Case for Al-Qai'da Links to the 2004 Madrid Bombings: A Key Assumptions Check," August 22, 2008.

4. Testimony by Abdelatif Mourafik, on July 7, 2004, in front of the Moroccan authorities referred to in DGP, CGI, *Diligencias 30,996*, 12.

5. ETAN, "Abu Musab al Zarqawi: Profile and Networks in Europe," March 2004, in *Sumario 20/2004*, vol. 39, 10,976–90.

6. "Abu Musab al Zarqawi: Profile and Networks in Europe," 7, in *Sumario 20/2004*, vol. 39, 10,982.

7. CGI, UCIE, "Informe sobre Operación Lago" [Report on Operation Lago], April 20, 2004; CGI, UCIE, "Informes del F.B.I., Departamento de Justicia U.S.A." [Report from the FBI, US Department of Justice], July 15, 2003; CGI, UCIE, "Cotejo de datos de los Servicios franceses" [Collated data from the French services], February 27, 2003. All these documents were sent to the National Court, Central Investigative Court No. 1.

8. In this respect, see the illuminating article by Peter Waldmann, "Revenge Without Rules: On the Renaissance of an Archaic Motif of Violence," *Studies in Conflict and Terrorism* 24, no 6 (2001), 436 and 446–47. On religiously inspired terrorism, see Mark Juergensmeyer, *Terror in the Mind of God: The Global Rise of Religious Violence* (Berkeley: University of California Press, 2001); and on suicide terrorism, see Assaf Moghadam, "Motives for Martyrdom. Al-Qaida, Salafi Jihad, and the Spread of Suicide Attacks," *International Security* 33, no. 3 (2008/2009): 46–78.

9. *Sumario 20/2004*, separate volume with declassified documents, 790–92, 793–96, and 797–99.

10. Testimony of Commissioner Mariano Rayón, Cortes Generales, *Diario de Sesiones del Congreso de los Diputados, Comisiones de Investigación*, VIII Legislatura, no. 3, *Sobre el 11 de marzo de 2004* [Journal of the sessions of the Congress of Deputies, commissions of inquiry, 8th legislature, no. 3, on the events of March 11, 2004] (2004), 23.

11. Ibid., 24.

12. Ibid., 35.

13. Ibid., 41.

14. CGI, "Informe del registro de Amer Azizi (Sumario 35/01)," 9 (emphasis added).

15. Beatrice de Graaf, "The Van Gogh Murder and Beyond," in *The Evolution of the Global Terrorist Threat: From 9/11 to Osama bin Laden's Death*, ed. Bruce Hoffman and Fernando Reinares (New York: Columbia University Press, 2014), 101–42.

16. Tawil, *Brothers in Arms*, 181–84.

17. *Sumario 20/2004*, vol. 97, 31–32, 316, and 848.

18. *Sumario 20/2004, Auto*, July 5, 2006, 64–65.

19. The information comes from the Moroccan authorities via an international rogatory commission on the May 2003 Casablanca bombings, whose results figured in *Sumario 9/2003*. Against Maymouni and Mourafik, there was also the dictated indictment of May 5, 2005; see *Sumario 20/2004*, vol. 173, 66,806–15.

20. Testimony by Abdelatif Mourafik, on July 7, 2004, before the Moroccan authorities referred to in *Diligencias 30,996*, 13.

21. Testimony by Mustafa Maymouni, July 18, 2003, before the Moroccan authorities referred to in *Diligencias 30,996*, 16.

22. *Sumario 20/2004*, vol. 99, 32,915.

23. On this see, see the established juridical facts in *Sentencia 22/2007*, 3 and 10.

24. *Sumario 20/2004*, vol. 99, 32,891

25. *Sumario 20/2004*, vol. 233, 90,730–90.

26. Former LIFG leader Norman Benotman, personal correspondence with author, Tripoli, March 22, 2010. He reiterated this information during a conversation in Madrid in November 2010. At the time, Benotman was accompanied by the individual who had received the phone call. Serhane ben Abdelmajid Fakhet had something important to say to this person, who then told my translator that they had to talk about "business."

27. On this matter, see Edurne Uriarte, *Terrorismo y democracia tras el 11-M* [Terrorism and democracy after March 11] (Madrid: Espasa Calpe, 2004), especially 9–36 and 61–81; Narciso Michavila, "Guerra, terrorismo y elecciones: incidencia electoral de los atentados islamistas en Madrid" [War, terrorism, and elections: Electoral impact of Islamist attacks in Madrid], DT 13/2005 (Madrid: Real Instituto Elcano, March 10, 2005), http://www .realinstitutoelcano.org/documentos/180/Michavilapdf.pdf; José R. Montero and Ignacio Lago, "Del 11-M al 14-M: terrorismo, gestión del gobierno y rendición de cuentas" [From 3/11 to 3/14: Terrorism, government management, and accountability], in *Elecciones generales 2004* [The 2004 general election], ed. José Ramón Montero, Ignacio Lago, and Mariano Torcal (Madrid: Centro de Investigaciones Sociológicas, 2007), 169–204; and William Rose, Rysia Murphy, and Max Abrahms, "Does Terrorism Ever Work? The 2004 Madrid Train Bombings," *International Security* 32, no. 1 (2007): 185–92.

28. Luis R. Aizpeolea, "Zapatero anuncia la retirada de las tropas de Irak en 'el menor tiempo posible'" [Zapatero announces the withdrawal of troops from Iraq in 'the shortest time possible'], *El País*, April 19, 2004, http://elpais.com/diario/2004/04/19 /espana/1082325601_850215.html; "Zapatero anuncia la retirada inmediata de las tropas de Irak" [Zapatero announces the immediate withdrawal of troops from Iraq], *El Mundo*, April 19, 2004, http://www.elmundo.es/elmundo/2004/04/18/espana/1082303152 .html; and "Zapatero anuncia la retirada inmediata de las tropas españolas de Irak" [Zapatero announces the immediate withdrawal of Spanish troops from Iraq], *ABC* (Madrid), April 19, 2004, http://www.abc.es/hemeroteca/historico-18-04-2004/abc /Ultima/zapatero-anuncia-la-retirada-inmediata-de-las-tropas-espa%C3%B1olas-de-irak_9621037869237.html.

Chapter 10

1. *Sumario 20/2004*, vol. 99, 32,891.

2. "Informe sobre Mohamed Belfatmi, sus relaciones con Amer Azizi y la célula de Abu Dahdah," 17–18; *Sumario 20/2004*, vol. 99, 32,891 and 32,895.

3. *Sumario 20/2004*, vol. 99, 32,914–15.

4. Ibid., 32,891.

5. Testimony by CNP official 18,403, instructor of *Diligencias Previas 396/2002* for the National Court, Central Investigative Court No. 5, Criminal Division, Section One, *Acta de juicio oral*, session of February 23, 2007, 85.

6. CGI, UCIE, "Informe general sobre conclusiones de la investigación de los atentados del 11 de marzo de 2004," July 3, 2006, 73.

7. This information on the vigilance and followings of a specialized CGI assignment on Amer Azizi between September and October 2001 appears in *Sumario 20/2004*, vol. 99, 32,914.

8. Ibid., 32,901–2.

9. "Declaración del imputado Driss Chebli" [Statement of the accused Driss Chebli], April 20, 2005, folios 3–4; reproduced in *Sumario 20/2004*, vol. 128, 46,574–75.

10. CGI, UCIE, *Diligencias 8470*, folio 7, in *Sumario 20/2004*, vol. 33, 9201.

11. *Sumario 20/2004*, vol. 99, 32,915.

12. Ibid., 32,676–77; and CGI, UCIE, *Diligencias 18,016*, June 25, 2003, 3.

13. "Declaración del imputado Driss Chebli," folio 4, in *Sumario 20/2004*, vol. 128, 46,576.

14. *Sumario 20/2004*, vol. 163, 61,740; National Court, Central Investigative Court No. 6, *Auto*, April 10, 2006, 1345.

15. "Declaración del detenido Abdulkarim A. Rahim Awleya" [Statement of the detained Abdulkarim A. Rahim Awleya], folio 3, *Sumario 20/2004*, vol. 33, 9281.

16. *Sumario 20/2004*, vol. 99, 32,898.

17. Ibid., 32,897. Lahcen Ikassrien was surprisingly absolved in 2006. However, in June 2014 he was again arrested and subsequently received a ten-year prison sentence, convicted of acting as ringleader of a jihadist cell styled as "Al Andalus Brigade," which was established in 2011 in Madrid with the purpose of radicalizing, recruiting, and sending individuals to Syria as foreign terrorist fighters, initially to join the ranks of Jabaht al-Nusrah and then of ISIL, later renamed the Islamic State. See National Court, Criminal Division, First Section, *Sentencia 25/2016.*

18. Translation into English from a Spanish translation of the letter rogatory released to Turkey on April 30, 2003, received by the Central Court of Instruction no. 5 of the National Court on December 2, 2003, 67 and 69.

19. Ibid., 61.

20. *Sumario 20/2004*, vol. 33, 8993.

21. *Sumario 20/2004*, vol. 99, 32,946.

22. Department of Defense, Joint Task Force Guantánamo US Naval Station, "Administrative Review Board Input for Guantánamo Detainee ISN: US9MO-000072DP (U)," November 8, 2004, 1 and 2.

23. *Sumario 20/2004*, vol. 99, 32,952.

24. *Sumario 35/2001*, 28,477–588; and *Sumario 20/2004*, vol. 163, 61,679–785.

25. *Sumario 20/2004*, vol. 99, 32,895.

26. *Sumario 20/2004*, vol. 48, 13,912–13.

27. DGP, CGI, UCIE, "Solicitando observación telefónica del número 619 213 092" [Requesting observation for telephone number 619 213 092], *Sumario 20/2004*, vol. 63.

28. Mouhannad Almallah Dabas initially was convicted for belonging to a terrorist organization in *Sentencia 65/2007*, derived from the National Court proceedings opened after the Madrid train bombings, but he was absolved of that crime in the *Segunda Sentencia 503/2008* released by the Supreme Court. He was considered a long-term collaborator of Abu Dahdah, as well as Fakhet and Mohamed al-Masri. He was also the owner of an establishment in Madrid on Virgen del Coro Street, where members of the 3/11 network met. In relation to all this, see *Sumario 20/2004*, vol. 72, 21,890; ibid., vol. 81, 25,204; ibid., vol. 85, 26,738; ibid., vol. 100, 33,447; ibid. vol. 123, 43,309; and ibid. vol. 140, 51,655. Dabas died in Syria in October 2013, while developing activities related to the al-Qaeda–affiliated jihadist organization Jahbat al-Nusra. This detail was confirmed to me by a police official familiar with Spanish-nationalized Syrians who have been implicated in jihadist terrorism, during an interview conducted in Madrid in November 2013.

29. *Sumario 20/2004*, vol. 114, 39,154; and vol. 163, 61,923–24.

30. DGP, CGI, UCIE, "Vínculos del 11-M con el GICM" [3/11 links with the MICG], folio 27, in *Sumario 20/2004*, vol. 97, 31,867.

31. DGP, CGI, UCIE, "Informe general de conclusiones, atentados del 11 de marzo, Sumario 20/04," 23–24.

32. In this sense, it is worth considering Serhane ben Abdelmajid Fakhet as a "middle manager" within al-Qaeda, as the idea has been elaborated in Peter Neumann, Ryan Evans, and Raffaello Pantucci, "Locating Al Qaeda's Center of Gravity: The Role of Middle Managers," *Studies in Conflict and Terrorism* 34, no. 11 (2011): 825–42.

33. NCTC, "The Case for Al-Qai'da Links to the 2004 Madrid Bombings," 2.

34. Ibid., 3 and 8.

35. "Investigaciones del piso de Leganés 03.04.04," 4–5; in *Sumario 20/2004*, 1192–3.

Chapter 11

1. Hegghammer, "Al-Qaida Statements 2003–2004," 42–44.

2. For a discussion on al-Qaeda strategy, see Bruce Riedel, *The Search for Al Qaeda: Its Leadership, Ideology, and Future* (Washington, DC: Brookings Institution Press, 2008), esp. 121–33; Bruce Hoffman, "Al Qaeda's Uncertain Future," *Studies in Conflict and Terrorism* 36, no. 8 (2013): 635–53; and Michael W. S. Ryan, *Decoding Al-Qaeda's Strategy: The Deep Battle against America* (New York: Columbia University Press, 2013).

3. Ahmed Rashid, *Descenso al caos. EE.UU. y el fracaso de la construcción nacional en Pakistán, Afganistán y Asia Central* [Descent into chaos: The United States and the failure of nation-building in Pakistan, Afghanistan, and Central Asia] (Barcelona: Península, 2008), 162–87 and 211–82.

4. *Sumario 20/2004*, vol. 163, 61,626–27; and vol. 234, 91,465.

5. "Qaeda Leader: Meetings Held to Carry Out bin Laden's Threats," Why-war. com, October 26, 2003 (defunct page; last accessed May 24, 2011), http://why-war.com /news/2003/10/26/qaedalea.html.

6. Atwan, *The Secret History of Al-Qa'ida*, 116.

7. In spite of this finding, it would not be out of the question to consider the possibility that the message came from Yemen, Egypt, or even Libya. See *Sumario 20/2004*, vol. 17, 4405.

8. Rashid, *Descenso al caos*, 290.

9. *Sumario 20/2004*, vol. 17, 4404–5.

10. Emphasis added. Given the length of this communique, I have omitted certain paragraphs irrelevant to the Madrid bombings. See *Sumario 20/2004*, vol. 17, p. 4404–5.

11. An insurgent strategy treatise written by Abu Hjir Abulaziz al-Muqrin, leader of Al-Qaeda in the Arabian Peninsula, offers a list of "human targets prioritized by order of importance." The Spanish appear third among Western nations, after the Americans and British. See Norman Cigar, trans., *Al-Qa'ida's Doctrine for Insurgency: 'Abd Al-'Aziz Al-Muqrin's A Practical Course for Guerrilla War* (Dulles, VA: Potomac Books, 2009), 129–31. Interestingly, the writings of al-Muqrin appeared in a publication called *Mu'askar al-Battar*, dedicated to operational matters, that had been circulated since 2003 and was consulted by members of the local 3/11 cell.

12. Interestingly, Moroccan Lahcen Ikassrien, who traveled from Spain to Afghanistan with Azizi and other members of al-Qaeda's Abu Dahdah cell before 9/11, was then captured and sent to Guantánamo before his transfer to Spain, where he has again been imprisoned since 2014—as already mentioned in chapters 2 and 10—during a conversation in Madrid at the end of 2013 with two other individuals inside his car, where an audio device was placed by the National Police, stated emphatically to his interlocutors: "Spain is the country which combats Islam the most, even more than America and Israel," see DGP, CGI, "Acta de Observación, Regrabación y Trasncripción," dated December 8, 2013, incorporated in National Court, Central Investigative Court 5, *Diligencias Previas 24/2013*.

13. On this point, I agree with Manuel Torres; see Manuel Torres, *Al Andalus 2.0. La ciberyihad contra España* [Al-Andalus 2.0: The cyberjihad against Spain] (Granada: Libros GESI, January 2014), esp. chap. 3, where he explains how the local 3/11 cell rapidly assumed a role that it had not foreseen in its original plans—that of propagandists, making their appearance through simple, low-quality videos at a time when there were no quick ways of publishing videos on the internet.

14. Fernando Reinares, *Patriotas de la muerte. Quiénes han militado en ETA y por qué* [Patriots of death: Who are the ETA militants and why] (Madrid: Taurus, 2001; 7th ed., 2011).

15. Canales and Montánchez, *En el nombre de Alá*; Irujo, *El agujero*, esp. chaps. 1 through 9; and Jordán and Horsburgh, "Mapping Jihadist Terrorism in Spain."

16. Uriarte, *Terrorismo y democracia tras el 11-M*, esp. 9–36 and 61–81; Michavila, "Guerra, terrorismo y elecciones"; Montero and Lago, "Del 11-M al 14-M," 169–204; Rose, Murphy, and Abrahms, "Does Terrorism Ever Work?"; Javier Jordán and Nicola Horsburgh, "Politics vs Terrorism: The Madrid Case," in *Playing Politics with Terrorism: A User's Guide*, ed. George Kassimeris (London: Hurst and Company, 2007), 203–19; and Rogelio Alonso, "The Madrid Bombings and Negotiations with ETA: A Case Study of the Impact of Terrorism on Spanish Politics," *Terrorism and Political Violence* 25, no. 1 (2013): 113–36.

17. Analysis of the hard drives on the computers used by the 3/11 operatives shows that they followed information published on various websites.

18. *Sumario 20/2004*, vol. 17, pp. 4406–7.

19. In this respect, see the hypothesis discussed in DGP, CGI, UCIE, "Informe general de conclusiones, atentados del 11 de marzo, Sumario 20/04," 82–86.

20. The English version of this surah comes from www.webislam.com/quran, accessed on May 25, 2013. See also "Los yihadistas en España."

21. Emphasis added. For an abbreviated text, see Unidad Central de Inteligencia, CGI, "Informe sobre el documento de las Brigadas Abu Hafs al-Masri encontrado en un ordenador intervenido en el registro de la vivienda de Jamal Ahmidan sita en la calle Villalobos núm. 51 de Madrid" [Report on the document from the Abu Hafs al-Masri Brigades, found on a computer in the search of the home of Jamal Ahmidan, located in Calle Villalobos no. 51, Madrid], 41–44; see *Sumario 20/2004*, vol. 156, 59,102–7.

22. Ibid, 3; *Sumario 20/2004*, vol. 156, 59,067.

23. These two recordings were recovered from the rubble of the destroyed flat in Leganés on the night of April 3, 2004. See DGP, CGI, UCIE, "Informe general de conclusiones, atentados del 11 de marzo, Sumario 20/04," 18–19.

24. Ibid., 23–24.

25. Brynjar Lia and Thomas Hegghammer, "Jihadi Strategic Studies: The Alleged Al Qaida Policy Study Preceding the Madrid Bombings," *Studies in Conflict and Terrorism* 27, no. 5 (2004): 355–75.

26. A translation of this recording is available at "An Account of the Syrian-Israeli Negotiations," Special Dispatch No. 69, MEMRI, January 27, 2000, http://www.memri.org/report/en/0/0/0/0/0/0/0/310.htm.

27. Ibid.

28. Ibid.

29. A translation of the audio that includes Osama bin Laden's statement is available at "Bin Laden in New Audiocassette: Makes a Promise in Advance to Accept and Uphold a Long-Term Truce [If America Offers It to Him] and at the Same Time Threatens New Attacks in the US," Special Dispatch No. 1074, MEMRI, January 20, 2006, http://www.memri.org/report/en/0/0/0/0/0/0/0/1586.htm.

30. Javier Jordán, "Analysis of *Jihadi* Terrorism Incidents in Western Europe, 2001–2010," *Studies in Conflict and Terrorism* 35, no. 5 (2012): 382–404.

31. This proclamation by Osama bin Laden, released with English and German subtitles, was made public days before Germany celebrated its general elections. See the transcribed version from the US government's Open Source Center at Juan Cole, "Bin Laden Message to Europe: Withdraw from Afghanistan," *Informed Comment*, September 26, 2009, http://www.juancole.com/2009/09/bin-laden-message-to-europe-withdraw.html.

32. "Al-Qaeda No. 2 Threatens More US Attacks," ABC News, www.abcnews.go.com/Blotter/al-qaeda-message-ayman-zawahiri-threatens-us-attacks/story?id=11262121.

33. See Grupo de Estudios en Seguridad Internacional, Universidad de Granada, "Referencias a España en la propaganda yihadista" [References to Spain in jihadist propaganda], http://www.seguridadinternacional.es/?q=es/content/referencias-españ-en-la-propaganda-yihadista#overlay-context=es/content/operaciones-policiales-contra-el-terrorismo-yihadista-en-espa%25C3%25B1%3Fq%3Des/content/operaciones-policiales-contra-el-terrorismo-yihadista-en-espa%25C3%25B1.

34. [Osama bin Laden], "Letter to Occupying Countries" [English version], Office of the Director of National Intelligence, posted March 1, 2016, https://www.dni.gov/files/documents/ubl2016/english/Letter%20to%20Occupying%20Countries.pdf.

Chapter 12

1. *Sumario 20/2004*, separate piece 29, annex II, document 8, and annex IV, document 2.

2. CGI, UCIE, "Acta de declaración de Hassan Bel Hadj" [Affidavit of Hassan Bel Hadj], *Diligencias 8470*, April 14, 2004, folio 3, in *Sumario 20/2004*, separate piece 5, 8276; and CGI, UCIE, "Declaración del detenido Hassan Bel Hadj" [Declaration of detainee Hassan Bel Hadj], folio 2, in *Sumario 20/2004*, separate piece 5, 8328.

3. DGP, CGI, UCIE, "Informe general de conclusiones, atentados del 11 de marzo, Sumario 20/04," 94.

4. *Sumario 20/2004*, vol. 162, 61,522–24.

5. *Sumario 20/2004*, vol. 42, 11,945–46 and 11,951–52.

6. Ibid., prepared piece 10 and separate piece 29, Annex II, docs. 15 and 16.

7. Rogelio Alonso and Fernando Reinares, "Maghreb Immigrants Becoming Suicide Terrorists: A Case Study on Religious Radicalization Processes in Spain," in *Root Causes of Suicide Terrorism: The Globalization of Martyrdom*, ed. Ami Pedahzur (London: Routledge, 2006), 179–98.

8. "Investigaciones del piso de Leganés 03.03.04," May 3, 2004, 50, in *Sumario 20/2004*, vol. 42, 11,968.

9. *Sumario 20/2004*, vol. 61, 18,591; vol. 81, 18,634 and 25,176; and vol. 162, 61,529–30 and 61,556–58 (emphasis added).

10. Reinares and García-Calvo, "Los yihadistas en España."

11. The text by Abdullah Azzam is reproduced in Malise Ruthven, *Islam in the World*, 3rd ed. (London: Granta Books, 2006), 407.

12. Jeffrey B. Cozzens, "Al-Takfir wa'l Hijra: Unpacking an Enigma," *Studies in Conflict and Terrorism* 32, no. 6 (2009): 489–510.

13. "Investigaciones del piso de Leganés 03.03.04," May 3, 2004, 35, in *Sumario 20/2004*, vol. 42, 11.953.

14. "The Case for Al-Qai'da Links to the 2004 Madrid Bombings: A Key Assumptions Check," 4.

15. *Sumario 20/2004*, vol. 161, 60,858.

16. Inspector-General Arief Dharmawan, assistant director of Indonesia's national counterterrorism agency, interview with author, Real Instituto Elcano, Madrid, November 25, 2013.

17. DGP, CGI, UCIE, "Informe general de conclusiones, atentados del 11 de marzo, Sumario 20/04," 104.

18. For a critical interpretation, see Casimiro García-Abadillo and Antonio Iglesias, *Titadyn: El informe científico del químico Iglesias: el estudio definitivo de los explosivos del 11-M* [Titadyn: The scientific report of the chemist Iglesias: The definitive study of the March 11 explosives] (Madrid: La Esfera de los Libros, 2009).

19. *Sumario 20/2004*, vol. 91, 29,165–69; vol. 98, 32,453–56; vol. 113, 38,935 and 43,682; and vol. 218, 84,743–79.

20. *Sentencia 6/2008*, 28 and 185.

21. See Joint Task Force Guantánamo assessment on Abu Faraj al-Libi, dated September 10, 2008, at the *New York Times* Guantánamo Docket, http://projects.nytimes.com /guantanamo/detainees/10017-abu-faraj-al-libi.

22. Bruce Hoffman, "The 7 July 2005 London Bombings," in *The Evolution of the Global Terrorism Threat: From 9/11 to Osama bin Laden's Death*, ed. Bruce Hoffman and Fernando Reinares (New York: Columbia University Press, 2014), 192–223.

23. "The Case for Al-Qai'da Links to the 2004 Madrid Bombings," 5–6 and 12.

Chapter 13

1. *Sumario 20/2004*, separate piece on financing, vol. 8, 2894.

2. Reuven Paz, "The Impact of the War in Iraq on the Global Jihad," *Current Trends in*

Islamist Ideology 1 (2005): 39–49.

3. "Declaraciones de Abdelatif Mourafik, el 7 de julio de 2004" [Statements by Abdelatif Mourafik, on July 7, 2004], before the Moroccan authorities, referred to in *Diligencias 30,996*, 12.

4. The Iraqi branch of al-Qaeda morphed a decade later into what starting in 2013 became known as the Islamic State of Iraq and Levant (ISIL); in 2014, it was renamed the Islamic State, as an organization competing with al-Qaeda for hegemony within global jihadism as a whole. See Charles Lister, "Profiling the Islamic State," Brookings Doha Center Analysis Paper no. 13 (Doha, Qatar: Brookings Doha Center, 2004), https://www .brookings.edu/wp-content/uploads/2014/12/en_web_lister.pdf.

5. *Sumario 49/2009*, vol. 5, 1404–5.

6. Ibid., 2.307; and National Court, Criminal Division, Second Section, *Sentencia 8/2011*, 24 and 45.

7. CGI, UCIE, *Diligencias 1*, January 2, 2007, 3; and *Sumario 49/2009*, vol. 5, 1392.

8. CGI, UCIE, *Diligencias 1*, 16; and *Sumario 49/2009*, vol. 5, 1405.

9. *Sentencia 65/2007*, 213–14.

10. CGI, UCIE, "Solicitud de órdenes de detención y mandamientos de entradas y registros" [Request for arrest warrants and orders for entries and records], January 2, 2006, 4; document incorporated into National Court, Central Investigative Court No. 6, *Diligencias Previas 309/2005*.

11. Interview with one of the CGI police officers who interrogated Abdelillah Hriz in Syria in Madrid, conducted by the author in Madrid, April 11, 2013.

12. Hriz was sentenced to eight years in prison in Sentence no. 53, dictated on December 18, 2008, by the Criminal Division of the Tribunal de Apelación in Rabat, Morocco (case no. 6-2009-28).

13. Mohamed Belhadj was sentenced to twenty years in prison in Sentence no. 8, dictated on January 28, 2010, by the Criminal Division of the Tribunal de Apelación in Rabat, Morocco (case no. 24-2009-27).

14. Hicham Ahmidan was sentenced to ten years in prison in Sentence no. 6, dictated on February 18, 2009, by the Criminal Division of the Tribunal de Apelación in Rabat, Morocco (case no. 5-2009-28).

15. CGI, UCIE, *Diligencias 1*, 3; corresponding to *Sumario 49/2009*, vol. 5, 1392.

16. *Sentencia 31/2009*; Supreme Court, Criminal Division, *Segunda Sentencia 1366/2009*; and National Court, Criminal Division, Second Section, *Sentencia 8/2011*.

17. CGI, *Diligencias 4475*, February 28, 2007, 8–9; and *Sumario 49/2009*, vol. 4, 808–9.

18. *Segunda Sentencia 1366/2009*, 39–40.

19. Interview with a senior officer (international terrorism specialist), stationed at the National Police Headquarters in Catalonia (interview held in Barcelona, December 18, 2012).

20. Translation of the declarations by Khaled Azig on November 19, 2005, provided by the Moroccan DGSN (Direction Générale de la Sûreté Nationale) and incorporated into *Sumario 49/2009*, vol. 6, 1298, 1317–19, and 1331.

21. Ibid., 1298 and 1301–3.

22. *Sumario 20/2004, Auto*, July 5, 2006, 64–65.

23. Jonathan Schanzer, *Al Qaeda's Armies: Middle East Affiliate Groups and the Next Generation of Terror* (Washington, DC: Washington Institute for Middle East Policy, 2005), 132–36; see also Mohammed M. Hafez, *Suicide Bombers in Iraq: The Strategy and Ideology of Martyrdom* (Washington, DC: United States Institute of Peace Press), 55 and 193–95. In December 2007, Ansar al-Sunna announced that it had returned to its previous name, Ansar al-Islam. See Springer, Regens, and Edger, *Islamic Radicalism and Global Jihad*, 127.

24. National Court, Criminal Division, Third Section, *Rollo de Extradición no. 151/2003*; and CGI, UCIE, "Solicitud de órdenes de detención y mandamientos de entradas y registros," 14, document incorporated into *Diligencias Previas 309/2005* of the National Court, Central Investigative Court No. 6.

25. DGP, CGI, UCIE, "Informe general de conclusiones, atentados del 11 de marzo, Sumario 20/04," 22–23.

26. This paragraph reproduces part of a transcript cited in chapter 11.

27. National Court, Criminal Division, First Section, *Sentencia 3/2010*, 7.

Chapter 14

1. A telling example of this line of argument can be found in Jaime Ignacio del Burgo, *11-M. Demasiadas preguntas sin respuesta* [3/11: Too many unanswered questions] (Madrid: La Esfera de los Libros, 2006). Del Burgo was a leading member of the Popular Party in the Spanish parliamentary commission that investigated the 3/11 bombings. According to an October 2006 Sigma Dos survey for *El Mundo* newspaper, 33 percent of respondents believed that ETA was involved in the Madrid train bombings, though this perception was shared by 65 percent of PP supporters and only 13 percent of PSOE supporters: "Un 67,5% de los ciudadanos piensa que aún no se sabe todo sobre el 11-M" [67.5 percent of citizens think that all has not been told about 3/11], *El Mundo*, October 16, 2006, http://www.elmundo.es/elmundo/2006/10/16/espana/1160967687.html.

2. A survey conducted by Elcano Royal Institute on March 2007, three years after the Madrid train bombings, showed that 6 out of every 10 adult Spaniards believed that the 3/11 attacks would not have taken place if Spain had not supported the United States in the 2003 invasion of Iraq. However, although 80 percent of respondents who voted for the PSOE in the March 2004 general elections agreed with that belief, only 40 percent of respondents who voted for the PP believed similarly. See: Barómetro del Real Instituto Elcano (BRIE), *14ª Oleada. Resultados de marzo de 2007* [14th Wave: Results from March 2007] (Madrid: Real Instituto Elcano, March 2007), 123, http://www.realinstitutoelcano .org/wps/wcm/connect/36e0640047a1f34cbacefa076e8e26e4/14BRIE_Informe _Completo.pdf?MOD=AJPERES&CACHEID=36e0640047a1f34cbacefa076e8e26e4.

3. "Informe solicitado en virtud de Auto de fecha 31 de marzo de 1997, Diligencias Previas 209/96, solicitado por el Juzgado Central de Instrucción número 5 de la Audiencia Nacional," 5, 10, and 11.

4. For a documented consideration of the action taken by police intelligence units regarding the al-Qaeda cell in Spain and its associated components, from the 1990s to March 11, 2004, at the level of investigative journalism, see Irujo, *El agujero*, 23–75.

5. José María Aznar, *Ocho años de Gobierno. Una visión personal de España* [Eight years in government: A personal vision of Spain] (Barcelona: Planeta, 2004). Some may think that it is easy to build these arguments now and quote this kind of statement after the fact. However, in January 2003, I completed a book that concluded: "Al-Qaeda has used Spain as one its main European bases. It is likely that the citizens and government of Spain will become targets of global terrorism." See Reinares, *Terrorismo global*, 131. On this book and its prediction, see Paul Ingendaay, "Terrorismo global" [Global terrorism], *Frankfurter Allgemeine Zeitung*, April 22, 2004, http://www.faz.net/aktuell/feuilleton/buecher/11-maerz-terrorismo-global-1160771.html.

6. José Antonio Alonso, interior minister from April 2004 to the spring of 2006, made the following statement to the Spanish parliament's interior committee when he took on the defense portfolio: "[T]his minister, his team and the entire government have been aware from the start that we should implement a set of measures which, while not eliminating the threat, would nevertheless make us more prepared to respond to this threat to our security, and therefore to our freedom and the democratic values that uphold it, to our lifestyle and our progress, and also to the security and freedom of our allies." See Fernando Reinares, "Tras el 11 de marzo: estructuras de seguridad interior y prevención del terrorismo global en España" [After March 11: Internal security structures and the prevention of global terrorism in Spain], in Charles Powell and Fernando Reinares, *Las democracias occidentales frente al terrorismo global* [Western democracies against global terrorism] (Barcelona: Ariel, 2008), 107.

7. Ibid., 108.

8. Ibid., 110–15.

9. Ibid., 115–19.

10. Ibid., 125–30.

11. Ibid., 120–24.

12. The Pew Global Attitudes Project, *The Great Divide: How Westerners and Muslims View Each Other* (Washington, DC: Pew Research Center, 2006), 4, 25, 57, and 60.

13. Fernando Reinares, "¿Coinciden el Gobierno y los ciudadanos en qué medidas adoptar contra el terrorismo internacional?" [Do the government and citizens agree on what actions to take against international terrorism?], Madrid: Real Instituto Elcano, *ARI* no. 78 (2006).

14. The data mentioned in this paragraph come from Reinares and García-Calvo, "Los yihadistas en España."

15. Data mentioned in this paragraph come from Carola García-Calvo y Fernando Reinares, "Procesos de radicalización violenta y terrorismo yihadista en España: ¿cuándo? ¿dónde? ¿cómo?", Madrid: Real Instituto Elcano, DT 16/2013, http://www.realinstitutoelcano.org/wps/portal/web/rielcano_es/contenido?WCM_GLOBAL_CONTEXT=/elcano/elcano_es/zonas_es/terrorismo+internacional/dt16-2013-reinares-gciacalvo-radicalizacion-terrorismo-yihadista-espana

16. See Carola García-Calvo y Fernando Reinares, "Pautas de implicación entre condenados por actividades relacionadas con el terrorismo yihadista o muertos en acto de terrorismo suicida en España (1996-2013)" [Patterns of involvement between those convicted for activities related to jihadist terrorism or killed in an act of suicide terrorism in Spain (1996–2013)], DT 15/2014 (Madrid: Real Instituto Elcano, 2014), http://www.realinstitutoelcano.org/wps/portal/web/rielcano_es/contenido?WCM_GLOBAL_CONTEXT=/elcano/elcano_es/zonas_es/terrorismo+internacional

/dt152014-garciacalvo-reinares-implicacion-condenados-terrorismo-yihadista-muertos
-terrorismo-suicida-espana-1996-2013.

17. National Court, Criminal Division, First Section, *Sentencia 78/2009*, 30.

18. *Sentencia 78/2009*, 7. For more detail on this plot, see Fernando Reinares, "The January 2008 Suicide Bomb Plot in Barcelona," in Hoffman and Reinares, *The Evolution of the Global Terrorist Threat*, 334–52.

19. Fernando Reinares and Carola García-Calvo, *Estado Islámico en España* (Madrid: Real Instituto Elcano, 2016).

20. Manuel Torres, *Al Andalus 2.0: La ciberyihad contra España* [Al-Andalus 2.0: The cyberjihad against Spain] (Granada: GESI, 2014).

Sources and Bibliography

Court and Attorney Records

Spanish Court and Attorney Records (Madrid)

National Court, Central Investigative Court No. 5
   Sumario 35/2001
   Sumario 9/2003
   Sumario 21/2006

National Court, Central Investigative Court No. 6
   Sumario 20/2004
   Sumario 49/2009

National Court, Central Investigative Court No. 1
   Diligencias Previas 79/2003

National Court, Central Investigative Court No. 5
   Diligencias Previas 53/2002
   Diligencias Previas 396/2002
   Diligencias Previas 24/2013

National Court, Criminal Division, First Section
   Sentencia 22/2007
   Sentencia 39/2007
   Sentencia 78/2009

Sentencia 3/2010
Sentencia 25/2016

National Court, Criminal Division, Second Section
Sentencia 12/2006
Sentencia 20/2006
Sentencia 65/2007
Sentencia 31/2009
Sentencia 8/2011

National Court, Criminal Division, Third Section
Sentencia 14/2001
Sentencia 26/2003
Sentencia 36/2005
Sentencia 6/2008

National Court, Criminal Division, First Section
Acta de juicio oral, February 23, 2007.

National Court, Criminal Division, Third Session
Acta de juicio oral, January 18, 2006.

National Court, Central Investigative Court No. 5
Testimony by CNP functionary no. 18403, instructor in preliminary investigation 396/2002.
"Declaración judicial de Abdula Jayata Kattan" [Affidavit of Abdula Jayata Kattan], February 4–5, 2004.

National Court, Central Investigative Court No. 6
Testimony before the judge by Basel Ghalyoun, March 24, 2004.
"Declaración del detenido Fouad el Morabit Amghar" [Statement of the detained Fouad el Morabit Amghar], March 30, 2004.
"Declaraciones ante el juez de Abdenabi Lebchina" [Statements to the judge by Abdenabi Lebchina], April 6, 2005.
"Declaraciones del detenido José Emilio Suárez Trashorras" [Statement of the detainee José Emilio Suárez Trashorras], May 22, 2004.

National Court, Criminal Division, Third Section
Rollo de Extradición no. 151/2003

National Court, Central Investigative Court No. 6
Auto, April 10, 2006.

National Court, Public Prosecutor
Conclusiones presentadas por el Fiscal a la Sección Segunda de la Sala de lo Penal de la Audiencia Nacional modificando un escrito inicial de 6 de noviembre de 2006, con fecha 4 de junio de 2007 [Conclusions presented by the Office of the National Court Attorney, June 4, 2007, to National Court of Spain, Criminal Division, Second Section, modifying a statement from November 2006].

Supreme Court of Spain, Criminal Division
Sentencia 556/2006
Segunda Sentencia 503/2008
Segunda Sentencia 1366/2009

US Court and Attorney Records (New York)

United States District Court, Southern District of New York
Indictment S(9) 98 Cr. 1023 (LBS)

Italian Court and Attorney Records (Milan)

First Court of Assize
Sentenza 10/2006

Third Court of Assize
Sentenza 38/2007

French Court and Attorney Records (Paris)

Tribunal de Grande Instance de París, 16ème chambre/1
No. d'affaire 0313739016, *Jugement du 11 juillet 2007* [Judgment of July 11, 2007].

British Court and Attorney Records (Manchester)

Crown Court at Manchester, T20087479, "The Honourable Mr. Justice Saunders, Regina v. Rangzieb Ahmed, Habib Ahmed, Mehreen Haji"
  Hearing Including Short Judgement, Verdicts and Mitigation, December 18, 2008.

Moroccan Court and Attorney Records (Rabat)

Rabat Court of Appeal, Court of Appeal
  Sentence no. 53 dictated on December 18, 2008 (case no. 6200928)
Rabat Court of Appeal, Criminal Division
  Sentence number 6 dictated on February 18, 2009 (case number 5200928)
Rabat Court of Appeal, Criminal Division
  Sentence no. 8 dictated on January 28, 2010, (case no. 24200927)

German Court and Attorney Records

The Attorney General of the Federal Republic of Germany
  "Ermittlungsverfahren gegen Mamoun Darkazanli, Sadel Borrmann, weitere, bisher unbekannte Personen wegen des Verdachts der Mitgliedschaft in einer terroristischen Vereinigung und der Geldwäsche; hier: Anzeige des spanischen Justizministeriums vom 17 Februar 2006," [Investigation into Mamoun Darkazanli, Sadel Borrmann, et al., previously unknown persons on suspicion of membership in a terrorist organization and money laundering; Spanish Ministry of Justice, February 17, 2006], July 14, 2006.

Police and Intelligence Documents

Spain

DGP, CGI, UCIE

  "Informe solicitado en virtud de Auto de fecha 31 de marzo de 1997, Diligencias Previas 209/96, solicitado por el Juzgado Central de Instrucción número 5 de la Audiencia Nacional" [Report requested under the order of March 31, 1997, preliminary investigation 209/26, requested by the National Court, Central Court of Instruction no. 5], April 14, 1997.

"Remitiendo Informe sobre Allekema Lamari" [Remitting report on Allekema Lamari], April 29, 1997.

"Informe ampliatorio a escrito de fecha 061101 en relación con una red de infraestructura en España de la organización terrorista Al Qaida vinculada a Osama bin Laden" [Supplemental Report, dated 11/1/06, regarding an infrastructure network in Spain of the terrorist organization al-Qaeda linked to Osama bin Laden], November 12, 2001.

"Informe del registro de Amer Azizi (Sumario 35/01)," [Log report of Amer Azizi (Sumario 35/01)], n.d. [likely written in November or December 2001].

"Informe de las investigaciones realizadas en torno a las visitas a España de Mohamed Atta y Ramzi Binalshibh" [Report of the investigations conducted around the visits to Spain of Mohamed Atta and Ramzi Binalshibh], October 15, 2002.

"Informe ampliatorio de las investigaciones realizadas en torno a las visitas a España de Mohamed Atta y Ramzi Binalshibh" [Expanded report of the investigations conducted around the visits to Spain of Mohamed Atta and Ramzi Binalshibh], October 16, 2002.

"Informe sobre registro del domicilio de Luis José Galán González, Yusuf Galán" [Report on the domicile registration of Luis José Galán González, Yusuf Galán], 2002.

"Informe sobre el Grupo Islámico Combatiente Marroquí (GICM)" [Information on the Moroccan Islamic Combatant Group (MICG)], undated document elaborated by the National Court judge [very likely written in 2003].

"Cotejo de datos de los Servicios franceses" [Collated data from the French services] February 27, 2003.

Diligencias 18, May 25, 2003.

Diligencias 18,016, June 25, 2003.

"Informes del F.B.I., Departamento de Justicia USA" [Information from the FBI, US Department of Justice], July 15, 2003.

"Remitiendo informe sobre la iniciación y continuación de investigaciones en España sobre los miembros de la organización o infraestructura de Osama bin Laden asentados en nuestro país" [Remitting report on the initiation and continuation of research in Spain on members of Osama bin Laden's organization or infrastructure settled in our country], October 17, 2003.

"Acta de declaración del ciudadano extranjero Ibrahín Afalah" [Affidavit of foreign citizen Ibrahín Afalah], March 17, 2004.

Testimony by Mohamed Chaoui (Jamal Zougam's brother by his mother), and by Mohamed Bakali, March 19, 2004.

Diligencias 8470, "Acta de declaración de Abdelouahid Berrak Soussane" [Affidavit of Abdelouahid Berrak Soussane], March 21, 2004.

"Acta de declaración de Hamid Ahmidan" [Affidavit of Hamid Ahmidan], March 21, 2004.

"Acta de declaración de Rosa María Aguayo de Inés" [Affidavit of Rosa María Aguayo de Inés], March 26, 2004.

"Formularios rellenados en campos de Al Qaida por mujahidín [*sic*] enviados desde España a través de Othman el Andalusi (Amer Azizi), hombre de confianza de Imad Eddin Barakat Yarkas a.k.a. Abu Dahdah" [Forms filled out in al-Qaeda camps by mujahedin sent from Spain through Othman al-Andalusi (Amer Azizi), confidant of Imad Eddin Barakat Yarkas a.k.a. Abu Dahdah], March 29, 2004.

"Acta de declaración de Hassan Bel Hadj" [Affidavit of Hassan Bel Hadj], *Diligencias 8470*, April 14, 2004.

"Informe sobre Mohamed Belfatmi, sus relaciones con Amer Azizi y la célula de Abu Dahdah" [Report on Mohamed Belfatmi, his relationship with Amer Azizi and the Abu Dahdah cell], April 16, 2004.

Diligencias 8470, folio 4, "Acta de declaración de Abdulkarim Rahman Awleya" [Affidavit of Abdulkarim Rahman Awleya], April 17, 2004.

Diligencias 8470, "Acta de declaración de Khalid Zeimi Pardo" [Affidavit of Khalid Zeimi Pardo], April 20, 2004.

"Informe sobre Operación Lago" [Report on Operation Lago], April 20, 2004.

"Declaración de Assad Mohamedeid abd el Maksoud" [Declaration of Assad Mohamedeid abd el Maksoud], April 20, 2004.

"Declaración del detenido Abdulkarim A. Rahim Auleya" [Affidavit of detainee Abdulkarim A. Rahim Auleya], April 20, 2004.

"Investigaciones del piso de Leganés 03.03.04" [Investigations of the Leganés apartment, March 3, 2004], May 3, 2004.

Diligencias 840/04, official correspondence, June 18, 2004.

"Declaraciones de Abdelatif Mourafik, el 7 de julio de 2004" [Statements by Abdelatif Mourafik on July 7, 2004], before the Moroccan authorities.

"Declaración del imputado Rabe Osman el Sayed" [Statement of the prosecuted Rabei Osman el Sayed], December 13, 2004.

Diligencias 37,552, "Acta de declaración de Mohamed el Ouazzani" [Affidavit of Mohamed el Ouazzani], December 15, 2004.

Diligencias 38,366, Diligencia Informe, December 17, 2004.

"Declaración del testigo protegido número 2323" [Statement of protected witness no. 2323], December 29, 2004.

"Informe sobre el documento de las Brigadas Abu Hafs al Masri encontrado en un ordenador intervenido en el registro de la vivienda de Jamal Ahmidan sita en la calle Villalobos núm. 51 de Madrid" [Report on the document from the Abu Hafs al Masri Brigades, found on a computer in the search of the home of Jamal Ahmidan, located in Calle Villalobos no. 51, Madrid].

"Solicitando observación telefónica del número 619 213 092" [Observation request for telephone number 619 213 092].

"Vínculos del 11M con el GICM" [3/11 links with the MICG].

"Declaración del detenido Hassan Bel Hadj" [Declaration of detainee Hassan Bel Hadj].

"Análisis del disco duro recuperado en la Carmen Martín Gaite, 40. Leganés (Madrid)" [Analysis of the hard drive recovered from 40 Carmen Martín Gaite Street, Leganés (Madrid)].

"Remitiendo traducción de la conversación ambiental mantenida por Rabei Osman El Sayed a.k.a. Mohamed el Egipcio, facilitada por las autoridades italianas" [Remitted translation of ambient conversation by Rabei Osman El Sayed a.k.a. Mohamed the Egyptian, provided by the Italian authorities]

"Declaración del imputado Rachid Bendouda" [Statement of the prosecuted Rachid Bendouda], February 7, 2005.

"Declaración del imputado Jaouad el Bouzroudi" [Statement of the prosecuted Jaouad el Bouzroudi], March 11, 2005.

"Delcaración del imputado Driss Chebli" [Statement of the prosecuted Driss Chebli], April 20, 2005.

Diligencias 8494, "Acta de declaración del detenido Abdelkrim Lebchina" [Affidavit of detainee Abdelkrim Lebchina], April 31, 2005

"Análisis de datos derivados de la investigación relativa a los hermanos

Oulad Akcha" [Analysis of data from the investigation on the Oulad Akcha brothers], May 2005

Diligencias Previas 16388, June 14, 2005

"Análisis de datos derivados de la investigación relativa a hermanos Ahmidan y Abdelilah el Fadual" [Analysis of data from the investigation on the brothers Ahmidan and Abdelilah el Fadual], June 2005

"Solicitud de órdenes de detención y mandamientos de entradas y registros" [Request for arrest warrants and orders for entries and records], January 2, 2006

"Informe general de conclusiones, atentados del 11 de marzo, Sumario 20/04" [General report of findings, March 11 attacks, Sumario 20/04], July 3, 2006

Diligencias 1, January 2, 2007

Diligencias 4475, February 28, 2007

Diligencias 30,996

"Acta de observación, regrabación y transcripción," December 8, 2013, *Diligencias Previas 24/2013*

DGP, General Commissary of Scientific Police
"Informe técnico-policíal núm. 116-IT-04" [Technical police report no. 116-IT-04], July 27, 2004.

DGP, Judicial Police Commissioner General, Central Unit on Drugs and Organized Crime
"Informe de 19 de agosto de 2004 de la Unidad Central de Droga y Crimen Organizado, de la Comisaría General de Policía Judicial" [August 19, 2004, report of the Drug and Organized Crime Central Unit of the Judicial Police Commissioner General].

DGP, Superior Headquarters of the Madrid Police, Provincial Information Brigade
Police statement by Fouad el Morabit Amghar, *Diligencias 8470*, March 28, 2004
"Acta de declaración de Mouad Benkhalafa" [Affidavit of Mouad Benkhalafa], *Diligencias 8470*, March 29, 2004.

DGP, Superior Police Headquarters of Valencia, Provincial Information Brigade
"Acta de declaración de Safwan Sabagh" [Affidavit of Safwan Sabagh], July 1, 2004.

Guardia Civil General Directorate, Information Service Headquarters
"Informe sobre el estado de las Diligencias Previas 367/01 y solicitud de comisión rogatoria internacional" [Report on the status of Preliminary Investigation 367/01 and request for international letters rogatory], September 16, 2002.

Guardia Civil Information Service Headquarters, Special Central Unit 2
Atestado número 01/2002, concluded April 17, 2002.

Italy

Questura di Milano, General Investigations and Special Operations Division, Antiterrorism Section
Procedimento penale n. 17596/04 r.g.n.r. mod. 21 [Criminal proceeding no. 17596/04 r.g.n.r. mod. 21], March 8, 2005

Morocco

DGSN (Direction Générale de la Sûreté Nationale)
Declarations by Khaled Azig on November 19, 2005

United States

National Counterterrorism Center (NCTC). "The Case for Al-Qai'da Links to the 2004 Madrid Bombings: A Key Assumptions Check." August 22, 2008.
Open Source Center. "Bin Laden Message to Europe: Withdraw from Afghanistan." *Informed Comment*, September 26, 2009.

US Department of Defense. "Verbatim Transcript of Combatant Status Review Tribunal Hearing for ISN 10013." US Naval Base Guantánamo Bay, Cuba, March 9, 2007.

US Department of Defense, Joint Task Force Guantánamo. "Administrative Review Board Input for Guantánamo Detainee ISN: US9MO000072DP (U)." November 8, 2004. http://projects.nytimes.com/guantanamo /detainees/72laacinikassrin/documents/5.

———. Assessment on Abu Faraj al-Libi. *New York Times* Guantánamo Docket. September 10, 2008. http://projects.nytimes.com/guantanamo /detainees/10017abufarajallibi.

———. "JTFGTMO Detainee Assessment on Abu Zubaydah." November 11, 2008.

European Union

Europol
"Valoración de amenaza sobre terrorismo extremista islámico, Sexta edición" [Threat assessment of Islamist extremist terrorism, 6th edition], January 29, 2004.

Council of the European Union. Joint Sitcen
Report SN 3358/05. Subject: "Al Qaeda Leadership." October 2005.

Parliamentary Inquiries

Cortes Generales, Congreso de los Diputados, *Comisiones de Investigación, VIII Legislatura,* "Sobre el 11 de marzo de 2004", 2004-2005 [Spanish Parliament, Congress of Deputies, Commissions of Inquiry, VIII Legislature, "On 11 March 2004", 2004–2005].

Diario de Sesiones del Congreso de los Diputados, Comisiones de Investigación, VIII Legislatura [Journal of the sessions of the Congress of Deputies, Commissions of Inquiry, VIII Legislature], sessions of May 27; June 16, 22, 23, and 30; July 1, 6, 7, 8, 13, 14, 15, 19, 20, 22, 27, 28, and 29; September 7 and 15; October 5, 14, 15, 19, and 25; November 3, 15, 17, 18, 22, 25, and 29; December 13, 15, and 22 (2004); March 8 and 16, April 5 and 19; May 5; June 8, 20, 22, and 30 (2005).

Diario Oficial de las Comunidades Europeas [Official Journal of the European Community], May 29, 2002, L 139/13.

Personal Interviews with the Author

Interview with intelligence officials dealing with external relations, then working for the EU Common Foreign and Security Policy community, in Brussels, in October 2007.

Interview with prison official competent on penitentiary vigilance held in Madrid between November 2008 and March 2009.

Interview with relevant CGI senior official in November 2009.

Interview with CIA sources present in Pakistan during the Haisori strike, in November and December 2009.

Interview with former LIFG leader Norman Benotman in Tripoli, Libya, on March 22, 2010.

Interview with former LIFG emir Abu Abdullah al-Sadeq in Tripoli, Libya, on March 23, 2010.

Interview with former LIFG leader Norman Benotman in Madrid in November 2010.

Interview with a CNP commissioner who participated in the investigation into Abu Dahdah's cell, Madrid, November 2008 and December 2012.

Interview with intelligence officials of two Western countries (one European) in December 2011 and February 2012.

Interview with senior officials of the Serbian police and the Serbian Ministry of Justice, about the arrest of Abdelmajid Bouchar on June 23, 2005, in Belgrade, May 15 and 16, 2012.

Interview with a senior officer, specialized on international terrorism, destined to the National Police Headquarters in Catalonia. Barcelona, December 18, 2012.

Interview with Commissioner Rafael Gómez Menor, in Madrid on December 20, 2012.

Interview with one of the CGI police officers who interrogated Abdelillah Hriz in Syria in Madrid, conducted on April 11, 2013.

Interview with Inspector General Arief Dharmawan, assistant director of Indonesia's national counterterrorism agency, Real Instituto Elcano, Madrid, November 25, 2013.

Interview with a police official familiar with Spanish-nationalized Syrians who have been implicated in jihadist terrorism, Madrid in November 2013.

Selected Secondary Sources

11M: retrato de los asesinos [11M: Portrait of the killers]. Cuatro, first broadcast on March 10, 2007.

Al-Qa'ida's Doctrine for Insurgency: 'Abd Al-'Aziz Al-Muqrin's A Practical Course for Guerrilla War. Translated by Norman Cigar. Dulles, VA: Potomac Books, 2009.

al-Suri, Abu Musab. "The Call to Global Islamic Resistance." In *The Canons of Jihad: Terrorists' Strategy for Defeating America*, edited by Jim Lacey. Annapolis, MD: Naval Institute Press, 2008.

Atwan, Abdel Bari. *The Secret History of Al-Qa'ida*. London: Abacus, 2006.

Bergen, Peter L. *Holy War, Inc.: Inside the Secret World of Osama bin Laden*. New York: Free Press, 2001.

Botha, Anneli. *Terrorism in the Maghreb: The Transnationalisation of Domestic Terrorism*. ISS Monograph Series 144. Pretoria: Institute for Security Studies, 2008.

Buesa, Mikel, Aurelia Vilariño, Joost Heijs, Thomas Baumert, and Javier González. "The Economic Cost of March 11: Measuring the Direct Economic Cost of the Terrorist Attack on March 11, 2004 in Madrid." *Terrorism and Political Violence* 19, no. 4 (2007): 489–509.

Canales, Pedro, and Enrique Montánchez. *En el nombre de Alá. La red secreta del terrorismo islamista en España* [In the name of Allah: The secret network of Islamist terrorism in Spain]. Barcelona: Planeta, 2002.

CNN. "Rare Photos Offer Look Inside Osama bin Laden's Afghan Hideout." March 12, 2015. http://www.cnn.com/2015/03/11/world/gallery/osambinladenrarephotos.

Filiu, Jean-Pierre. *Les neufs vies d'AlQaida* [The nine lives of al-Qaeda]. Paris: Fayard, 2009.

Gunaratna, Rohan, and Anders Nielsen. "Al Qaeda in the Tribal Areas of Pakistan and Beyond." *Studies in Conflict and Terrorism* 31, no. 9 (2008): 775–807.

Gunaratna, Rohan, and Aviv Oreg. "Al Qaeda's Organizational Structure and Its Evolution." *Studies in Conflict and Terrorism* 33, no. 12 (2010): 1043–78.

Hafez, Mohammed M. *Suicide Bombers in Iraq: The Strategy and Ideology of Martyrdom*. Washington, DC: US Institute of Peace Press, 2007.

Hastert, Paul. "Al Qaeda and Iran: Friends or Foes, or Somewhere in Between?" *Studies in Conflict and Terrorism* 30, no. 4 (2007): 327–36.

Hoffman, Bruce. "Al Qaeda's Uncertain Future." *Studies in Conflict and Terrorism* 36, no. 8 (2013): 635–53.

Hoffman, Bruce, and Fernando Reinares, eds. *The Evolution of the Global Terrorist Threat: From 9/11 to Osama bin Laden's Death.* New York: Columbia University Press, 2014.

Irujo, José M. *El agujero. España invadida por la yihad* [The hole: Spain invaded by jihad]. Madrid: Aguilar, 2005.

Jordán, Javier. "Analysis of *Jihadi* Terrorism Incidents in Western Europe, 2001–2010." *Studies in Conflict and Terrorism* 35, no. 5 (2012): 382–404.

Jordán, Javier, and Nicola Horsburgh. "Mapping Jihadist Terrorism in Spain." *Studies in Conflict and Terrorism* 28, no. 3 (2005): 169–91.

———. "Politics vs Terrorism: The Madrid Case." In *Playing Politics with Terrorism: A User's Guide*, edited by George Kassimeris, 203–19. London: Hurst and Company, 2007.

Kepel, Gilles. *The War for Muslim Minds: Islam and the West.* Cambridge, MA: Harvard University Press, 2004.

Lia, Brynjar, and Thomas Hegghammer. "Jihadi Strategic Studies: The Alleged Al Qaida Policy Study Preceding the Madrid Bombings." *Studies in Conflict and Terrorism* 27, no. 5 (2004): 355–75.

Moghadam, Assaf. "Motives for Martyrdom: Al-Qaida, Salafi Jihad, and the Spread of Suicide Attacks." *International Security* 33, no. 3 (2008/2009): 46–78.

Montero, José R., and Ignacio Lago. "Del 11-M al 14-M: terrorismo, gestión del gobierno y rendición de cuentas" [From 3/11 to 3/14: Terrorism, government management, and accountability]. In *Elecciones generales 2004* [The 2004 general election], edited by José Ramón Montero, Ignacio Lago, and Mariano Torcal. Madrid: Centro de Investigaciones Sociológicas, 2007.

National Commission on Terrorist Attacks upon the United States. *The 9/11 Commission Report.* New York: W. W. Norton, 2004.

Neumann, Peter, Ryan Evans, and Raffaello Pantucci. "Locating Al Qaeda's Center of Gravity: The Role of Middle Managers." *Studies in Conflict and Terrorism* 34, no. 11 (2011): 825–42.

Riedel, Bruce. "The Mysterious Relationship Between al-Qa'ida and Iran." *CTC Sentinel* 3, no. 7 (2010): 1–3.

———. *The Search for Al Qaeda: Its Leadership, Ideology, and Future.* Washington, DC: Brookings Institution Press, 2008.

Rose, William, Rysia Murphy, and Max Abrahms. "Does Terrorism Ever Work? The 2004 Madrid Train Bombings." *International Security* 32, no. 1 (2007): 185–92.

Sageman, Marc. *Understanding Terror Networks*. Philadelphia: University of Pennsylvania Press, 2004.

Sánchez, Juan J. *Las bombas del 11-M. Relato de los hechos en primera persona* [The 3/11 bombs: A first-person account of the facts]. Madrid: Amazon, 2013.

Tawil, Camille. *Brothers in Arms: The Story of Al-Qa'ida and the Arab Jihadists*. London: Saqi Books, 2010.

Torres, Manuel. *Al Andalus 2.0: La ciberyihad contra España* [Al-Andalus 2.0: The cyberjihad against Spain]. Granada: Libros GESI, 2014.

Vidino, Lorenzo. *Al Qaeda in Europe: The New Battleground of International Jihad*. Buffalo: Prometheus Books, 2005.

Waldmann, Peter. "Revenge Without Rules: On the Renaissance of an Archaic Motif of Violence." *Studies in Conflict and Terrorism* 24, no. 6 (2001): 435–50.

Webster, Justin, and Ignacio Orovio. *Conexión Madrid. Cómo y por qué Serhane y Jamal se convirtieron en terroristas yihadistas* [The Madrid connection: How and why Serhane and Jamal became jihadist terrorists]. Barcelona: Debate, 2009.

Index

Proper names starting with "al," "el," and "es" are alphabetized by the subsequent part of the name (e.g., "al-Masri" appears under "m").

GPSR Authorized Representative: Easy Access System Europe, Mustamäe tee
50, 10621 Tallinn, Estonia, gpsr.requests@easproject.com

www.ingramcontent.com/pod-product-compliance
Lightning Source LLC
Chambersburg PA
CBHW032128020426
42334CB00016B/1085